LEADING PRACTICE AND MANAGING CHANGE IN THE MATHEMATICS DEPARTMENT

A Resource Book
for Subject Leaders
in Mathematics

LEADING PRACTICE AND MANAGING CHANGE IN THE MATHEMATICS DEPARTMENT

A Resource Book
for Subject Leaders
in Mathematics

Edited by
Sue Johnston-Wilder
Clare Lee

tarquin publications

Cover Image
Quasicrystal. Computer model of a quasicrystal generated by the addition of nine equally-spaced particles behaving like waves (showing wave- particle duality). The waves met at the centre of the yellow "sun", producing a quasicrystal. Within the sun the pattern approximates to a mathematical Bessel function; there is regular repetition, concentric circles forming about the centre. As the pattern moves outwards from the sun, this order is lost, with similar structures appearing at irregular intervals. The yellow "slice" is one repeating unit of the pattern. The quasicrystal was modelled by Professor Eric Heller, Harvard University, USA.
Credit: ERIC HELLER/SCIENCE PHOTO LIBRARY

© The Authors

Paperback ISBN: 978-1-907550-01-0

Cased ISBN: 978-1-907550-02-7

E-Book ISBN: 978-1-905273-31-7

Published by   Tarquin Publications
              99 Hatfield Road
              St Albans Al1 4JL, UK

              www.tarquinbooks.com

All rights reserved. No part of this publication may be reproduced, stored in a retrieval system, or transmitted, in any form or by any means, electrnic, mechanical, photocopying, recording or otherwise without the prior permission of the publisher.

CONTENTS

Chapter	page
Foreword	vii
Introduction	1
1. Leading Mathematics - an Opportunity to Influence *Sue Pope*	5
2. Mathematics, Joy and Rigour *Barbara Jaworski*	15
3. Learning Theories in the Mathematics Classroom *Steve Lerman and Richard Cowley*	33
4. In the Mathematics Classroom with Learning Theories *Richard Cowley and Steve Lerman*	47
5. Taking a Lead with Pedagogy *Anthony Broadly, Clare Lee, Tim Rattigan and Anne Watson*	59
6. Taking a Lead on Developing Professional Practice – Coaching and Mentoring *Clare Lee, Anthony Broadly, Tim Rattigan, Anne Watson*	75
7. Using Research Evidence to Innovate, Change and Improve Learning *Peter Johnston-Wilder*	87
8. Using Assessment Data to Enhance Professional Practice *Mick Marks and Clare Lee*	105
9. Leading Assessment for Learning Mathematics *Clare Lee*	123
10. Organising the Teaching of Mathematics for Children and Young People who have Additional to Typical Needs *Melissa Rodd*	139
11. Using ICT to Enhance Professional Practice *Dave Miller*	159
12. Using ICT to Enhance Learning in Mathematics *Sue Johnston-Wilder*	183
Epilogue	211
Index	213

FOREWORD

The book is intended for new and aspiring subject leaders. It is particularly timely as schools are becoming more autonomous and subject leadership thus increasingly important. Subject leaders need to hold a vision for mathematics in their schools and beyond. They need to be able to articulate their goals to mathematics colleagues and to school management, as well as be able to map out what they see as an effective mathematics department in their school, which could bring their vision to reality. Subject leaders should be excellent practitioners themselves but much more. They need to be able to make explicit what it means to be an effective teacher, provide strategic leadership to cope with day-to-day situations as well as take on board new ideas, while inspiring and mentoring their colleagues.

This book is about leading practice and about how to manage changes to bring about a vision for a mathematics department. It includes invaluable discussion of theoretical and practical issues – both necessary for articulating clear goals and actions to reach them.

Drawing on contributions from experts in mathematics education all with extensive experience of leading mathematics departments, the book touches on a range of crucial topics including:

- the theoretical underpinnings of what constitutes mathematical knowledge and what this means in practice;
- what the theorists have to say about how people learn mathematics and how this manifests itself in the classroom;
- the problems and challenges in taking a lead on mathematics using voices of experienced subject leaders;
- how coaching, mentoring and action research can serve as important tools in managing change;
- what assessment can mean, how it can be deployed to measure

progress and how it can be exploited to enhance learning;
- how pupils progress in mathematics along different trajectories and can achieve in different ways;
- the difference ICT can make to a mathematics department, the potential of ICT to enhance pupil learning and practical strategies to increase its use by teachers.

I am delighted that the National Centre for Excellence in the Teaching of Mathematics (NCETM) has been associated with and supported this book from its inception. The book brings together the authentic voices of those who are leading mathematics in school with those who are leading thinking in mathematics education. I would like to congratulate the two authors, Sue and Clare, for their efforts that have reached such a successful conclusion and for turning their own vision into a reality.

Professor Celia Hoyles OBE

London Knowledge Lab, Insitute of Education, University of London and Director of the National Centre for Excellence in the Teaching of Mathematics

1
LEADING MATHEMATICS – AN OPPORTUNITY TO INFLUENCE

Sue Pope

Mathematics is an exciting and creative subject. It has evolved out of the human need to understand and manage circumstances and resources and solve problems. Mathematics is a truly global language; its development has been closely allied with trade, commerce, industry and war. Mathematical thinking is part of what it means to be human and includes making sense of information, seeking patterns, asking questions like 'how true?', 'what happens if?', and taking delight in things that are surprising and things that are predictable.

Like many mathematics teachers and others who enjoy and value mathematics you are probably dismayed when a friend, acquaintance or parent/guardian/carer says, 'I was never any good at maths'. No-one would ever say this about English! However, we live in a culture where an inability to 'do' mathematics and a disregard for its importance in our technological, and increasingly global, society is perfectly acceptable. As a teacher of mathematics you have the opportunity to plant the seeds that might counter this lack of esteem for mathematics and to build secure foundations for developing a healthy relationship with this increasingly important subject.

As a subject leader you have day-to-day responsibility for a team of teachers of mathematics and consequently the opportunity to influence the developing attitudes of learners in your school/college/institution towards mathematics. I propose that this challenge needs to be at the heart of every subject leader's agenda for change. There are exciting possibilities in this realisation and that is what this chapter is about. Throughout this chapter I will pose questions that you may wish to consider. I suspect that they are the sort of questions that you might be asked in an interview! More importantly they are the sort of questions that enable you to position yourself during challenging times. Sometimes you need to be able to articulate your beliefs in order to justify particular approaches that you are advocating or positions you are adopting.

How do you work with your colleagues to optimise the opportunity to influence attitudes towards mathematics?

Firstly, how do you ensure that senior leaders in your institution appreciate the importance and significance of developing positive attitudes towards mathematics and provide you with the support you might need? After all, they are concerned with raising standards. Can you be sure that improved attitudes will raise standards? There is considerable evidence that where learners are given the opportunity to develop genuine understanding (e.g. Watson, 2007) and can see how the mathematics they do in school is relevant to their interests and every day life (e.g. Boaler, 1997), attainment improves relative to a traditional 'drill and practice' regime.

This is not to suggest that developing fluency in technical competence should not be part of the mathematics agenda; rather that the agenda should not only be about developing technical competence. There is some evidence that teachers think 'having fun' by playing games in lessons will improve learners' attitudes. Whilst this may help, just like drill and practice, it will not be enough on its own. Learners need to be challenged to think and be given opportunities to use and develop their mathematics in unfamiliar and challenging contexts. It is the difference between developing 'instrumental understanding' or 'relational understanding' (see Skemp, 1971). The latter is far more powerful, enabling learners to make connections within mathematics and have the confidence to use their mathematics in a wide range of contexts.

Secondly, how do you engage with all the learners in your institution so they become active participants in learning mathematics and develop as mathematicians? Many learners may come to your institution with pre-conceived ideas about themselves in relation to mathematics. How do you work with these learners' notions to engender positive, confident attitudes that will sustain them through challenging and engaging experiences and result in them being committed to achieving their mathematical potential and eager to learn new mathematics when the opportunity and/or necessity arises? There are some ideas for how you could do this in this book but you will probably also want to refer to Wells (1995) or Johnston-Wilder and Mason (2005) or the websites of the professional subject associations for mathematics.

How do you lead a team of professionals committed to teaching mathematics as effectively as possible?

As a subject leader the expectation is that you are an effective practitioner – you know how to manage the learning environment, get the best out of learners and keep on top of the administrative demands of the job. You will have a well developed sense of what makes effective practice and have the confidence to take risks in order to improve the learning experiences of young people. You have convinced the institution's senior management that you have the potential to manage the subject team and to lead. This does not mean imposing your vision and beliefs on others. Every member of your team will have their own vision of what effective practice is, and whilst they may not resonate with yours they need to be respected, valued and nurtured. Working collaboratively with your team will help to ensure the development of shared values and understandings.

In order to lead you need to know where you are going. As a team leader you will be most effective if the team are fully involved in developing the vision and planning the route to achieving it. Working with your team on 'the raison d'être' or 'what are we trying to achieve?' will enable you to identify priorities for development and galvanise the team to action. This approach will help you to ensure that new initiatives (whether internal or external) are embraced as an opportunity, rather than 'yet another change'. Being clear about what you want to achieve empowers you and your team to manage incorporating initiatives into your vision for the learners in your institution. To optimise the opportunities for all learners in your institution it is essential that you adopt a positive disposition towards the challenges you will encounter.

One challenge that faces many mathematics subject leaders is that you may not have a full complement of dedicated, qualified teachers with mathematics as their specialism or your team may include some senior teachers or non-specialist teachers. How can you influence their practice and support them in being as effective as possible? It may be that non-specialists would benefit from the support offered by taking advantage of TDA funded CPD opportunities for experienced non-specialist teachers of mathematics. Such opportunities would enhance their personal knowledge and understanding of mathematics and develop their mathematics specific pedagogy. For senior teachers you need to be clear about involving them in decision making and ensuring they know what your expectations are for their work in mathematics. Invariably they are busy and highly experienced people. However, you are responsible for their work in mathematics. It may be that you will need to ask for support from other senior managers or external agencies such as the local authority.

Another way to add to the store of subject and pedagogic knowledge within your department is to work with people who are training to teach. If your team is not involved in supporting people who are training to teach at your local higher education institution, or through the SCITT or GTP schemes, you will probably find that investigating how you can get involved could re-invigorate your department. Working with beginning teachers is an investment in the future of the teaching profession and whilst the trainee teachers are likely to need a considerable amount of support, they will bring energy, enthusiasm and, probably, some new ideas. Training new teachers can provide opportunities for the teachers that they work with to reflect on their practice (perhaps asking, Why did I do that? Why do I do that?) and encourage them to articulate the rationale for their professional behaviours.

Beginning teachers also provide an opportunity for innovation. Do you want everyone in the team to begin to work with particular resources? The trainee teacher(s) could, with support, develop a unit of work using dynamic geometry or graphing calculators and work alongside each teacher in the team adapting the resources for their group of learners. Cultivating beginning teachers or supply teachers as team members will help when it comes to recruiting new team members. People who have worked as part of your team, albeit temporarily, are the best ambassadors for mathematics in your institution. Whilst it may be some time since you trained as a teacher, it is well worth recalling the challenges, frustrations and disappointments, in order that you can be realistic in your expectations and empathise with the considerable personal upheaval that becoming a teacher involves. As an established teacher, one of the most exciting and rewarding aspects of the job is that you never stop learning and there is always room for improvement and development.

As the subject leader for mathematics you are a middle manager with a responsibility for the quality of the mathematics education of every person in the school. As well as the day-to-day work with your team, you are accountable to the school's senior leadership. You need to be an ambassador for your team and an advocate for mathematics. You will influence decisions around the amount of money you have to spend on resources, the recruitment of new staff, the timetable for mathematics – when is mathematics taught and who is teaching it?, the environment in which you work – do you have a dedicated suite of rooms which include interactive whiteboards in every room and an ICT suite or trolley of laptops? If not, how can you go about securing such an environment in your school? It is surprising how much money can be found for things that the senior management team see as important.

You will also have a direct influence on how mathematics is perceived in the school. Do you contribute to whole school curriculum development initiatives? Is mathematics at the forefront of school liaison and transition arrangements? Is there a whole school approach to mathematics across the curriculum? For example in relation to the use of calculators, methods of calculation, conventions for mathematical diagrams such as bar charts and pie charts, techniques for manipulating equations, correct mathematical vocabulary, etc.

How do you position mathematics at the heart of the school curriculum?

Many teachers feel that they have insufficient time to adequately address all the content that is prescribed in the National Curriculum (1999, 2007) and the non-statutory framework for mathematics (SNS 1999, 2008). Just suppose that the senior management said, 'We are removing mathematics from the curriculum'. If mathematics is an essential part of every learner's entitlement – how would you ensure that mathematics is taught through other areas of the curriculum? How would you ensure that specialists in other areas understand sufficient mathematics that will enable learners to build secure mathematical foundations? What opportunities are there for developing mathematical understanding in Art & Design, Citizenship, Design &Technology, English, Geography, History, MFL, Music, PE, PSHE, RE, Science and in cross-curricular project based learning?

Although the above scenario is very unlikely to happen, it hopefully gave you a chance to consider some of the opportunities that exist within other subject areas that may be worth exploring. Given the perceived time pressures, how do you exploit opportunities across the curriculum and structure the scheme of work to minimise repetition, to bring aspects of mathematics together and to develop a secure understanding of mathematics through rich learning experiences?

Is mathematics essential to the curriculum because it is about developing problem solving skills and logical and critical thinking? There are many other subjects that would claim to do the same thing. How is mathematics different? By articulating what is special about mathematics and how it is distinct from

1. AN OPPORTUNITY TO INFLUENCE

other subjects you will help to ensure its rightful place at the heart of the curriculum. You might like to start with the importance statement from the new programmes of study for secondary mathematics which includes 'mathematical thinking as a habit of mind' and 'mathematics as a uniquely powerful way to describe, analyse and change the world'.

The new secondary curriculum has as overarching aims: successful learners, confident individuals and responsible citizens. Schools are challenged to consider how their curriculum (the entire planned learning experience) can be tailored to meet learners' individual needs, provide a coherent experience for each and every learner and exploit local resources and opportunities. Schools are asked to consider three key questions:

- What are we trying to achieve?
- How do we organise learning?
- How well are we achieving our aims?

The QCDA website includes a number of resources to support schools in 'disciplined innovation' using these three questions and a number of case studies from schools who have already begun to implement the new curriculum: *www.qcda.org.uk*.

The curriculum can be accessed in a number of different ways including personal learning and thinking skills, functional skills and through whole curriculum dimensions:

- Identity and cultural diversity
- Healthy lifestyles
- Community participation
- Enterprise
- Sustainable futures and the global dimension
- Technology and the media

The programme of study defines an entitlement of experience for all learners. Rather than labelling learners and restricting access, the richness of the entire programme of study needs to be made available to all. Whilst this may seem daunting, particularly if you are used to teaching level by level i.e. certain topics can't be introduced because the learner hasn't mastered 'the basics', it can also be liberating. How do you introduce Pythagoras' theorem in an accessible manner to all in KS3? How do you introduce notions of trigonometry* to all in KS4?

The programme of study for each subject is presented in the same way, which will support subjects in working together to plan compelling learning experiences.

---

* What is trigonometry about? I suggest is has to do with distances in circles.

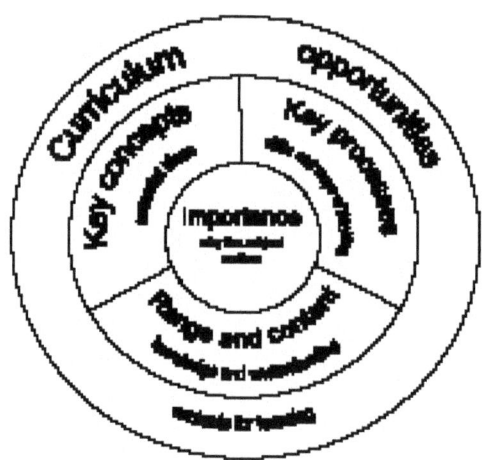

The mathematics importance statement in the new secondary curriculum (QCA, 2007) emphasises mathematics for the individual, for society and as part of our global identity and cultural heritage. The key concepts are the essential ideas that underpin the study of mathematics: competence, creativity, applications and implications of mathematics and critical understanding. They include the historical and cultural roots of mathematics, mathematical modelling, the personal construction of new mathematics and the use of mathematics in society. A significant shift in emphasis in the new curriculum is towards developing learners' process skills in mathematics – these include representing, analysing, interpreting, communicating and evaluating. They incorporate the functional skills and need to be developed alongside technical competence. In previous versions of the national curriculum considerable detail has been given about the content that is to be taught. This is not the case with the new curriculum where the content can be written on a side of A4 paper and is made up of broad 'overarching' statements. The content is described as the context through which the process skills are developed and the key concepts are to be experienced. For the first time in the National Curriculum there is an indication of how mathematics is to be taught through the curriculum opportunities:

- Develop confidence
- Range of tasks – open, closed, explore mathematics in depth, combine different aspects
- Range of contexts – different subjects, society issues, economic well being and financial capability
- Work collaboratively
- Familiarity with resources including ICT

Schools are being encouraged to 'not throw the baby out with the bathwater' but to begin by considering 'what are we trying to achieve?'. This discussion feeds into the development of a shared vision mentioned at the beginning of this chapter. By interrogating the opportunities of the new curriculum with an agenda in mind, it will be easier to identify priorities for 'disciplined innovation'. This means making changes which are compatible with your agenda and the new curriculum but which incorporate thorough evaluation of impact. There is considerable potential to collaborate with other subjects and to design learning experiences which are complementary rather than repetitive. Typically, topics in mathematics are visited regularly if not annually. If insufficient time is allowed for learners to develop genuine understanding and extend their knowledge at each visit the spiral curriculum becomes the circular curriculum with learners never having the opportunity to make progress as their previous failures are reinforced.

In some schools that have embarked on implementing the new curriculum, mathematics has chosen not to participate. Pupils who experience a stimulating curriculum elsewhere are likely to be less responsive if mathematics is 'the same as it ever was'. Mathematics needs to play a full part in curriculum development to ensure that opportunities to promote and enrich mathematics are fully exploited. Attitudes towards mathematics need careful cultivation if learners are to have high aspirations and the motivation to achieve them. A negative attitude can last a lifetime. A positive attitude provides the self confidence and motivation to keep going, however difficult the task might be.

How do you organise learning?

The environment within which mathematics is taught and the resources available to support teachers' endeavours are significant factors that influence learners' responses. An attractive, stable environment with clear routines is crucial to establishing a 'safe' climate for learning. A dedicated suite of rooms with one member of staff responsible for each room helps to ensure maintenance of good quality stimulating displays which make a positive contribution to learner engagement. I recall a secondary teacher explaining to me the benefits of display. One year he had an attractive display on co-ordinates in his classroom. He deliberately chose not to teach co-ordinates to any of his classes that year. Despite this, they were all very successful in the end of year assessments which included co-ordinates.

If learners are to be able to make informed choices about which resource to use, in which activity, it is crucial that they are introduced to a wide range of mathematical equipment and resources. This includes mathematical and generic software including (as a minimum) graph plotting, statistical presentation and analysis, dynamic geometry and Logo.

The most common arrangement for teaching mathematics is to set on the basis of prior attainment. Learners then have access to, what is considered, an appropriate mathematical diet. Typically this means that they do not have access to the entire programme of study and, for many, expectations are not sufficiently aspirational. Indeed a learner in a set for low attainers has little chance of 'escape' as they never experience and have the opportunity to learn 'harder' concepts. Learning does not happen in a linear fashion; some highly talented mathematicians admit to weaknesses with arithmetic. We all know pupils who are brilliant at some aspects of mathematics yet struggle with other areas. All learners need the opportunity to surprise their teachers and themselves with their capabilities.

How well are you achieving your aims?

As the leader for mathematics you will be held to account for the impact of the work of your team. This will be through performance management, the school's monitoring programme and Ofsted. You need to be an advocate for your team, confident of the quality and the commitment of the work of your colleagues to learners and mathematics. Do the learners and their parents/guardians/carers appreciate the work you do? Are they able to participate in and contribute to the development of mathematics in the school? Many primary schools have regular communication with their children's homes, informing them of the areas of mathematics that will be met that term, the methods children might be introduced to and ways in which parents/guardians/carers might help. Is it possible to introduce something similar at secondary?

Often the priority in school is on academic attainment – whilst high standards are important this shouldn't be at the expense of positive attitudes. An attitude is likely to last a lifetime and is very difficult to change. A positive attitude will enable learners to sustain their study of mathematics to achieve as highly as they can.

Sunset and sunrise

As we draw to a close of this first chapter I wish you well in your role as subject leader for mathematics. Your potential for day-to-day influence on the mathematics experience of every learner in your school is huge – use it well.

The subsequent chapters in this book will provide you with insight into important aspects of mathematics education that will enable you to become more effective in your role. You will be better able to support your colleagues in achieving their professional aspirations and enabling young people to develop as mathematicians.

The fact you are reading this book means you recognise the importance of your own professional development. If you have not done so already, I commend three things to you in order to support you in remembering just how worthwhile your role is:

- Join a professional subject association for mathematics and benefit from joining a community committed to making mathematics better for all learners.

- Enrol with the National Centre for Excellence in Teaching Mathematics (NCETM), the portal has a wealth of material to support you in your role and opportunities to participate in discussions with teachers and monitor your professional development.

- Complete some accredited further study in mathematics education e.g. a Masters' degree.

Further reading

Gates, P. (2001) *Issues in mathematics teaching*. London: Routledge Falmer.

Mason, J. and Johnston-Wilder, S. (2005) *Developing thinking in algebra*. London: Paul Chapman Publishing.

Noyes, A. (2007) *Rethinking School Mathematics*. London: Paul Chapman Publishing.

Ollerton, M. and Watson, A. (2001) *Inclusive Mathematics 11-18*. London: Continuum.

Johnston-Wilder, S. & Mason, J. (2005) *Developing thinking in geometry*. London: Sage Publications.

Graham, A. (2006) *Developing thinking in statistics*. London: Paul Chapman Publishing.

References

Boaler, J. (1997). *Experiencing School Mathematics: Teaching Styles, sex and setting*. Buckingham: Open University Press.

DfES (2000) *Framework for teaching mathematics KS3*. London: HMSO.

Skemp, R. (1971) *The Psychology of Learning Mathematics*. London: Penguin Books.

Watson, A. (2007) *Raising Achievement in Secondary Mathematics*. Maidenhead: Open University Press.

Wells, D.G. (1995) *You are a mathematician*. London: Penguin Books.

National Curriculum *www.qcda.org.uk/curriculum*

National Strategy *www.dcsf.gov.uk/standards/nationalstrategies*

2
MATHEMATICS – JOY AND RIGOUR

Barbara Jaworski

Why did you become a subject leader in mathematics? Why mathematics?
Why and in what ways is mathematics important to you?
What was it that brought you into mathematics in the first place?
How do you yourself feel about mathematics?

As a former subject leader in mathematics in a secondary school, and in many other roles that I have played in mathematics education since then, I have no doubt as to why I am in mathematics education, and it boils down to two words – *joy* and *rigour*. I enjoy engaging in mathematics; I like its beauty and elegance, I appreciate the challenge of a mathematical problem and particularly the feeling of success when I contribute to its resolution. I value the ways in which we can express ideas succinctly and precisely in mathematics and appreciate the importance of a clearly defined language, its associated rules and the necessity for proof. The feelings of joy in stimulation, challenge and success are allied to recognition of the centrality of rigour and its manifestations in definitions, forms of expression and styles of proof.

I am going to say more about what I mean by joy and rigour, but let me start by saying that if we can enable our pupils to experience the joy and value the rigour of mathematics then we are doing a good job as educators.

What is it that you enjoy about mathematics? Do you know what teachers in your department enjoy about mathematics?

The authors of the Cockcroft report, produced in 1982, revolutionary in its time and still relevant in many respects today, wrote "Mathematics is a difficult subject both to teach and to learn" (para 228, p.67). Wide experience in learning mathematics and in working with learners of mathematics supports the statement that mathematics is found difficult by many pupils. This is fine – playing the piano is difficult, making a successful soufflé is difficult, building bridges that do not fall down is difficult. Many things that are worth doing are difficult but this does not mean we cannot enjoy the challenge and the engagement, and indeed our success in achievement. Mathematics is also difficult to teach. The challenge here is not *just* to present mathematics to learners in a way that is clear and easy to understand (where often the teacher is the one doing all the work), but really to *seek out the essence* of what we are trying to teach and to bring all our powers of motivational analysis to constructing a classroom environment that maximizes opportunity for pupils also to appreciate this essence. Most of the rest of this chapter is about what I understand this to mean.

In 2003, the Swedish National Agency for Education presented a report called *The Joy to Learn – Focus on Mathematics*.[1] One important finding in their report was that many pupils in Swedish schools experience mathematics as boring, and not challenging or joyful – probably not so different from many pupils in UK classrooms. In a study of disaffection in secondary mathematics classrooms in the UK, Elena Nardi and Susan Steward found that pupils on whom the study focused "apparently engage with mathematical tasks in the classroom mostly out of a sense of professional obligation and under parental pressure. They seem to have a minimal appreciation and gain little joy out of this engagement". Nardi and Steward go on to say,

> Most pupils we observed and interviewed view mathematics as a tedious and irrelevant body of isolated, non-transferable skills, the learning of which offers little opportunity for activity. In addition to this perceived irrelevance, and in line with previous research that attributes pupil alienation from mathematics to its abstract and symbolic nature, pupils often found the use of symbolism alienating. (Nardi & Steward, 2003, p. 361. Emphasis in original.)

These authors point also to the school experience of the pupils they studied. Pupils resented what they perceived as *rote learning* activity, *rule-and-cue* following, and some saw mathematics as an "elitist subject that exposes the weakness of the intelligence of any individual who engages with it." Other researchers in the UK have looked closely at pupils' experience in the classroom and talk about underachievement in mathematics in relation to, for example, the effects of *setting* on pupils' opportunity and performance; to ethnic and social groups who have difficulty with school expectations, particularly in terms of language; to the kinds of tasks and activity presented in classrooms and the emphasis on testing (e.g. Boaler, 1997; Houssart, 2004; Lee, 2006; Watson, 2006). Thus we see pupils who are alienated due to the intrinsic nature of mathematics and pupils who underachieve in mathematics because of the practices and social norms within schools where they are taught.

If we focus on the need to share joy in mathematics as a solution, the question arises – what is needed for teachers to be able to awaken the 'joy to learn mathematics' in their pupils? I would claim that the answer lies, first and foremost, in how we, as educators, think of and promote mathematics itself. What areas of mathematics do we like and appreciate? Which ones stimulate us and give us pleasure? For example, we might think of the golden section, aspects of fractal geometry, ideas of infinity, algebraic conciseness in expressing an idea, a dissection proof for Pythagoras theorem, symmetry… Whatever it is that brings us personally to appreciation of mathematics, we need to exercise some of the passion from our own joy of mathematics in creating learning opportunities for our pupils.

Now for my second key word: *rigour*. The Cockcroft report, again, said "Mathematics provides a means of communication which is powerful, concise and unambiguous" (para 3, p. 1). The reason why mathematics is powerful, concise and unambiguous is to do with its logical consistency, its means of

---

[1]. See Straesser, Brandell, Grevholm, & Helenius (2004).

expressing generality and its use of abstraction to capture the essence of ideas. It uses elegant forms of expression to capture complex relationships and succinct pieces of logic to prove complicated propositions. G. H. Hardy is reported as saying "A mathematician, like a painter or a poet, is a master of pattern" (Davis & Hersh, 1981, p. 173). Recognition of pattern, expression of generality in pattern and abstraction from pattern are essential to being mathematical and doing mathematics. Rigour lies in the expression of generality and what is allowable as proof. Logical consistency demands rules, and rules have to be applied according to agreed systems of logic. Understanding and gaining fluency with rules is both central to mathematical success and part of what makes mathematics difficult to learn. Reducing mathematics to the rules, however, leaves the subject bereft of meaning, joy or passion. People who find mathematics hard and boring might do so because all they see is the rules: the rules lack connection to the exciting ideas for which they are invented, and tedious exercises to practice disembodied rules can be mind-numbing. However, practicing the rules, like arpeggios, is essential to bringing out the beauty of the music. So a central challenge for teaching mathematics is how to embody the rules of mathematical engagement in a way that is exciting and challenging and joyful.

A classroom story[2]

Look at Figure 1 here.

What is it?

What shape is it?

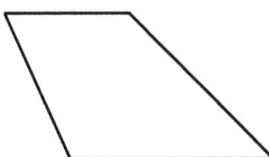

Figure 1: The teacher's drawing

What would be your reaction to someone who said it was a square?

A class of 12 year olds had been asked by their teacher to name the above shape, which he had drawn on the board. Someone said that it was a trapezium. Some pupils agreed with this, others disagreed.

The teacher said, 'If you think it's not a trapezium then what is it?' One boy said, tentatively, 'It's a square…'.

There were murmurings, giggles, 'a square?!'. But the boy went on '…sort of flat.'

The teacher looked puzzled, as if he could not see a square either. He invited the boy to come out to the board and explain his square. The boy did. He indicated that you had to be looking down on the square – as if it were on your book, only tilted. He moved his hand to illustrate.

'Oh' said the teacher. 'Oh, I think I see what you mean…does anyone else

---

[2]. Jaworski, 1988, pp. 287/8.

see what he means?' There were more murmurings, puzzled looks, tentative nods.

The teacher drew onto the shape, modifying it to produce Figure 2 below.

There were responses of oooooh yes (!) and nods around the class.

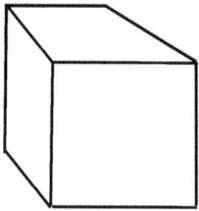

Figure 2: The revised drawing

What started out potentially as a right/wrong answer – trapezium or not trapezium – turned into an opportunity for the class to extend its visions of two dimensional space. Seeing the apparent two-dimensional figure in three-dimensions opened up other correct answers to the original question. The teacher, at first not seeing what the boy was getting at, nevertheless provided opportunity for explanation. The boy was encouraged to explain, possibly motivated and made to feel good about his contribution, and the class was encouraged to respect and value what was offered. Mathematically, perceptions of relations in shape and space were extended for this class as well perhaps as a shift from expectations of simple right/wrong answers. The teacher's intervention opened up the situation for the pupils, engaging their curiosity and offering challenge.

Curiosity and challenge

Have you noticed, when you travel, how many fellow travellers are engaging with puzzles of some sort? Whether crosswords, Sudoku, or other kinds of puzzles in puzzle books, there seems to be avid engagement in puzzling. It seems that we like to puzzle things out. For as long as I can remember, *The Guardian* on Saturdays has offered Chris Maslanka's puzzle corner, and one of the things I have liked about it is that some explanation is usually provided. Often a puzzle has a mathematical solution and I feel inordinately pleased if I have worked it out! The author has engaged my curiosity and offered me a challenge. I feel pleasure, joy in my success. How can I, as a teacher, bring the experience of such joy to pupils' engagement in mathematics in the classroom?

I remember observing a lesson in which the class of 12 year olds was invited to engage with a problem ostensibly about penning sheep. A farmer had 36 panels of fencing, each of length 1 m. to fashion a sheep pen in a field against a wall. What was the largest area of grass he could fence in? Most groups agreed that the best case was a pen of 9m by 18m. So then the teacher said, "Oh dear, before building the fence, one panel was destroyed by rain and wind. So in the end he had only 35 panels. What should he do then?" Two groups in the class were having an argument. One group said the best pen would be 9m by 17m. The other said there was a better answer, if you had 8.75m by 17.5m. The first group objected: "you can't have 8.75 of a panel"!! The teacher opened up a discussion: "what do the answers mean"? Pupils had the opportunity to contrast the mathematical with the practical: the latter giving the bigger area, the former providing a more workable solution. As pupils left the room at the end of the lesson, one said to the teacher, "That was brilliant miss!"

In this classroom activity, groups had worked on 'puzzling' in a mathematical problem related to a context in which their curiosity was engaged. Pupils had puzzled out their own solution and then defended it in the light of challenge from their peers. Their engagement was evident in their bright faces, excited voices and wide participation. It seemed here that for one group, the mathematical solution was what mattered, never mind the sheep. For the other group, the practical situation was what the problem was about. The difference in viewpoint, and each group's commitment to their own solution, gave the teacher an opportunity to encourage debate and point to the factors involved in different solutions.

In Table 1 below, I have related curiosity and challenge to joy and rigour as I see them.

	Joy	Rigour
Curiosity	Through having my curiosity stimulated, I experience joy in my motivation to engage. My curiosity leads me into the problem and fires my dealing with challenge. Curiosity is itself a powerful stimulant.	Curiosity provides an incentive to engage with the mathematics and make sense of the rigour needed to engage successfully. Because I see a need for the rigour, I do not turn away from it.
Challenge	Challenging me in *productive* ways – i.e., I can engage with the challenge and need to put my mental (and maybe social) skills into the task – gives me joy in worthwhile and possibly productive engagement and outcome.	Rigour is challenging. I need some real motivation to engage with the challenge of rigour and this can come from the joy that I experience from engagement and the desire for success that motivate dealing with rigour.

Table 1: Joy, Rigour, Curiosity and Challenge

One of the reviewers of this chapter responded as follows to the ideas above "I started to think about 'time' here. That allowing pupils to be curious and challenged may need time when they are apparently doing nothing because they are thinking or trying things out. The joy comes from spending that time and succeeding in meeting the challenge. Therefore it is time well spent, time when pupils 'grow mathematically.' This then links to your discussions of time later on".

The practical and the mathematical both in their own ways stimulate curiosity and offer challenge. Ultimately, it does not matter from which source the challenge and stimulus come, so long as the result is deeper, more serious engagement with mathematics involving joy and rigour. We get, here, into a meta-level of consideration – beyond the usual concerns of the teacher in planning for a lesson. This is why this discussion is especially important for the subject leader. When the SL appreciates the more general principles behind activity and links this to particularities of designing activity for classrooms, the result can be especially fruitful for mathematics within a school. I shall return to these ideas a bit later.

Mathematics 'versus' the real world

In *penning sheep*, we saw a task set in a (perhaps pseudo) real world context. The context there might be seen to have been fruitful in generating mathematical discussion. However, real world contexts do not always prove to be fruitful in generating *mathematical* thinking. A difference in perception – mathematics versus real world – is sometimes at the heart of issues in or about learning mathematics. In 1979 Margaret Brown (1979, p. 362) reported from research into 11-12 year old children's solutions to problems involving number operations. One question asked:

> A gardener has 391 daffodils. These are to be planted in 23 flowerbeds. Each flowerbed is to have the same number of daffodils. How do you work out how many daffodils will be planted in each flowerbed?

The following interview took place between a pupil YG and the interviewer MB:

YG You er... I know what to do but I can't say it...

MB Yes, well you do it then. Can you do it?

YG Those are daffodils and these are flowerbeds, large you see... Oh! They're being planted in different flowerbeds, you'd have to put them in groups...

MB Yes, how many would you have in each group? What would you do with 23 and 391, if you had to find out?

YG See if I had them, I'd count them up... say I had 20 of each... I'd put 20 in that one, 20 in that one...

MB Suppose you had some left over at the end when you've got to 23 flowerbeds?

YG I'd plant them in a pot (!!)

It seems clear that for YG the practical situation was predominant in his or her thinking and the strategy offered was quite reasonable in practical terms. Mathematically we might be looking for something different – for example $391 \div 23$, from which the answer is 17. It is important to recognize that this answer is to the mathematical question $391 \div 23$, not necessarily to the question asked above. In fact a mathematical modelling operation has to be undertaken to fit these two together. Often however, such an operation is treated implicitly as if the two situations are isomorphic. Offering the daffodil question in a classroom could open up opportunity for different solutions to emerge, so that issues like this could be discussed with the pupils. Otherwise, how can pupils become aware of relationships between the mathematical and the practical, the real world and the world of mathematics?

Barry Cooper and Máiréad Dunne report a striking outcome from their research into children's solutions to questions in the national mathematics tests: that is that children from working-class families do less well on average than children from middle-class families on items that involve everyday situations. They report on an item in an SCAA test in 1994. We see a copy of the item in the figure below.

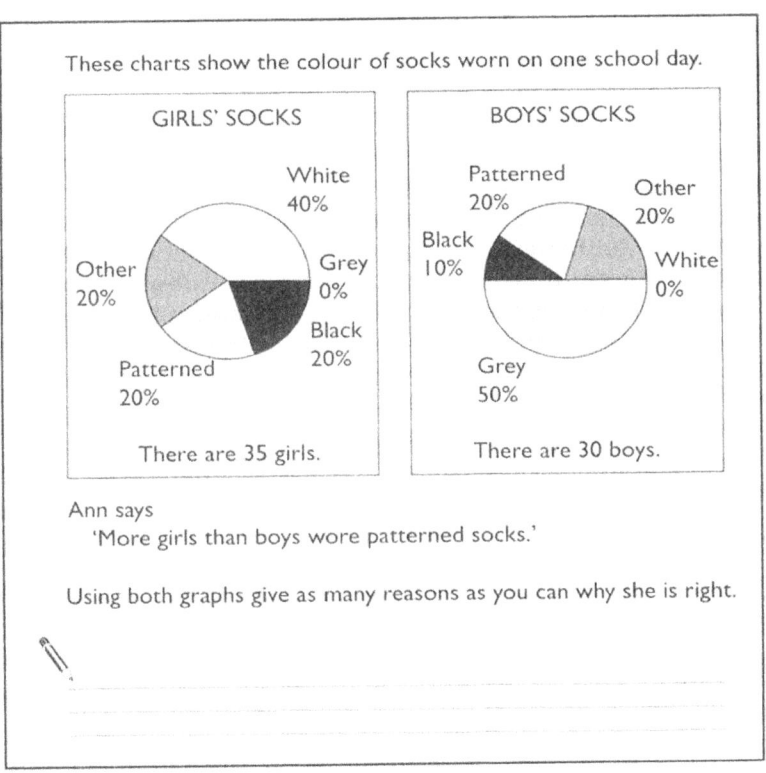

Figure 4.1 The socks item: interpreting statistical diagrams (SCAA 1994)

Cooper and Dunne report from responses of two children, Diane and Mike ("a girl of high measured 'ability' from a professional middle-class background and a boy of average measured 'ability' from a working-class background", p. 43), to the question above. Although Diane considers the practicalities involved, she is able to cut through the everyday context and perceive that the required answer is that Ann is right "because although it's the same proportion, there are more girls" (p.47). Mike "fails to avoid this trap" (p. 47). I quote here from the interview with Mike in which he starts by reading the text of the test item.

Mike These charts show the colour of socks worn on one school day. [pause] That says that they, the girls, wore more patterned socks than the boys, but it says they both, they both had the same [sounding puzzled].

BC So, what do you think then? What do you want to say? [pause]

Mike Is it – I think, really, boys just wear, like, plain old sporty socks, white socks – unless they're, like, teachers' pets – with the socks up here, and things – socks all the way up to their knees. [pointing to his knees during this] But the girls, the girls seem to have more pattern on their socks – they're white and they've got patterns on all of them. The boys just have plain old sporty things with something like sport written down them. Not much of a pattern.

BC So you want – you don't agree with that then?

Mike No.

BC OK, What about this bit here? [Interviewer points to the 35/30 statements.] There are 35 girls. There are 30 boys. Does that make a difference?

Mike It might do [pause] in one way. Or another. But [pause] I mean, really, you've got five more girls that boys and, like, they're just going for it.

I have chosen this as an example, not to suggest that Mike's responses are typical of working-class children, but to exemplify the kind of response that is possible to such a question. How might a teacher deal with such a response? If the nature of the question draws a child into a practical situation which obscures the mathematical answer that is sought, how reasonable are the expectations that a child will give the mathematical answer?

If we want children to think mathematically in practical situations what can we do as teachers to prepare them to see the mathematics and perceive the question being asked?

Narratives

Above, I have offered narratives, stories from different sources – two from my own experience, two from the literature. I will refer to them respectively as "it's a square", "penning sheep", "daffodils" and "socks". Each narrative captures for me certain aspects of the classroom mathematical milieu that relates to the issue I highlighted above: *a central challenge for teaching mathematics is how to embody the rules in mathematical engagement* (rigour) *in a way that is exciting and challenging and joyful*.

Joy might come from a number of sources including pleasure in thinking and engagement with others and the challenge of argument and also the pleasure in engaging with mathematical concepts and seeing inside relationships. The four narratives seem to afford opportunity to notice aspects of these. Rigour lies in the relating of concepts and clear delineation in definition and argument. I challenged myself to try to say what aspects of joy and rigour I find encapsulated in these narratives – why are they important enough to include in this book?

In "It's a square", I see the teacher taking the opportunity, when it arises, to *open up* mathematics. In one stroke, he values the thinking of one pupil, encourages a respectful and collaborative ethos in his classroom and enables attention to, perhaps otherwise unconsidered, mathematical relationships. On the one hand, it is important for pupils to recognize particular geometrical figures, like a trapezium, and distinguish them from other figures, such as squares or parallelograms. This is delineation: mathematical thinking requires clear mathematical arguments for how a trapezium is different from a square – what are the properties that distinguish? This is going beyond visual perceptions and recognition to property articulation and definition – the rigour. However, a rehearsal or noting down of properties and definitions might not occasion much joy. The visual perception in seeing how the apparent trapezium (two dimensions) could be seen as a square (in three dimensions) affords a moment of joy – the rising "oooooh yes!" of the pupils' response. Such new perceptions open up new possibilities – ultimately perhaps an entry to different geometries such as projective geometry.

Of course, this narrative is only the beginning; there are many questions to follow. How would I follow up this situation if it happened in my class? What are our goals as teachers, with respect to our pupils, to the curriculum, to assessment scores and so on? How can we work in ways that foster serendipitous moments while ensuring pupils work on the rigour of mathematical concepts? How can we use class time most fruitfully in relation to all our objectives? I come back to these questions later in the chapter.

In the sheep penning narrative, I see a deep tackling of rigour alongside joyful engagement in mathematical argument that relates concepts and real world issues. The problem, which appears in many text books in this or some other form, is designed to address different combinations of factors of a number and relate these to area and perimeter of plane shapes. Its contextualization in penning sheep introduces a (pseudo) real world situation to enable thinking about the mathematical concepts. Here, we see some pupils engaging with the mathematics – perhaps forgetting the sheep – and others analyzing their possible results in terms of the situation in which the problem was posed. Both seem important, and the argument that ensued took the pupils deeply into mathematical properties (the rigour) and their relation to a real world situation. I saw the pupil's words, "That was brilliant miss", to capture his pleasure in the argument which I would like to think captured also some enjoyment in mathematical understanding that was secure enough to allow the depth of argument. We might also see opportunities here for opening up ideas of mathematical modelling and the difference between a pure mathematical solution and one that fits a given real world situation.

Issues relating to a real world situation and its relation to mathematical concepts can be seen in both *daffodils* and *socks*. It seems that YG in *daffodils* and Mike in *socks* were both caught up in the real world context to which the problem refers. The exclamation marks at the end of the quoted dialogue in *daffodils* perhaps recognizes that the pupil's answer was not what the interviewer was expecting or hoping for. It was not a mathematical answer. But perhaps many humans in the situation described would do what YG suggested – *put them in a pot*. How is YG to know that the problem is not actually about daffodils? Similarly, for Mike, in the socks problem; he seems to have trouble separating the mathematical question from everyday issues to do with choice of socks. Could those setting this question have anticipated such a response? Given the research of Cooper and Dunne, those in a responsible position for setting such questions should now perhaps be more aware of how the problem might appear for some pupils, rather than seeing it just from their own point of view.

There seem to be two sides to the issue. A goal of these problems can be seen to be to situate mathematics in some recognizable everyday context, so that the context might help pupils to understand what is required mathematically. However, for some pupils, the context is powerfully dominant, with mathematics taking a second place, leaving them little opportunity for mathematising the situation. I have been in many classrooms where well meaning tasks, situating mathematics in a context familiar to pupils, have resulted in activity that was only peripherally mathematical. In many cases, pupils were having a good time talking through the issues in the everyday situation, perhaps tackling meaningful and important social issues, but not really doing mathematics. Thus the situation provided fun in social terms, but the fun was not mathematically related and little rigour was evident. This, I think, contrasts with the fun and rigour in *penning sheep*.

Questions for a teacher

The questions I asked earlier are relevant for all teachers and especially for subject leaders who have a responsibility for the kind of mathematical ethos generated in classrooms in a school. I think therefore, that the questions are worth repeating.

- How would I follow up this situation (it's a square) if it happened in my class?
- What are our goals as teachers, with respect to our pupils, to the curriculum, to assessment scores and so on?
- How can we work in ways that foster serendipitous moments while ensuring pupils work on the rigour of mathematical concepts?
- How can we use class time most fruitfully in relation to all our objectives?

How would I follow up this situation (it's a square) if it happened in my class?

Of course, there are many ways of responding to a pupil who gives a surprising comment or answer. One thing I have learned to do is pause. Pausing allows thinking time for the teacher, and perhaps allows pupils also to think. Pausing allows the teacher to show that mathematics requires thinking about while a quick and ready answer might foster a belief that quick and ready answers are the norm in mathematics. Pausing allows me to consider alternative forms of action to the one which might seem most natural.

One of the problems in mathematics is the perception that questions have right or wrong answers and there is nothing in between. The answer "trapezium" is one right answer, but not the only one. For it to be the only one, the questioner would have had to be much more precise about what was required: e.g. "given a two-dimensional shape with just two sides parallel...". Definitions of plane shapes require such precise language, and pupils need to be able to appreciate such definitions and the constraints they impose on what is possible. Such awareness rules out the possibility of different interpretations. Perhaps a teacher can lead discussion in the classroom to distinguish such cases. We might see the opportunity presented here to afford discussion of the rigour of definition versus the perception of alternative perspectives.

What are our goals as teachers, with respect to our pupils, to the curriculum, to assessment scores and so on?
Teachers are under enormous pressure to conform to the curriculum, the strategy, the tests and the examinations. We owe it to our pupils to ensure they have the very best opportunity to achieve in all the different kinds of assessment with which they are faced. It is not surprising therefore if sometimes teachers lose sight of what brought them to mathematics in the first place. Perhaps their own joy in mathematics has abated over the years. Perhaps they would like more time to take diversions from the strict day to day following of routines and rules. Perhaps there is some wish that circumstances could be different; a recognition that the status quo is not conducive to teaching mathematics as they dream might be possible. However, perhaps again, it is too hard to go against imposed norms, whether they come from external forces or are part of socio-historical ways of being in school.

I took part in a research project recently in which mathematics educators from a university worked with teachers from a range of schools (lower primary to upper secondary) to develop mathematics teaching and learning in classrooms.[3] In workshops, we engaged in mathematics together through a variety of mathematical problems designed to provide an interesting and challenging environment for doing mathematics – an *investigative* ethos.[4] One upper secondary teacher spoke vehemently against the possibility of using such problems in his teaching. He claimed that the syllabus was too demanding, and there was just not enough time for investigative problems. Yet he acknowledged the *fun* of engaging with these problems in the workshops. A suggestion was that the investigative problems had no place in the regular syllabus-directed teaching; they would need extra time, time that was not available.

So, incorporating *fun* into teaching needs extra time? Certainly I would question this, since I have seen many teachers offer tasks in ways that engage pupils in mathematically challenging activities from which they gain enjoyment. Enjoyment comes from being drawn into the mathematics along with their peers and, although challenged, feeling accessibility and possibility for success. The challenges need to be seen by pupils as relating to the mainstream syllabus and of relevance to tests and examinations – not 'extras'

---

3. See Bjuland & Jaworski (2009) for an account of this project and some of the issues it generated for teachers.
4. See Jaworski (1994) for a study of an investigative approach to teaching mathematics.

designed for social amelioration. Pupils are quick to see though the latter. So, the seeking-out or design of syllabus-related tasks might be seen as a crucial factor along with thoughtful response to pupils' questions and suggestions.[5]

How can we work in ways that foster serendipitous moments while ensuring pupils work on the rigour of mathematical concepts?
By serendipitous moments, I mean moments that arrive 'out of the blue' that offer opportunity to work on mathematical ideas in a fruitful, perhaps novel context that brings relevance to the mathematics. This context can be a mathematical context as well as an everyday context. In 'It's a square' above, we saw a pupil relating a mathematical context to the real world in terms of his own exercise book. The combination, seized on by the teacher, allowed further development of a mathematical idea. In "penning sheep", the argument that arose between two groups allowed the teacher to get pupils to examine their solution critically and develop their judgement on the suitability of a mathematical solution to the context to which it relates, mathematical or real world.

There seem to be two possibilities to address – one is planning for the serendipitous moments, and the other is seizing them when they arise. In the second case, *seizing the moment* is first a case of recognition: recognizing that there is a moment to be seized and being prepared to go with it, perhaps to abandon the carefully prepared tasks for a lesson. Recognition is something to cultivate. John Mason (e.g., 2002) talks about "noticing in the moment": when we are sufficiently aware of a concept or issue, we notice it when it arises and the noticing gives us the opportunity to act differently. This is where the pause is valuable: it allows us to register the noticing, and make a quick decision as to how to move on. It allows us to avoid always taking the well worn path, and only thinking afterwards what else might have been possible.

However, experience helps too. A teacher, planning a task for his lesson, said to me that he would offer the task in a particular way, expecting that pupils would ask a certain question – because in his experience, pupils always did ask that question. The question gave him opportunity to draw pupils' attention to mathematical choices in working on the task. True to his expectations, as I observed in the classroom, pupils did ask the question and the desired discussion took place.[6] Responding to serendipitous moments, seizing the moment, can lead to possibility to create such moments in the future.

Regarding rigour; seizing the moment can lead to an interlude in what has been planned. The interlude may, or may not, provide opportunities to emphasise rigour. However, when experience from seizing the moment leads to pre-planning on a future occasion, the 'what is planned' around the moment can certainly have a rigorous foundation. When the serendipitous moment can be re-created in the future, it provides opportunity for rigour to be built in at an appropriate point.

---

5. The *Journal of Mathematics Teacher Education* published a special issue on design of tasks and issues relating to their purpose and use in classrooms (JMTE, 2007, Volume 10, issues 4/5/6).
6. For details see Jaworski, 1994, pp. 146-7.

How can we use class time most fruitfully in relation to all our objectives?
This is not an easy question to answer. I believe it means challenging pupils to engage with mathematics so that they experience both joy and rigour. How we do this is something for every teacher and every department to work at in a serious way. Quite some years ago, Richard Skemp distinguished two kinds of mathematical understanding – relational and instrumental. He writes:

> By the former (relational) is meant what I … have always meant by understanding: knowing both what to do and why. Instrumental understanding I would until recently not have regarded as understanding at all. It is what I have in the past described as 'rules without reasons', without realizing that for many pupils and their teachers the possession of such a rule, and ability to use it, is what they mean by 'understanding'. (Skemp 1989, p.2)

Instrumental understanding enables pupils to do what is asked in the short term, and is very specifically focused. Outside the very local conditions of the particular understanding, pupils may be unable to apply or sometimes even recall what they have understood. Some times instrumental understanding is referred to as rote or *procedural* learning.[7] On the other hand relational understanding involves a conceptual appreciation of what is involved in and underpins the particularities addressed. This allows the learner to relate ideas within and across topics and apply them in different contexts and circumstances. Relational understanding is often linked to conceptual learning. It seems to me that to experience joy and appreciate rigour in mathematics learners need to experience some degree of relational understanding and conceptual learning. Just knowing what to do in certain circumstances can be frustrating and limiting. Many pupils see through this, and realise they are being denied what really matters. Often they put this down to their own deficiencies because this is how it is often presented – putting pupils in 'lower' sets if they cannot manage what is demanded in the 'higher' sets, for example. Clare Lee (2006, p. 6), reporting on research in which she focused on developing pupils' use of mathematical language, wrote:

> Many pupils come to the classroom with the idea that they have a predetermined and fixed level of ability. In mathematics they are often worried that this level is low. [This] may have been reinforced by 'setting' or 'grouping' procedures in schools, but in other ways as well. The approaches that I am advocating depend on the idea that everyone can become better able to use mathematical ideas by addressing the particular difficulties in learning that they have. This may be a new idea to the pupils. If in the past a pupil had tried but failed to learn mathematics, it is unsurprising if he or she gives up trying. In these circumstances the choice for pupils may seem to be between appearing to be lazy and not trying, or trying and giving the impression of being stupid. It seems, on balance, to be a sensible decision when pupils decide they would rather be thought lazy than stupid.

---

7. See for example Brown, 1979 p. 354.

If what pupils see as a result of their school mathematical experience is that their choice is between seeming lazy or stupid, then we are certainly failing them.

So, what is a teacher to do?

There is no prescription, but I offer some thoughts on how I have tried to tackle the issue.

I ask, what is the mathematics I have to teach (according to the curriculum)? I try to go beyond the textbook presentation to really try to analyse what are the central concepts (the essence), and particularly where pupils might have difficulty. Of course, sometimes I have to work hard at the mathematics myself, to ensure I understand it.[8]

- I look at how others have addressed these concepts – the textbook author, other writers, what I can find on the web. I think about what I need in order to understand and ways in which this mathematics excites or stimulates me. I look for interesting problems that can engage and challenge pupils. I think about possible questions or prompts I might use to get pupils thinking.[9]

- I try to think of my pupils and how they might respond – which ones will need more help, support, challenge? Any class, even in a system with finely divided sets, is mixed ability: I ask how I can respond to different learning needs and preferred approaches to learning.

- I devise a set of tasks resulting from my own thinking and analysis and drawing on the various resources I have used. I bring these to the classroom and use my own energy and personality in presenting them in an interesting and challenging way that stimulates pupils to engage.

- In the classroom I try to encourage collaborative working between pupils, support and respect for each other, and a classroom ethos of serious mathematical engagement, dealing with challenge together and providing support relevant to the needs.

- I reflect on outcomes related to pupils' engagement and understanding, and whether I need to modify tasks for further use or organise activity differently another time.

Of course, all of this is VERY demanding of the teacher. As teachers we too need support and challenge. The subject leader therefore has a very important role to play in encouraging and stimulating teachers of mathematics within a school.

In what ways can a subject leader approach this task?

---

8. Some years ago the Centre for Mathematics Education at the Open University produced a series of booklets for teachers who wanted to update their own mathematics. These are still relevant today. The Project Update site provides free access to these materials. *http://labspace.open. ac.uk/course/view.php?id=4780*
9. See Watson and Mason, 1998.

Inquiry in mathematics, learning and teaching

Before fully discussing inquiry I will start by coming back to joy and rigour. I assume that even those teachers who have become disillusioned over the years once experienced the joy and appreciated the rigour of mathematics. How is it possible to re-awaken this where necessary? Perhaps there are newer teachers in a school who are still excited and motivated who can be brought into the creating of an ethos of joy and rigour within a mathematics department. It seems to me that a collaborative, inclusive approach has most chance of success. And a key word or concept that I personally recommend is "inquiry".

Inquiry means to ask questions and seek answers; to recognise problems and seek solutions; to wonder, imagine, invent and explore. It can mean these things for ourselves as teachers in designing activity for the classroom and reflecting critically on the outcomes. It can mean these things also for our pupils as they engage with mathematics. A book that I find exceptionally valuable, written by Stephanie Prestage and Pat Perks (2001), is called *Adapting and Extending Secondary Mathematics Activities: New tasks for old*. In it, Prestage and Perks look at traditional tasks such as one finds in a text book, and suggest an alternative slant on the task so that it offers pupils something to think about or explore; engaging pupil in mathematical inquiry. An example is:

> Pythagoras Theorem
> What right angled triangles can you find with an hypotenuse of 17cm?
> (Page 25)

The authors make the point that such a task is different from traditional exercises which ask more direct questions with single right or wrong answers. They write:

> Solving the problem requires the algorithm to be used many times as a pupil makes decisions about the number and types of solutions. This is better than a worksheet any day, and requires little preparation. (Prestage and Perks, 2001, p. 25)

In my experience, when pupils engage with such tasks they experience joy in their engagement, as in penning sheep, and mathematics becomes more *real*, more accessible, something they believe they can engage with and have success. And this is also related to rigour: pupils start to see why it is important to do things in certain ways; they recognise inter-relationships between mathematical topics and gain insights to justification and proving.

I mentioned above "reflecting critically on the outcomes". This is an essential part of the inquiry process. We need to keep in mind what we are trying to achieve and review critically what we seem to have achieved. How have pupils engaged with the tasks we offered them? Mathematically speaking, are they able to do the mathematics involved? For example, can they apply Pythagoras' theorem suitably in finding lengths in triangles? Can they solve a quadratic equation? Can they work with the unitary method in ratio problems? Can they find the reflected image of a shape when the mirror line is not horizontal or vertical? And what about deeper levels of understanding: do pupils engage with the mathematical concepts that underlie what they are doing? To what extent? And how do we know? I am thinking here of Skemp's two kinds of understanding. To what extent are pupils developing relational understanding of the mathematics with which they engage in the classroom?

Reflecting critically leads to 'metaknowing' (Wells, 1999). *Meta*knowing is knowing about knowing, being more aware of what we know and what we need to know, and conscious of issues or tensions in our activity. Sometimes, issues and tension arise because we cannot achieve what we want to achieve due to the system within which we operate; the school system, the educational system, the social system more widely which includes parents and youth culture. Ways of doing and being within a school can be both empowering and constraining; the curriculum and examination structures which are often externally imposed can also constrain what is possible – or perhaps seem to do so. Parents can be both supportive and critically demanding. Youth culture influences how young people see themselves and what therefore they are prepared to do and engage with. Such factors and their associated empowerment/constraint affect all teachers within a system, although some may see it differently from others. It seems therefore worthwhile for teachers together to explore what is possible, how to engage in ways that seem fruitful while coping with or circumventing the constraints. This suggests having some *collaborative inquiry* in which teachers support each other in thinking about innovative ways of working with pupils and in reflecting on outcomes.

The NCETM (National Centre for Excellence in Teaching Mathematics) supports teachers in engaging in inquiry or small-scale research in classrooms. For example, a project with which I am currently involved includes 4 schools in which teachers are exploring how to challenge young people to be enthusiastic about mathematics in the GCSE-A Level interface. These teachers are each devising an innovative programme for a selected group of pupils and exploring the outcomes for the pupils involved and in terms of those going on to A Level mathematics and further mathematical studies.[10] As the teachers and the university team talk with each other about what is happening in the schools, what is planned and the outcomes that are being experienced, we intrinsically address joy and rigour. There is joy in the way the teachers express themselves about mathematics and their pupils, and their critical reflection addresses ways in which innovation is achieving its aims with respect to mathematical learning outcomes in which rigour is fundamental.

A key element here is collaboration across schools and between teachers and university academics. Together we bring diverse knowledge and expertise to the project. Such diversity is valuable in providing expertise and experience to deal with the different facets of the project. Teachers are the experts in their school environments, and in working with current systems in education. The university academics bring knowledge about doing research and of the wider educational literature that can inform practice. By discussing and reflecting together, each one can develop understanding of issues and we can support each other in seeking resolution. Undertaking inquiry within such a

---

10. Further information can be obtained from the director of the project Dr Rod Bond at Loughborough University: R.M.Bond@lboro.ac.uk

supportive structure both motivates and helps sustain development. When several teachers within one school are involved, shared understandings of school practice and expectations and individual ideas for innovative practice, together with input and encouragement from university colleagues, can lead both to enhancements in thinking and practice and a strength to deal with issues. The initiative for such activity has to come from somewhere, and the subject leader is one obvious source.

What is needed to make this possible? Perhaps a first step is for the subject leader to start to engage personally in inquiry into learning and teaching and encourage pupils to inquire in mathematics in the classroom. In meetings with other mathematics teachers, opportunity can be taken to introduce some anecdote from the classroom to stimulate discussion. An inquiry task can be introduced for discussion between teachers. A short article, perhaps from the NCETM website,[11] or from a journal like *Mathematics Teaching*, or *Mathematics in Schools*, can be read and discussed between teachers. The subject leader might contact an academic in mathematics education at the local university or college teacher education programme to come and discuss possibilities for development. It seems essential for the subject leader to want to promote a positive environment for teaching and learning mathematics in the school; an environment in which both teachers and pupils express joy in mathematics and in which the rigour of mathematics is centrally addressed.

So joy and rigour, curiosity and challenge; how can these concepts start to be part of the ethos of a mathematics department? When I was head of mathematics in a secondary school, I persuaded my colleagues to join with me occasionally in a problem-solving session – sometimes in school, sometimes out of school in a more social environment. One or more of us found some interesting problem or problems to work on, and inevitably our joint engagement led to questions, discussion, sometimes to argument, usually to new insights, and overall to pleasure in mathematical engagement. Like the teachers in the workshops mentioned above, we found it fun to engage. Engagement brought us closer in spirit and philosophy, and we could discuss some of the serious issues of engaging pupils in our classrooms. This is just one way of developing an ethos in which joy and rigour, curiosity and challenge become familiar friends and clearly relate to doing mathematics and enjoying it.

---

11. Websites: NCETM: http://www.ncetm.org.uk/, ATM: http://www.atm.org.uk/, MA: http://www.m-a.org.uk/

References

Bjuland, R. and Jaworski, B. (2009) Teachers' perspectives on collaboration with didacticians to create an inquiry community. *Research in Mathematics Education*. Vol. 11, No. 1.

Boaler, J. (1997) *Experiencing School Mathematics: Teaching Styles, sex and setting*. Buckingham: Open University Press.

Brown, M. (1979) Cognitive Development and the Learning of Mathematics. In A. Floyd (Ed.). *Cognitive Development in the School Years*. pp.351-373. London: Croom Helm. Cockcroft.

Cooper, B. and Dunne, M. (2000) *Assessing Children's Mathematics Knowledge: Social Class, sex and problem solving*. Buckingham: Open University Press.

Cockcroft, W. H. (1982) *Mathematics Counts. Report of the Committee of Inquiry into the Teaching of Mathematics in Schools*. London: HMSO.

Davis, P. J. and Hersh, R. (1980) *The mathematical experience*. London: Penguin Books.

Houssart, J. (2004) *Low Attainers in Primary Mathematics: The Whisperers and the Maths Fairy*. London: Routledge Falmer.

Jaworski, B. (1994) *Investigating Mathematics Teaching: A Constructivist Enquiry*. London: Falmer Press.

Jaworski, B. (1988) 'Is versus seeing as': Constructivism and the mathematics classroom. In D, Pimm (Ed). *Mathematics Teachers and Children*. pp. 287-296. London: Hodder and Stoughton.

Lee, C. (2006) *Language for Learning Mathematics*. Buckingham: Open University Press.

Mason, J. (2002) *Researching your own Practice: The Discipline of Noticing*. London: Routledge/Falmer.

Nardi, E. and Steward, S. (2003) T. I. R. E. D? A profile of quiet disaffection in the secondary mathematics classroom. *British Educational Research Journal*, Vol. 29, No. 3.

Prestage, S and Perks, P. (2001) *Adapting and Extending Secondary Mathematics Activities: New tasks for old*. London: David Fulton.

Skemp, R. (1989) *Mathematics in the Primary School*. London: Routledge.

Straesser, R., Brandell, G., Grevholm, B. & Helenius, O. (2004) *Educating for the future: Proceedings of an international symposium on mathematics teacher education*. Gothenburg University, Sweden: The Royal Swedish Academy of Sciences.

Watson, A. (2006) *Raising achievement in secondary mathematics*. Maidenhead: Open University Press.

Watson, A. and Mason. J. (1998) *Questions and Prompts for Mathematical Thinking*. Derby: Association of Teachers of Mathematics (ATM).

Wells, G. (1999) *Dialogic Inquiry: Towards a Sociocultural Practice and Theory of Education*. Cambridge: Cambridge University Press.

3
LEARNING THEORIES IN THE MATHEMATICS CLASSROOM

Steve Lerman and Richard Cowley

In these two chapters we look, first, at some of the theories of how children learn, with a special focus on mathematics, and then in the second chapter we look at the impact of what teachers, and especially teacher leaders, come to believe and know about learning on teaching and learning in their Department. Whilst the study of child development and of learning in particular is the same for everything children encounter, there are special problems raised by mathematics, such as the degree of abstraction, the role of symbols, and the engagement with infinity.

We believe time spent considering theories of learning is absolutely vital for any practising or pre-service teacher. It is especially important for someone who is to take responsibility for running a mathematics department and leading colleagues to ways of improving pupils' learning and enjoyment of mathematics. Although, as we will argue in these two chapters, connections between theories of learning and what is implied for teaching are by no means clear, nevertheless teaching has to be informed by what we understand as learning. To take an example, it was once thought, at least by lazy students such as the first author of this chapter, that if one played a tape recorder under one's pillow through the night, playing French irregular verbs, multiplication tables, or English kings and queens, one would wake up with all that knowledge embedded in the mind next morning. Were this to have proved correct, the job of the teacher would be to prepare suitable tapes. This piece of fanciful thinking at least points to the need to consider what learning is, before determining what kinds of teaching would be called for.

In this first of two chapters we will sketch an historical trajectory of recent theories of learning before focusing on just four, the ones we consider most relevant to today's classrooms. We will try and justify our choice. Following this we will discuss what these learning theories might reveal about life in our mathematics classrooms; considering each perspective in its historical turn, comparing and contrasting on the way. Our main focus will be on how pupils learn but, inevitably, we will periodically consider implications for how teachers learn too; specifically, how teachers learn about how pupils learn. In the following chapter we will complete our thread of thoughts about teachers' learning.

A partial historical approach
We begin with a brief account of behaviourism, also called reflexology and associationism, partly because there are many features of this theory present in schools today but also because engaging with the ideas of Piaget and of

Vygotsky has to start with a recognition that they began their work as a response and rejection of behaviourism, the dominant psychology of (child) development at the time, the early 1920s, albeit in quite different ways. In starting there we are not looking at the Platonic view of learning as a process of recalling, through Socratic dialogue, the knowledge of the forms that each person's immortal soul knew before birth, but forgot in that process. Nor are we looking at empiricism. We also will not have anything to say about multiple intelligences, computer science models or neuroscience. Beginning with behaviourism we will concentrate on Piaget's and Vygotsky's psychological theories, the ideas coming from apprenticeship learning and the sociological theories of Basil Bernstein.

Before embarking on the investigation, however, we must address the question of why there isn't just one answer to the question: "How do children learn?" In mathematics we are used to precision and non-ambiguity, making up a language with what can be called a strong grammar (Bernstein, 1999), making it harder for us than others perhaps to realise that we are dealing with a different domain when we consider pedagogy, in our case the teaching of mathematics. The objects we deal with in mathematics are abstract, they are symbols, and the rules of how we work with them are determined. They certainly never answer back! And this is precisely the problem.

In developing theories about learning, teaching, or indeed any aspect of human behaviour, we are trying to interpret the something that we ourselves are, at the same time, engaged in. What is more we are interpreting the behaviour of people who are themselves in the process of making sense of the world. Inevitably, therefore, we will encounter interpretations, not certain knowledge. We will have competing theories, unlike in mathematics where, for example, the discovery of non-Euclidean geometries led to the enlargement of the notion of geometry, to include Euclidean as just one way amongst many of setting up axioms. In education when a new theory comes along it ends up sitting alongside the previous theories. So, although behaviourism is a theory from a century ago that carried research on training rats and dogs to hypotheses about human learning, it still has its advocates. Education is a social science, not a science, and the multiplicity of discourses about any social science is typical; we are working with weak grammars where things are not specified unambiguously in language.

Behaviourism

Behaviourism is associated with psychologists such as Pavlov, Thorndike, Watson and Skinner. It is a materialist theory, meaning that it is based on the notion that actions of all kinds are reactions and responses to what is going on around the individual and can be observed. What is in the mind is a result of the internalisation of what has been established as a response to something material. In other words it carries the assumption that there are no philosophical differences between publicly observable processes (such as actions) and privately observable processes (such as thinking and feeling). Behaviourism draws on the well-known and still used tools of reinforcement and punishment.

Both Piaget and Vygotsky considered behaviourism inadequate to explain any higher cognitive functions in humans. It might be considered to have something to say about basic aspects of learning, such as practising techniques in sport or learning multiplication tables. One can always give pupils a multiplication table to use, but in the service of more complex tasks it is after all very useful to know the answer to 6 x 7 without needing to think about it, an immediate response to a stimulus. But there are other elements of behaviourism present in teachers' strategies, the gold stars and smiley faces we give for good work and detentions or extra homework when we are not satisfied. These positive and negative reinforcements are still essential tools of many teachers.

Piaget and Vygotsky

We will consider the theories of these two great developmental psychologists together in constant comparison of those theories. We do this, rather than examine them separately, for a number of reasons. First, they were both born in 1896 and entered the field in the early 1920s. Vygotsky died in 1934, Piaget living much longer, to 1980. Second, as we said above, their theories were partly inspired by a move away from behaviourism, although in different ways. Third, in the writings produced by Vygotsky during his short life he addressed Piaget's work directly, indicating where he agreed and where he disagreed with Piaget's ideas. It seems that Piaget did not encounter Vygotsky's work until long after the latter's death. Finally, in a speech given at a conference "The Growing Mind" held to celebrate the centenary of the birth of Piaget and Vygotsky, where the audience consisted of Piagetian and Vygotskian scholars, Jerome Bruner said that Piagetian researchers should read Vygotsky's work as it provided a challenge to their ideas and the same for Vygotskian scholars, that they should read Piaget. Bruner added that trying to put the two theories together would not work; they were too contradictory. We will follow Bruner's advice in the following comparison.

Social and cultural background

A comparison of the places and social milieus into which Piaget and Vygotsky were born and lived their early years may shed some light on how they arrived at their very different psychologies. Piaget was born into a wealthy, educated family in Neuchâtel in the French-speaking part of Switzerland. His father, Arthur Piaget, was a professor of medieval literature at the University of Neuchâtel. Piaget was a precocious child who developed an interest in biology and the natural world, particularly molluscs, and even published a number of papers before he graduated from high school. In fact, his long career of scientific research began when he was just ten, with the 1907 publication of a short paper on the albino sparrow. It was while he was helping to mark some instances of intelligence tests that Piaget noticed that young children consistently gave wrong answers to certain questions. Piaget did not focus so much on the fact of the children's answers being wrong, but that young children kept making the same pattern of mistakes that older children and adults did not. This led him to the theory that young children's thought or cognitive processes are inherently different from those of adults.

Vygotsky was born into a middle-class Jewish family on November 5th, 1896 in Orsha, a small town in Belorussia, now known as Belarus. However, soon afterwards his father was appointed department chief of the United Bank of Gomel and the family moved. Vygotsky's mother had trained to be a teacher but saw her priority as being at home to provide a stimulating and enriching environment for her eight children. Vygotsky completed his primary education at home with his mother and a private tutor and then entered public school for his secondary education. Possessing an exceptional reading speed and memory he was an excellent student in all subjects although his passion was drama and poetry. Vygotsky graduated from secondary school with a gold medal at the age of 17. Although a brilliant student, there were doubts whether he would be accepted to the University of Moscow, due to the anti-Semitic quota system which limited the number of Jewish students admitted and the courses they could take. However, although Vygotsky was successful in the ballot and entered the University he was barred from studying philosophy and initially studied medicine, but soon switched to law. Vygotsky continued his self-directed studies in philosophy and when he graduated in 1917 with a law degree he returned home to teach literature and philosophy. Later, he attended the Institute of Psychology in Moscow (1924–34), where he worked extensively on ideas about cognitive development, particularly the relationship between language and thinking. Vygotsky died of tuberculosis in 1934, leaving a wealth of work that is still being explored. Vygotsky was also a highly prolific author: his major works span 6 volumes, written over roughly 10 years, from his *Psychology of Art* (1925) to *Thought and Language* [or *Thinking and Speech*] (1934/1986).

The opposition to behaviourism of both Piaget and Vygotsky has already been mentioned and they both also reacted strongly to the way so many millions went obediently to their death during the First World War at the command of their leaders and hence were concerned to highlight the autonomy of the individual. They both entered the field of psychology from prior studies: zoology and philosophy in Piaget's case and philosophy, art and literature in Vygotsky's.

Key driving forces
Piaget's prior studies in zoology led him to bring into his theory the notion that individual development repeats the process of the development of the species, defined as *ontogeny replicates phylogeny*. This idea can be seen in, for example, his argument that where mathematical concepts were troublesome for the development of knowledge, individual pupils will also face difficulties: negative numbers, and the gap between algebraic equations with the unknown on just one side and algebraic equations with the unknown on both sides are examples. His interest in philosophy, particularly writings on epistemology, led him to propose a change of approach to understanding what counts as knowledge and how people come to know anything, that is, the fundamental problems in epistemology. He proposed that one should study the actual process of how children come to know, how they acquire knowledge, what he called *genetic epistemology*; genetic in this case means origins rather than what is in one's DNA. Piaget placed the individual at the heart of his theories;

the work of learning must be carried out by the individual making sense of the world for her/himself. Thinking precedes language, which performs an organising and externalising function. These last two fundamental underlying focuses can be seen as emerging from Piaget's own early life experiences and his view of the world.

Turning now to Vygotsky, we can point first to his interest in language and culture as being a critical factor in the approach he took to developmental psychology. We should just note that 'culture' was not considered a social variable in Marxism. Marx argued that prejudice and differences between cultures (and genders) would wither away after the revolution, which would be essentially about social class. From a late 20th century perspective we would recognise the essential role of culture in Vygotsky's theories and indeed his approach is often called cultural psychology. For Vygotsky it was clear that the languages he spoke, Russian, Yiddish and Hebrew, performed quite different functions and offered different views on life: Russian was the public and academic language; Yiddish was the everyday language of Jews in those days, carrying within it centuries of suffering and dislocation; and Hebrew was the ancient language of the bible and of prayer. Thus, language carries meaning and identity, it precedes us and we are immersed in it from the first day of birth, if not before; it makes us who we are. Second, like Piaget, Vygotsky was also keenly interested in creativity, as illustrated by his first book, The Psychology of Art. Vygotsky's opposition to behaviourism was different from Piaget's. Vygotsky considered that the materialist perspective was fundamentally correct and wanted to build on it, rather than oppose it completely, towards higher thinking. We must also indicate the Marxist roots of Vygotsky's approach. In the years after the revolution and before Stalin took over, and perhaps earlier, there was a flowering of the arts, the sciences, indeed all of social and cultural life in Russia. Much of these developments were stimulated by the desire to identify how Marxism might inform a particular field. In developmental psychology the story was the same, and so we will need to indicate the role of Marxism as we elaborate Vygotsky's psychological theories. Finally, Vygotsky contracted tuberculosis quite early on and he was aware that he did not have too many years to live. As a consequence he wrote a great deal about his ideas and theories and the consequences of those theories but did not have the time to carry out research on them. That was left to people who studied with him and his followers. We are fortunate that Piaget lived a long life and the body of research on his theories is enormous.

Opposing behaviourism
Behaviourism is often represented by a stimulus-response link, this link being established and reinforced as we described above:

Stimulus  **Response**

Piaget severed the link by inserting the interpreting individual. When any stimulus appears the individual responds to it from within his or her prior set of experiences and interprets that new stimulus. We can represent this as follows:

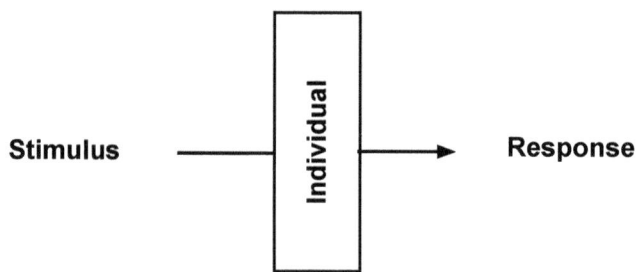

Vygotsky argued, on the other hand, that the response to any stimulus is always mediated or interpreted, it is explained, and its use is elaborated: by a parent; by a sibling; by a peer; by a text; and of course by teachers. Thus the stimulus-response link is replaced a mediating triangle:

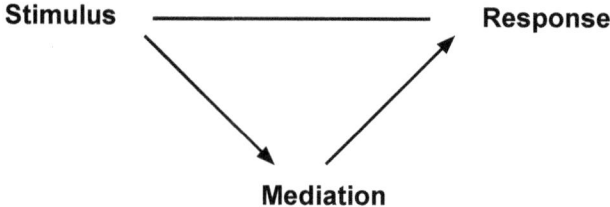

This is the essence of what is called cultural psychology. The mediation is always relative to time, culture, belief and so on. In principle, therefore, people can have quite different conceptions of the 'same' stimulus in different cultures (and in practice, see for example Pinxten's (1994) study of Navajo Indian conceptions of shape and space).

We will now move away from taking Piaget's and Vygotsky's theories together. Firstly we will elaborate Piaget's theories further in their own right, then we will return to Vygotsky, and pull out some similarities and differences between the two at the end of that section. This is the appropriate order since Vygotsky himself contrasted his work with Piaget's.

Piaget's developmental psychology

For Piaget, learning is the process of cognitive reorganisation by the individual, in response to interactions. Interactions can be physical, textual, or social, the latter being the most frequent and influential. The child must therefore be active or else learning will not take place. This view of learning is at the heart of the move in the 1950s to make primary schools places where children could experience things for themselves: sandpits; water tubs; home corners, and the whole notion of child-centred learning became popular currency in the language and organisation of schools, although studies suggested that the approach was not taken up as widely as popular perception had it at the time. In the secondary mathematics classroom this has substantial implications too, although dealt with at the abstract level, whose meaning for Piaget we will explain below. Traditional formal teaching actually inhibits learning; pupils will mimic the teacher but because they have not constructed the ideas for themselves they will not have understood and will not retain what the teacher

3. LEARNING THEORIES IN THE MATHEMATICS CLASSROOM

has shown them. Teachers should provide activities, with which pupils can engage, make conjectures about ways of doing the tasks and possible answers and have them modified through interactions with teacher, other pupils and/or books. Investigative ways of working and the SMILE era of individualised learning (also in other such projects: KMP; SMP etc.) were also stimulated by that theoretical approach, although we should add that these developments were influenced also by writers like Gattegno (e.g. 1974) and the interest in problem solving from Polya (1957) and Mason, Burton and Stacey (1982).

When an individual encounters an experience she assimilates or accommodates to it. The former means that the experience is absorbed into the child's prior conceptual framework. Coming across a banana 'tree' for the first time, one might assimilate it into one's tree schema: it has a trunk, large leaves and a flower followed by fruit later in the year. The plantation owner might then point out that it is in fact a plant, a member of the grass family. Now the tree schema has to change, the individual accommodates to the new experience, restructuring her knowledge. Now any encounter with a tree-like object needs to be examined further. The term *cognitive conflict* is used here to describe situations that the teacher sets up specifically to lead to accommodation in a pupil. A small group of low achieving pupils were found to be adding 3 digit numbers using the column algorithm but starting from the hundreds. This is not a problem if one has a method for adding backwards if there is something to be carried from the tens or units, but these pupils did not have such a method. No amount of practising had shifted these pupils to start from the units. Whilst there are several moves a teacher might make at this point, this teacher chose to try and set up cognitive conflict by getting them to add the same numbers on a calculator. Finding a different answer, produced from a tool they trusted, made them reconsider their method.

Based on his early biological studies and his studies of children's development, Piaget argued that children do not think like adults, resulting in what he described as 'development leads learning'. Children develop through biological stages, a process of maturation, and teaching cannot accelerate development across those stages. Thus, children must be ready for what the teacher offers as learning activities or else the child will not be able to learn and the teacher has to judge whether the child is ready. These stages, and the approximate ages the child remains in each stage, are as follows:

sensory motor stage:	birth to 2 years, when the child learns to organise actions
pre-conceptual:	2 to 4 years, when the child's concepts lack the generality of accepted concepts
intuitive:	4 to 7 years, when a child can think about actions but cannot make mental comparisons
concrete operational:	7 to 11 years, when the child can think logically about objects and events from direct experience
formal operational:	12 years onwards, when the person has the capacity for abstract thought

In education generally and mathematics education in particular these ideas have been developed as constructivist theory, sometimes further specified as radical constructivist theory (see Glasersfeld, 1991).

Vygotsky's developmental psychology

As we said above, the child learns what the world means from others through mediation; hence Vygotsky's theory is called cultural psychology. He saw the process of learning, of acquiring knowledge, as one of internalisation.

> Every function in the child's cultural development appears twice: first, on the social level, and later, on the individual level; first, between people (interpsychological), and then inside (intrapsychological)... All the higher functions originate as actual relations between human individuals. (Vygotsky, 1978, p. 57)

By referring to higher functions Vygotsky refers to the difference between development that is biological and development that is cultural. When he refers to biological, though, it is not meant in the same sense as Piaget, as maturational stages. He is referring to what one might call the 'animal' aspects of human development. Elsewhere he says that sociocultural development begins from the first day of a child's life. Becoming human, in the fullest sense of the word, only happens in interaction with others. Vygotsky was very interested in the phenomenon of the wolf child, the appearance of people who have developed without contact with humans, perhaps through severe neglect, or the chance survival in a forest (hence the name), and also in work with the higher primates because he was concerned to understand how human development is distinguished from animal development. Whilst the higher primates can be taught to recognise up to 200 words they do not take these back to their community and pass them on to the next generation. Amongst humans there is a ratchet effect of culture. We each begin from where society has reached; we do not need to construct all knowledge for ourselves.

Late in his life, Vygotsky developed the notion of the *zone of proximal development* (*zpd*), based on some ideas of his predecessors but made distinctively his own. Vygotsky was dissatisfied with IQ tests, which were developed in his time, as useful measures of any child's state of development because, he said, two children may gain the same mark but as learning is always a dynamic process one child may be about to 'reach out' for further knowledge whilst another child may not. He termed the space of emerging development and learning as the zpd.

> The zone of proximal development... is the distance between the actual developmental level as determined by independent problem solving and the level of potential development as determined through problem solving under adult guidance or in collaboration with more capable peers. (Vygotsky, 1978, p. 86)

This does not mean that, as a child enters the classroom, the teacher needs to assess the size of the bubble that surrounds the child; it is not a physical space but a symbolic one. In fact it is only in a learning activity that the zpd emerges (or not) in any individual or class of children. For instance,[1] a teacher might say "Mummy gives 2 oranges to 3 children. What should they do?" One child might respond, "Cut them into halves and give one half back to mummy". Another child might then respond "Cut the fourth piece up as well." In this way, a conversation begins in which the children hear unexpected responses that pull them forward in their learning, their zpd has emerged in the learning interactions. For Vygotsky, in contrast to Piaget, learning leads development.

In these descriptions, one can see the essential role of the teacher in Vygotsky's view of education. Whilst we can't say that when a teacher teaches children will learn, we can say that whenever children are learning there is a teacher teaching ('teacher' here is taken to include parents, more informed peers, teachers, textbooks and so on). In fact, many neo-Vygotskian writers put teaching/learning together.

In the quote above, Vygotsky refers to adult, or other, guidance. He elaborated that to say that development in the zpd begins with the child mimicking, then the child managing alone but with guidance, and then alone. Understanding develops in this way through stages to acquisition of the concept. The child also internalises the teacher's voice. So, young children will be heard talking to themselves using the voice of a parent for example, to control their actions. Eventually they stop speaking aloud, but that external control has become an internal voice, not disappeared. This is one of the many points in his writing where Vygotsky indicated that he disagreed with Piaget, who said that external speech actually disappears.

For Piaget, children proceed from the concrete to the abstract; Vygotsky drew on a Marxist notion to argue for the ascent from the abstract to the concrete. Piaget's formulation will be familiar to us all as it underpins the structure of schooling in the UK and many other places. Children are expected to build on a whole range of physical experiences to extract the essential underlying abstraction. Vygotsky wrote about the interaction between the everyday experiences, which he called the spontaneous, and the scientific. In school 'scientific' concepts are taught, and children need to be encouraged to recall spontaneous ideas and experiences that come under the scientific notion, making the abstract concrete. Programmes following this approach, developed in Russia by Davydov and Galperin, amongst others, build from the general structures of mathematics, such as greater than and lesser than, to the specific numbers and lengths that children already know.

Apprenticeship learning

Psychologists had a monopoly on learning until the last 20 years or so. Psychology focuses on how the individual develops, and cognitive psychology addresses how the thinking individual develops those characteristics of higher thought - memory, reasoning and knowledge acquisition. Other intellectual fields have something to say too, however, and in the next two sections we will look at ideas coming from anthropology and sociology of education.

---

1. This example was given by a Russian teacher working in a Vygotskian school.

Anthropologists study the social life of groups of people. For decades their focus was on studying and then translating the social and cultural life and mores of distant societies around the world into the dominant language and concepts. More recently they have turned to sub-groups within societies, such as dieters in Weight Watchers or port wine workers in Portugal. Jean Lave is an anthropologist who began her interventions into education through her studies of the mathematics learning of people apprenticed into the tailoring trade in Africa. She found a number of important features of their learning.

The skills they learnt that Lave saw as school-mathematical were seen by the apprentices as skills for tailoring – knowledge is situated, in a work setting or as school-mathematics for example. We know that transfer of (mathematical) knowledge from school to out-of-school does not just happen and Lave's analysis explains why. This aspect of her theory has led to the term situated cognition (Lave and Wenger 1991).

Those mathematical skills are just a part of the process of becoming tailors – learning is part of identity and not separable from it, and that applies to the classroom too. Indeed Lave describes learning as increasing participation in a social practice. Although she was not at first referring to learning in school, both Lave and many others (see Watson & Winbourne, 2007 for example) have now done so, seeing significant messages for the whole process of learning in studying how apprenticeships function.

Put simply, 'participate' means acquiring the norms, knowledge, ways of being and meanings that are typical of that group in that place at that time. But a community of practice also develops over time through changes by participants.

The expert, or master of the practice as in the tailoring situation, does not deliberately teach. Most of the learning of the apprentices is implicit, by example. Now this element does contrast somewhat when one looks at schoolteachers whose job, after all, is to consciously teach. But the point about implicit learning is highly relevant. It also raises questions about how people learn about teaching.

Thinking of teaching mathematics as about supporting pupils to absorb or acquire the social norms of the mathematics classroom and the mathematical norms of specific language, ways of thinking, ways of arguing/reasoning that are mathematical, and so on, are very powerful. We can sum it up as pupils becoming apprenticed into being school-mathematical. This move in terms of learning theories is an interesting and important one, because it moves the process of learning from a cognitive act by the individual to a mode of participation in a way of being mathematical that is the responsibility of the teacher, and the mathematics department, the school, the curriculum, and so on, all mediated through the teacher. Boaler's (1997) book was a study of two similar schools over a 3-year period where one had a well-focused textbook-based programme and the other was based around problem solving activities; she found that there were quite different forms of participation and senses of what it meant to be mathematical in those two schools. These differences were not issues of cognition, knowledge acquisition or abilities; they were the products of the two different communities of practice regarding doing mathematics.

Sociology of education – learning as social reproduction

From decades of experience of 'traditional' mathematical classrooms we are well aware that most pupils do not succeed. There is a strong correlation of social class with that failure, with working class pupils under-achieving. Interestingly, where a more pupil-centred system was introduced, the same phenomenon was found (Lubienski, 2000). So what is it about mathematics teaching that always seems to reproduce social advantage and disadvantage? Psychological theories don't help here, with their focus on normal development. Sociology usually concerns itself with the macro issues of political and social change, and in the case of sociology of education issues such as which sections of the middle classes are influencing educational change. Some sociologists of education also address the links between these macro issues and the micro issues of what are the effects in the classroom. Here we will discuss the work of Basil Bernstein as precisely one of those sociologists. Bernstein's theory is extensive and powerful. His framework enables a symmetrical analysis of all kinds of forms of pedagogy, traditional, child-centred (what he calls liberal-progressive), critical (in the sense of critical theory) or others.

The key argument he makes, based on an analysis of forms of power and control, centres around two forms of framing interactions in classrooms, that he terms invisible and visible pedagogies (see for example Bernstein, 2004). The former is typical of child-centred classrooms, where teachers tend to be oblique when giving instructions: "Would you mind standing up please and reading from the top of page 4". This is not intended as an invitation which pupils can refuse if they wish, even though it sounds like it. Rather it is an order framed in an invisible way. A second example, given by Bernstein in the 2004 chapter mentioned above, is a fictitious encounter between a teacher and a pupil who has drawn a person with hands that have three fingers. The teacher's comment, "Tell me about it" or "Oh, that's very exciting" (p. 201), gives the child no idea that there might need to be some adjustment made to the picture (unless the child's surname is Picasso!). Another teacher, drawing on a more visible pedagogy, might say, "That's a lovely man, but he's only got three fingers" or in another picture "That's a very good house, but where is the chimney?" (*op cit*).

Bernstein explains how working class pupils will be less likely to 'read' the teacher's invitation to read from the top of page 4 as in fact an order, and will not gain anything from the first art teacher's lack of guidance. It seems that middle class pupils acquire a more *elaborated* linguistic code in their home lives, whereas working class pupils acquire a more *restricted* code. As a consequence middle class children can read what is being expected of them, both in terms of general behaviour and in terms of the content of knowledge and hence are advantaged from the start of their schooling. This is circumstantial, though; given the resources (small classes, teachers with appropriate knowledge) all pupils can acquire the elaborated code. However, teachers are not generally aware of the need to teach the elaborated code to some pupils and the resources required are not available.

Although it must be said that traditionally organised teaching is far from dead, on the contrary it remains the most common throughout UK schools as compared to other forms of pedagogy, at least in principle most teachers of mathematics would say that a child-centred, liberal-progressive approach is best for pupils. Something can be done about the disadvantage that is sustained and reproduced through invisible pedagogies, though, and research shows that where pedagogy is in part more visible, leading later to a move to more invisible, working class pupils can gain the required linguistic code that can lead to success. Pedagogy consists of a number of elements: pacing, sequencing, assessment, setting out rules, and so on. If some of these are moderated to ensure explicitness, where all pupils are made aware of what is expected, both in terms of social norms in the classroom (such as respecting all pupils' attempts to answer challenging questions) and of specifically mathematical ways of being (such as being ready to be challenged for justification by other pupils on the answers proposed), disadvantage can be overcome, although Bernstein does suggest that this needs to happen as early as possible in the child's trajectory through schooling.

Final comment

We have looked at four theories of learning, the ones we consider most relevant to teaching and learning today. We referred above to what teachers will decide they believe to resonate with their experience. We are never neutral about social life! Readers will of course have been thinking about the connections with classroom practice and the following chapter will address those connections directly.

References

Bernstein, B. (1999) Vertical and Horizontal Discourse: an essay. *British Journal of Sociology of Education*, 20(2).

Bernstein, B. (2004) Social Class and Pedagogic Practice. In S.J. Ball (Ed.) *The RoutledgeFalmer Reader in Sociology of Education* (pp. 196-217), London: RoutledgeFalmer.

Boaler, J. (1997) *Experiencing school mathematics: Teaching styles, sex and setting*. Buckingham: Open University Press.

Gattegno, C. (1974) *The Common Sense of Teaching Mathematics*. New York: Educational Solutions.

Lave, J. and Wenger, E. (1991) *Situated Learning Legitimate peripheral participation*, Cambridge: Cambridge University Press.

Lubienski, S. T. (2000) Problem Solving as a Means toward Mathematics for All: An Exploratory Look through a Class Lens. *Journal for Research in Mathematics Education*, 31(4)

Mason, J., Burton, L. & Stacey, K. (1982) *Thinking Mathematically*. Oxford: Blackwell Publishers

Pinxten, R. (1994) Anthropology in the Mathematics Classroom? In S. Lerman (Ed.) *Cultural Perspectives on the Mathematics Classroom*, Dordrecht: Kluwer Academic Publishers.

Polya, G. (1957) *How to Solve It*. New York: Doubleday Anchor Books.

Von Glasersfeld, E. (1991) *Radical Constructivism in Mathematics Education*. Dordrecht: Kluwer Academic Publishers.

Vygotsky, L. (1978) *Mind in Society*, Cambridge. MA: Harvard University Press.

Vygotsky, L. (1986) *Thought and Language*. edited by Alex Kozulin. Cambridge, MA: The MIT Press.

Watson, A. & Winbourne, P. (Eds.) (2007) *New directions for situated cognition in mathematics education*. New York: Springer.

4
IN THE MATHEMATICS CLASSROOM WITH LEARNING THEORIES

Richard Cowley and Steve Lerman

In this chapter, we take learning theories into the classroom, considering them as lenses through which we interpret mathematical activity. In our view, the problem of the uncertainty of knowledge about how humans learn is a key catalyst for creating interesting professional activities for the development of mathematics teachers and for enriching the experience of a leader in a mathematics department. It is difficult to imagine a good teacher operating without a learning theory to help them rationalise their actions. To illustrate this point, we will, to start with, narrow our focus onto the notions of learning objective, teacher intervention and learning outcome. At present, there is considerable pressure on mathematics teachers to make learning objectives explicit and to be able to ensure learning outcomes. How do we come to an agreement about how to ensure learning outcomes? Even more complex, how do we decide what evidence we will accept that learning outcomes have been ensured?

Indeed, this raises questions about what learning objectives and outcomes really are. Consider this example; a pupil writes:

$$3.7 \times 10 = 3.70$$

We will all recognise a misapplication of the rule to add a zero when multiplying by 10 (although a radical constructivist, e.g. Von Glasersfeld, 1991, would claim there is no way to know what the pupil is thinking for sure). However, if we follow through with our assumption, we notice that the rule has been applied to multiply a decimal number when the rule only applies to integers; but how do we respond? We could imagine, for the sake of this discussion, that we are teaching and we observe the pupil write this. Just after the episode, pupil-time is frozen but teacher-time goes on and we have a chance to plan our intervention; in effect, planning a mini-lesson. Adopting the common discourse of lesson planning, we identify a learning objective, devise an intervention and decide to assess the learning outcome. We already have philosophical problems here because all planning, to a certain extent, is about predicting the future and different learning theories would say different things about this.

A behaviourist perspective

A behaviourist perspective might lead to a plan such as this:
- the learning objective is that, in future, the pupil will move the digits one place to the left when multiplying decimals by 10;

- the intervention is the instruction, when we *multiply a decimal by ten, we move the digits one place to the left*, followed by a demonstration of the correct way to multiply 3.7 by 10;
- assessment is by watching to check that the pupil is applying the correct method.

We have emphasised the word correct here because the notion of a wholesome correct method is associated with a behaviourist perspective on learning mathematics; pupils must implement the taught method without variation as and when required. This is a behaviourist approach because correct performance is associated with learning; there is no reference to understanding. A further implication is that, if implemented effectively, the plan is a perfect prediction of a future in which the pupil will get questions like this one correct, without fail. Behaviourism is a positivist belief system in which discovering the right stimulus will lead to the desired response every time; implying that full understanding of complex human psychology can make the future predictable.

Of course, we cannot be sure that the teacher here is seeing learning from a behaviourist perspective unless we ask for a rationale for the plan. A behaviourist rationale might be:

- Pupils who follow instructions will get the questions right, enjoy a positive relationship with the teacher and receive merits for their efforts.
- Pupils who fail to follow instructions will get the questions wrong, endure the wrath of the teacher and be given extra work to do corrections or additional questions.

If we briefly move our focus off the pupil and on to the teacher; we might ask how teachers developed their rationale and how they learned to plan in this way. Assuming they were taught to teach like this by a behaviourist, they would be following instructions, "When a pupil writes: $3.7 \times 10 = 3.70$, we tell the pupil to…" Jonathan Kozol (2006) observed a fourth grade mathematics lesson in the United States (equivalent to Year 5 in the UK) about building runways.

> "When we count the edges around the runway," said a worksheet that was on the children's desks, "we find the perimeter. When we count the number of squares in a runway, we find the area… Today we are going to conduct an inventory of all the different perimeters." (page 7)

Here both the pupils and the teachers are following instructions in order to ensure the pupils get the right answers to the problems. A major criticism of this approach is that an understanding of the concepts would be accidental because the activity does not get to the essence of what perimeter and area are. What would the pupils do with a curved shape that did not have "edges" to count? Would they know it had a perimeter?

Consideration of any learning theories challenges us to articulate and our assumptions and clarify our perspectives on classroom episodes. In the next few paragraphs, we will continue to develop our analysis of the place value and multiplication by 10 problem above, considering how various learning theories might help and challenge us to explain our lives as mathematics teachers. However, we do not expect everyone to agree with this analysis or this interpretation about how these perspectives might be applied. This is an important point when considering how a teacher with leadership responsibilities for mathematics in a school might encourage teachers to engage with learning theories and what the purpose of such engagement would be. The first author of this chapter cannot tell the second author which learning theory his experience should resonate with and vice-versa; that would be ridiculous. Likewise, there will be a multitude of experiences and resonances amongst any group of mathematics teachers, even in the same school.

A constructivist perspective

What if we adopt Piaget's idea that the individual interprets the stimulus, bearing in mind that we have two individuals, the teacher and the pupil? First of all for the teacher, given the same observation, there is no set response; prior experience of this pupil, other pupils, approved methods and so on will come into play, which creates a unique dynamic between this teacher and this pupil at this moment in time. From this perspective, the teacher has an immediately complex problem. Can the teacher know what the pupil is thinking? Let us assume for a moment that the teacher knows that the pupil has misapplied the rule because the pupil has already explained that "to multiply by 10, you add a nought." This might be the plan:

- The learning objective is that, in future, the pupil will shift all of the digits one place to the left relative to the decimal point and will understand why that works.

- Here are some possible interventions:

    - the teacher reviews the answer of $3.7 \times 10 = 3.70$ making various attempts to stimulate cognitive conflict; for example, focussing attention on the digit 3 of 3.7, "What is ?" and "30 is more than 3.7";

    - the teacher guides the pupil through the process of shifting all the digits one place to the left relative to the decimal point explaining why the shift of places works;

    - the pupil will revisit the original rule and understand an explanation of why the rule works with integers (because the insertion of a zero in the units place pushes all the other digits one place to the left, multiplying them all by 10);

    - the pupil will apply the exact same rule to decimals (placing a zero in the units place to push the 3 into the tens column to get 30.7) and see that this doesn't work either.

- Assessment is by watching the various responses of the pupil (hesitancy, affirmation, tension, relief and so on); interpreting them and hoping the interpretations are right; listening to the pupil's own explanations. Ultimately though, the teacher will check that the pupil is applying the correct method, apparently behaviourist. However, the difference is that this teacher is focussed on the idea of a cognising individual and will not necessarily accept the performance of a method or implementation of a rule as evidence of understanding; they will look for further evidence.

A constructivist, faced with the problem of a pupil writing $3.7 \times 10 = 3.70$, would recognise the need for some cognitive reorganisation and assume that a previous step or element of knowledge on which correct new knowledge depends is missing. Such a teacher might use intuition to retrace the pedagogical steps to this outcome or might make recourse to an accepted authoritative document such as the National Numeracy Strategy Framework (DfEE, 1999). In the framework, "Multiply and divide decimals mentally by 10…" appears in the Year 6 objectives. The Year 4, 5 and 6 supplement of examples (pages 6 and 7) offers a possible progression in "Multiplying and dividing whole numbers, then decimals, by 10, 100 and 1000". Starting from "understand that when you multiply a number by 10, the digits move one place to the left" in Year 4, and working through with the same rule for integers less than 1000; including multiplication and division by 10 and 100; through describing patterns created by multiplication and division by 10, 100 and 1000 in Year 5, and on to multiplication by 10, 100 and 1000 in Year 6 including decimals, still using the rule/algorithm of moving digits. Even an imaginary child who has never been told the rule "add a nought to multiply by 10" is likely to notice such a rule once presented with this list:

$$26 \times 10 = 260$$
$$260 \times 10 = 2\,600$$
$$2600 \times 10 = 26\,000 \quad \text{DfEE, 1999, Section 6, p.7}$$

It would not be fair on the constructivist perspective to leave the discussion of their perspective at this point though. The need to get pupils constructing their own knowledge leads to other considerations. A constructivist would think beyond this particular episode; realising that misunderstandings of the decimal number system are not easily reconstructed and noticing that this pupil has no real sense of the numbers in the problem. Further experiences would be planned to facilitate the pupil's reconstruction of their understanding; for example, metric measurement, cross-curricular work (perhaps measuring in P.E. during the athletics season), solving money problems, investigating what happens when we multiply and divide decimals by 10, 100, 1000 and so on, or trial and improvement games such as "Guess my pocket money" (Appendix 1). Many interesting, exciting and engaging activities have been created by innovative teachers to address this kind of teaching problem from a constructivist perspective.

A cultural psychological perspective

Whilst a constructivist would retrace steps, seek the missing links and probe the pupil's understandings, attempting to diagnose and prescribe, wondering all the time whether the pupil was ready to understand the next bit of mathematics or not, a cultural psychologist such as Davydov would question

4. IN THE MATHEMATICS CLASSROOM WITH LEARNING THEORIES 51

the entire structure of a curriculum that leads to this kind of error and would seek to address the underlying concepts and generalisations of real number (not integer), multiplication and division; seeing place value and the number system as a specific application of multiplication and division. Both teachers would engage in discussion with the pupil and/or facilitate discussion between pupils offering new experiences to address the situation, but the aims would be different. The Piagetian would seek to prompt a reconstruction of the knowledge of the cognising individual; the Vygotskian would seek to mediate a whole new perspective, building from generalisations to specific examples.

From a cultural psychological perspective, the introduction of arithmetic in the early years using only integers, is a mistake which can lead to early conceptualisation of number as cardinality. This leads to an atomised curriculum with the phenomenon of cognitive conflict inevitable as pupils are forced to reorganise one schema (Skemp, 1971) after another because the early foundation of general concepts is not formed carefully enough. This is the fundamental difference between Piaget and Vygotsky. For Piaget (1926, 1928), generalisation will come later; pupils will gradually generalise their understanding of multiplication, for example, as they experience first integers, then fractions, decimals, algebra and so on. For Vygotsky (1978, 1986), generalisation will come first and be applied to specific examples as pupils come across them. For Piaget, generalisation will not come until abstract thought is posssible from 12 years old onwards during the formal operational stage of development; development leads learning. For Vygotsky, learning leads development and young children can and do cope with abstract concepts, for example, conceptualising the counting numbers demands abstraction. The research of Davydov (1992) and others provides evidence that problems such as our illustration do not occur when general concepts are formed before specific cases are considered. The Piagetian needs to retrace the steps of historical discovery of mathematical ideas when teaching individuals, the ontogeny replicates phylogeny we mentioned in the previous chapter is countered by Vygotsky's idea that we can start from where society has reached; we can ignore the struggles of the past if we conceptualise mathematics in general terms as it stands now. The cultural psychologist would ensure that the concept of multiplication presented in the first place was going to be able to encompass all practical situations in which multiplication might be met.

A historical and cultural analysis of this trick (adding a zero to multiply by ten) at first reveals an origin in place value and number bases, for example, in base five, shifting digits one place to the left has the effect of multiplying by 5. Further analysis reveals that the concepts of number bases and place value have their origins in multiplication and measures; when a unit of measure is tediously small, multiples of it might be used instead. Hence, in working out how many tiny cups of water can be poured from a giant jug, children decide to work out how many medium sized glasses of water can be poured from the jug and then how many cups from the glass. See Schmittau (2003) or Davydov (1992) for a more detailed account of this activity.

An apprenticeship perspective

If we turn now to take an apprenticeship perspective on our teaching problem, we must ask more about the situation. Is this an exercise of questions of all the same type designed to facilitate practice of a technique or method; or is it a one off calculation during a practical activity; or is it an investigation into what happens when we multiply by ten; or some other mathematical activity? And here is a central concern, what is to be regarded as a mathematical activity? A teacher with an apprenticeship perspective on our teaching problem would ask, "What is the nature of mathematics?" and "What does it mean to be mathematical?" and "Is this pupil being mathematical?" and "What can I do to make this situation mathematical?" If we return to our habit of planning learning objectives, interventions and assessment of learning outcomes, we might compose the following general plan:

- the learning objective is to

    - become mathematical in the way we want people to be mathematical;

    - be able to carry out this particular calculation amongst others;

    - to understand how this method fits into the wider set of mathematical knowledge and how carrying it out constitutes being mathematical;

- the intervention will depend on what the teacher sees as being mathematical and will involve being mathematical, in that sense, with the pupil;

- in learning through apprenticeship, assessment is implicit if the learner chooses to participate or is allowed to participate by the teacher; the implication is that the teacher creates situations in which activities are mathematical, according to their perspective on what that means, and pupils become increasingly mathematical in that situation.

Clearly, there is a variety of perspectives on how mathematical this particular method or skill is; using place value to multiply decimal numbers by 10. One teacher might decide that this particular trick of the trade fits into a finite set of shortcuts that a school mathematician has to become familiar with in order to access the rest of mathematics. Another teacher might decide that this is not what mathematics is about and that the whole curriculum needs to be reorganised. Either way, using the lens of apprenticeship learning to look at our classrooms leads us to ask questions about what we are expecting of children in more general terms; what kind of people we are asking them to be when they do/learn mathematics? Lave and Wenger expressed this perfectly:

> One way to think of learning is as the historical production, transformation and change of persons. (Lave and Wenger, 1991, p.51)

Now it would be a grand claim that our pupil will be significantly transformed by our one up-and-coming interaction on multiplying a decimal number by ten. However, the general way we deal with this situation and how we might expect pupils to act out being mathematical will need to have some consistency if learning from this perspective is to occur. Here is the power of this perspective: it takes us beyond a consideration of how to teach particular topics or techniques, or how to intervene in particular situations, to encourage us to ask what is being mathematical all about.

A sociological perspective

For Bernstein (1996), language has functions beyond individuals expressing their ideas and interacting to learn and create; language rules have the power to limit the meanings that can be expressed in a given situation and to define identities. Of language, Bernstein writes:

> ...the device is not neutral, [and it] may have some intrinsic regulatory function. (Bernstein, 1996, p. 27)

Returning to our teaching problem, each perspective we have examined seems to lead to a particular range of pedagogies. Bernstein's framework allows us to analyse each and consider a wider range of contextual variables as we do so. Such an analysis of our teaching problem would be highly complex and is beyond the scope of this chapter but we can say some things here. The role of the individual, the freedom to develop ideas and the scope to grow are significantly different in each of the pedagogies we have described; this applies to pupils and teachers. Language and social context interact to regulate what is possible for pupils and teachers in classrooms but a sociological perspective helps us to understand what is happening and act knowledgeably.

Bernstein's framework can help reveal a wider range of the assumptions we inevitably make in our classrooms and challenge us to question them. To illustrate this point, recall the proposition made earlier in the section on constructivist perspectives that pupils might gain more of a feel for decimal numbers through solving money problems. Consider this in the light of Cooper and Dunne's (2000) study of key stage 3 test questions in mathematics. The researchers examined pupils' performance on questions set in everyday (or pseudo-everyday) contexts, compared to questions set in purely mathematics contexts, questions such as the following:

> A drink and a box of popcorn together cost 90p. 2 drinks and a box of popcorn together cost £1.45. What does a box of popcorn cost?

This is of course the 'same' task as:

> Solve simultaneously: $x + y = 90$ and $2x + y = 145$

The researchers found that some students answered with responses like the following:

> I said to myself that in a sweetshop a can of coke is normally 40p so I thought of a number and the number was 50p so I add 40p and 50p and it equalled 90p

This illustrates the need to teach our pupils how to learn from contrived or real life practical contexts and not to automatically assume that meaning is more easily communicated in this way.

Final thoughts about teachers' learning

Our presentation of learning theories as an historical account in our earlier chapter, and our progressive story of perspectives on teaching problems in this chapter, might lead to a false inference that these learning theories get better and better; in some way superseding each other. To ensure this is not the message, we would like to reiterate our earlier point that in education when a new theory comes along it ends up sitting alongside the previous theories. Whilst we would reject behaviourism as lacking explanatory power and limiting for teachers, we would consider the other learning theories presented here all have something worthwhile to say about learning in mathematics classrooms; for teachers as well as for pupils.

As teachers we will draw on our learning theories when designing activities, responding to learners and reviewing progress but we will also be learning ourselves through our participation in these processes. It is worthwhile briefly giving some consideration to how learning theories might help us better understand how we learn as our learning also has an impact on the mathematics classroom. This is where the responsibilities of a leader in a mathematics department can be seen to be complex; finding ways to take a lead on learning for pupils and for teachers.

It is currently considered good practice to have schemes of work in place in mathematics departments. These should adhere to the requirements of statutes such as the National Curriculum, be informed by non-statutory advice such as the Numeracy Strategy Framework for Teaching Mathematics and be developed through self-evaluation. No matter how detailed a scheme of work is, even to the extent of including detailed lesson plans, individual teachers will interpret and this will lead to the activity of pupils varying across classrooms. Ensuring a consistent experience and curriculum entitlement for all pupils is one of the responsibilities of a subject leader.

What is it that leads to teachers' different interpretations and decisions in their own classrooms? An engagement with learning theories can lead us to a concept of consistency that is to do with learning about children's learning rather than to do with prescriptive planning and automatic responses to categories of classroom scenarios. For example, if Numeracy Strategy recommendations are to be taken into consideration some critical evaluation should take place first.

We have already illustrated how Piagetian developmental psychology has clearly influenced the recommended teaching sequence for multiplication by powers of ten. Is the Framework consistently informed in this way? What is to be made of the placement of an arithmagon problem (Appendix 2) as an example of a context for forming and solving linear equations? Is it intended that the ingenious alternative approach used by one pupil is to be deemed the wrong method (a behaviourist perspective)? We hope not but it is easy for such a prescriptive interpretation to take hold of any mathematics department, especially those under pressure to make significant improvements in external examination results at the same time as being under intense scrutiny from Ofsted or HMI. Learning theories offer us a starting point on the rare occasions we have an opportunity to step back from these pressures to contemplate how to develop. Adopting an apprenticeship perspective, for example, might alert us that:

> Conditions that place newcomers in deeply adversarial relations with masters, bosses or managers; in exhausting over involvement in work; or in involuntary servitude rather than participation distort, partially or completely, the prospects for learning in practice. (Lave and Wenger, 1991, p.64)

Equally, adopting a sociological perspective might help us to understand why it is that sometimes the wider context has such qualities that it compels us to jettison our better judgement, hopefully only temporarily. We believe that the ability to adopt these alternative perspectives is potentially highly empowering for teachers at all levels.

Conclusion

So we have learning theories as lenses offering complementary or opposing interpretations of the mathematics classroom, how children learn and how teachers learn, or we have learning theories as the foundation of teaching approaches and curriculum organisation. Either way, learning theories offer a way in to thinking about the complexity of our task as teachers. As Cobb (2006) proposes, learning theories can be thought of "as sources of ideas to be appropriated and adapted" (p.2). In the academic world in which learning theories are developed or discovered, the theorists adhering to various views are rarely sworn enemies; they work together and this process helps develop their thinking; this is how an understanding of learning theories can enhance the quality of experience for mathematics teachers and mathematics learners in a school so that there is a recognition that each individual is operating under a field of learning theories that is changing shape as their thinking develops. Learning theories pervade every aspect of a teacher's work whether we are conscious of them or not; they regulate the formation of assumptions we make when we plan, implement and evaluate. Questioning assumptions and considering alternative learning theories helps us see more when we work with our pupils; helps us understand each other's motives as teachers; and helps us envisage new possibilities in our classrooms.

The only principle that does not inhibit progress is: anything goes. (Feyerabend, 1978, p.23)

References

Bernstein, B. (1996) *Pedagogy, Symbolic Control and Identity*. Lanham, MD.: Rowman and Littlefield.

Cobb, P. (2006) Supporting a Discourse About Incommensurable Theoretical Perspectives in Mathematics Education. *Philosophy of Mathematics Education Journal* No. 19 (December 2006), Editor: Paul Ernest. ISSN 1465-2978 (Online) http://www.people.ex.ac.uk/PErnest/ .

Cooper, B. and Dunne, M. (2000) *Assessing Children's Mathematics Knowledge: Social Class, sex and problem solving*. Buckingham: Open University Press.

Davydov, V. V. (1992) The psychological analysis of multiplication procedures. *Focus on Learning Problems in Mathematics*, 14(1).

DfEE (1999) *The National Numeracy Strategy Framework for teaching mathematics from Reception to Year 6*. London: DfEE publications.

DfEE (2001) *Key Stage 3 National Strategy Framework for teaching mathematics: Years 7, 8 and 9*. London: DfEE publications.

Feyerabend, P.K. (1978) *Against Method: Outline of an Anarchistic Theory of Knowledge*. London: Verso Books, New edition (April 1978).

Kozol, J. (2006) Confections of Apartheid Continue In Our Schools. In *Education Digest* Vol 71 (6).

Lave, J. and Wenger, E. (1991) *Situated Learning Legitimate peripheral participation*. Cambridge: Cambridge University Press.

Piaget, J. (1926) *The Language and Thought of the Child. London*: Kegan Paul.

Piaget, J. (1928) *Judgement and Reasoning in the Child*. London: Kegan Paul, Trench, Trubner & Co Ltd.

Schmittau, J. (2003) Cultural-Historical Theory and Mathematics Education. In Alex Kozulin et al. *Vygotsky's Educational Theory in Cultural Context* (pp.225-245), Cambridge: Cambridge University Press.

Skemp, R. (1971) *The Psychology of Learning Mathematics*. London: Penguin Books.

Von Glasersfeld, E. (1991) *Radical Constructivism in Mathematics Education*. Dordrecht: The Netherlands: Kluwer Academic Publishers.

Vygotsky, L. (1978) *Mind in Society: Development of Higher Pyschological Precesses*. Cambridge, MA: Harvard University Press.

Vygotsky, L. (1986) *Thought and Language*. edited by Alex Kozulin. Cambridge MA: The MIT Press.

Appendix 1: Guess my pocket money

- Player A chooses an amount of pocket money up to £10.00 and secretly writes it down.
- Player B has to guess how much pocket money A has.
- Each time Player B guesses, player A has to say whether the guess is too high or too low.
- The guessing continues until player B guesses correctly.

The teacher encourages pupils to use logical trial and improvement methods and to find the most significant figures first.

Appendix 2: Arithmagons

In the supplement of examples of the Key Stage 3 National Strategy Framework for teaching mathematics: Years 7, 8 and 9, (DfEE, 2001) on page 123; under Algebra: Equations, formulae and identities; we have, "As outcomes, Year 8 pupils should, for example:…consolidate forming and solving linear equations with an unknown on one side". There is the following example.

> In an arithmagon, the number in a square is the sum of the numbers in the two circles on either side of it.

In this triangular arithmagon, what could the numbers A, B and C be?

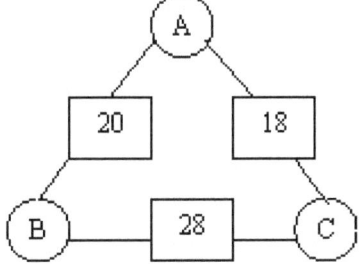

Let x stand for the number in the top circle. Form expressions for the numbers in the other circles, $(20-x)$ and $(18-x)$. Then form an equation in x and solve it.

$(20 - x) + (18 - x) = 28$

$38 - 2x = 28$

$2x = 10$

$x = 5$

So A = 5, B = 15, C = 13.

One pupil presented with this problem without an explanation of how to solve it noticed that the difference between 20 and 18 is 2 so the difference between B and C must also be 2. For that pupil, the new problem was to find two numbers with a sum of 28 and difference of 2. B then C and finally A were each evaluated mentally.

5
TAKING A LEAD WITH PEDAGOGY

Anthony Broadly, Clare Lee, Tim Rattigan and Anne Watson

This is the first of two chapters focusing on 'taking a lead'. There are many issues in taking a lead on pedagogy in a mathematics department. In these two chapters, two heads of successful mathematics departments (AB & TR) discuss their roles with a leading figure in mathematics education (AW). Another of the authors (CL) takes the role of interviewer asking questions, moving the discussion on and summing up the conversation. This chapter shows how the heads of department have worked for the successes they have gained, what they count as success in leading on pedagogy and where they have found problems and difficulties. Three of the people in this conversation have worked together on research exploring how previously lower attaining pupils can be included in the mainstream curriculum and how addressing the challenge of including these pupils helps such pupils to see themselves as learners who can "do maths". This research is referred to within the conversation.

Both heads of department have a track record of innovations within their departments that have resulted in their pupils achieving high standards. They debate what it means to take a lead and to persuade reluctant members of their department to try out new ideas and see if the ideas can be put to good use in practice. The heads of department have been successful but, as will become apparent when reading the conversation, they have had their problems as well. Not all members of their departments want to be part of innovative ways of working and although the heads of departments' beliefs and principles would suggest working in certain ways, they are reluctant to impose such ways on colleagues.

These heads of mathematics have had questions to answer within their departments that will resonate with many new and aspiring subject leaders. They have many new ideas but it is not possible to make huge changes all at once, so where should they start? What are the key ideas that must be discussed and decided? What about part-time teachers, people who work part-time in the school or part-time in the department? How about those teachers whose subject knowledge is less than would be ideal, for whatever reason? The time that departments get to work and talk together is very limited so how should they make best use of the time that they have?

In this conversation, the heads of department explain how they have tried to work within these constraints, what they have successfully accomplished and where they are still working and puzzling. Taking a lead on pedagogy will never be straightforward and taking a lead in a mathematics department presents its own significant challenges. There is much to think about and to decide both for yourself as head of department and in discussion with your team of teachers.

Good pedagogy in mathematics

In order to establish what it means to take a lead on pedagogy, we started by discussing what we meant by good pedagogy in mathematics:

AB: Good pedagogy provides an opportunity to explore ideas and to make conjectures and to test those conjectures.

TR: Good pedagogy is about providing the opportunities, and at an appropriate time the support, so that the pupils can engage in mathematical activity. One of the most difficult things is to define what is meant by mathematical activity and what such activity entails. Within any department there will be disagreement about what is mathematical activity and different views about what it means to be mathematical.

AW: I want to ask what is the justification for taking the view that mathematics is about exploring and conjecturing, when that is not the general view of many mathematics teachers or the models of assessment that we have at the moment?

AB: The justification for saying that as mathematics teachers we want pupils to explore and conjecture goes back to our definition of what it means to be a mathematician. As a head of department I spend most of my time with my team working on ways to develop the pupils as mathematical thinkers. If we are teaching mathematics then we should be teaching pupils what it means to be a mathematician. Although we realise that many of those that we teach will not become mathematicians, I believe we should provide all of our pupils with an opportunity to see what being a mathematician is like and to experience the ways of thinking and processes that mathematicians use. Over time my team has formed the view that if we develop pupils' ability to be mathematical thinkers then performance criteria will be met. The pupils will be able to sit examinations and do well in tests, as a result of being able to tackle problems by thinking about them. My team and I are certain that this is the case, and our results show that our pupils are achieving well.

TR: I believe that by teaching pupils to be able to think and to work mathematically, they should be able to access a wider range of questions and tackle a wider range of tasks because they appreciate the underlying concepts; therefore their performance in tests and examinations will improve. My team has spent a long time discussing what those mathematical processes are and what it means to be a mathematician. I am pleased to say that this has actually become the most important thing to discuss. The teachers in my team know and value mathematical processes and thinking. However every day, when we look at examination papers and we listen to the concerns of our senior management team, the ability to think mathematically and enjoy mathematics for its own sake are not necessarily the things that seem to be valued. We believe, and we have evidence, that teaching the pupils to be mathematical does have a positive impact on our results.

AB: We prepare our pupils to access mathematics by expecting them to have conversations and share their ideas and really tease out and explore thought processes that otherwise can just get lost in thinking 'what's the answer?' We know we have to get the context and what we expect the pupils to do right, but the most important thing is that they think about the material we offer them in the right way. As a department we attack any innovation or initiative by discussing it in the same way as we ask the pupils to do with mathematical ideas; asking what this means for us, what are the opportunities and what are the barriers and how the new ideas can be fitted in with our priorities and values.

Mathematical thinking and experiencing, exploring and conjecturing are clearly the most important facets of the pedagogy that AB and TR are developing within their department. It is also clear that this is not an either/or situation; the heads of department have both nurtured their pupils' abilities to think mathematically and prepared them to succeed in examinations.

Making a start

However, when they started as heads of department this was not the case, so the next part of the conversation explores how they started to develop such pedagogy in their departments:

AW: Another school I know decided to start to think about developing their pupils as mathematicians. They settled on a list of six or seven ideas from Leone Burton's book (Burton, 2004) in which she looks at professional mathematicians and discovers what exactly they do in their working lives – that is, they do not sit at desks proving theorems neatly and privately all day. The department constructed a poster that said 'Mathematicians do the following things…'. The poster was displayed in every classroom and it was the frame the department took for their initial thinking.

AB: We also adopted a frame for our initial thinking when I took over as head of department. We took three 'R's, reflective, resourceful and resilient (Claxton, 2002) as our starting point. There is a fourth 'R', reciprocity but we did not adopt this because we were not sure what it meant! We asked, how do we enable our pupils to display these three characteristics? We developed the content and structure of the mathematics that the pupils would be asked to engage with and also the way that they were asked to work together. Different strands have developed at different rates over the last four years because of changes within the team and where my thoughts and the thoughts of others in the department have been going at the time.

AW: The teachers in the team take general aims that they have developed and discussed and turn those into lessons. Hence there is a range of different things going on, all about developing their pupils' ability to engage with mathematics. I think there is an 'R' that is missing and that is 'Repertoire'. There is a sense that teachers have to have a repertoire of approaches. From my observations there are a range of different things that happen in any classroom all designed to promote and support pupils' engaging in mathematics.

TR: I would expect there to be a variety of approaches in any one teacher's lessons. Sometimes the teacher will want to focus on discussion because that is important but at other times it will be different. I would expect discussion to play a part in most lessons but there may be times when teachers decide that they want the pupils to reflect individually or to try things out individually. It depends on what the teachers want the pupils to learn about and how they want them to learn. There are lots of different pedagogical practices to implement; different teachers will teach in different ways.

All teachers within each of the two departments use a variety of approaches depending on their own and their classes' preferences and experiences. Each approach is designed to develop the pupils' ability to engage in mathematical thinking and processes and through that, learn mathematics.

Negotiating a shared vision

Whether the team's vision of what it means to work mathematically is framed by thinking about what mathematicians do or by thinking about good learning behaviours, an ethos is built within the department that values some ways of working and not others. So whose ethos is developed? Is it the head of department's own ethos and expectations or is it negotiated?

AB: The triggers for developing the ethos in the department have been mine. This is partly because I have the time and the freedom to think around things and introduce ideas. However I remain aware that I do not want to railroad people into thinking certain things and having to do things in certain ways because I say so. If I did that I might as well be a document or a prescriptive textbook. My expectation has not been that the teachers do things my way, rather that we approach ideas together in order to develop ways of doing things that fit within certain agreed guidelines. I have my own ideas about the way things should be, but the teachers do not always follow what I think and use their own ideas. I think this is important. I see my job as providing a framework that allows for differences whilst giving each pupil as high a quality mathematical experience as possible. I trust that I have a team that is capable of having conversations about, and supporting one another in developing the pupils as mathematicians.

TR: How do you deal with someone who seems to be planning and emphasising something that conflicts with your overall vision? How do you address that?

AB: Recently we have been looking at lesson objectives. What makes a lesson objective useful and powerful? How do you make a lesson objective so that the pupils will end up addressing higher order thinking skills? How could you improve learning objectives so that you can develop key questions that will allow the pupils to use higher order thinking skills and to think widely and deeply about the mathematics that they are doing? We found that some of the less experienced members of the department felt that developing their learning objectives meant making them slightly more obscure. It seemed that they felt that if nobody had a clue what the objectives meant, they would make the pupils use high order thinking skills. I asked the department to work in pairs to develop new lesson objectives initially and then we moved to new groups of four. I made sure that I had more experienced people in both groups, so the conversation could flow and I trusted the team to thrash the ideas out together and develop some understanding.

TR: I do not imagine that if I asked people to show me their lesson objectives tomorrow that they would all be absolutely perfect, but I do think there has been a development process within the department. It comes back to what do I expect the teachers to do. I do not expect them to be perfect every single time as that would be impossible. As teachers, we are all on a journey to develop, to learn how to teach better all the time. Teachers will develop and learn if they are allowed to discuss and see different ways of teaching and learning. Just as with the pupils, telling them is not the best way.

The department ethos and expectations are developed over time through shared thinking and negotiation led by the experience and expertise of the head of department. Heads of department have a duty to use the time that is made available to them to continue to develop their expertise through reading, discussion with teachers and heads of department both inside and outside school and other experiences such as studying for higher degrees and taking part in research with local university departments.

Working inclusively

However, how does expertise built by teachers within the department get shared? How does a head of department ensure that different approaches are understood and used throughout the department? In the next extract, the heads of department discuss the difficulties of including teachers who for one reason or another find it hard to see themselves as part of the team:

TR: Part of my job is both to value and share teachers' different approaches. As head of department I have to enable teachers to see different pedagogical approaches, to broaden their own repertoire and ways in which we would expect pupils to develop repertoires of their own. We have tried several different models to enable the sharing of good practice and different ideas have worked with differing success. The most successful idea has been to involve PGCE students. Teachers may have historically seen PGCE studentsas an excuse, or an opportunity to have a cup of tea. We have tried to use these pupils explicitly as a vehicle for developing mathematical discussion within the faculty. We team teach with the students and explicitly discuss what and how we want to teach and what we as a team want both the PGCE students and the school pupils to learn. We have tried other things that have not been so successful because of pressures of time. Currently ordinary teachers get six hours a fortnight when they could observe other teachers but they can only do that if they choose not to do their planning, preparation or assessment.

AB: We have planned teacher review cycles in my department. This is not the same as formal observations where you get a view from someone outside the department. In our teacher review meetings, teachers plan a lesson together using a framework that fits with our principles. They then observe each other teach the lesson and review how that went afterwards.

The planning and reviewing is done together, often using faculty meeting time to do this.

AW: Anthony, I have been present at some of your department meetings and I know that you are an amazingly good listener. You set up a task, the idea that is going to be talked about, and then you shut up and let everyone else talk. Very often you are the last person to talk and you show an immense amount of trust in the people in your department. You always seem to have a really good task for teachers to talk about that enables them to develop their understanding. Even so I suspect that, like most departments, there may be some who teach mathematics who are not fully part of the team.

AB: There are some teachers whose specific context makes it difficult to include them in the team. For example a part time teacher who is not working on the days when you have meetings cannot be involved in the conversations and they miss out on that learning experience. I always have one to one meetings with them to try to catch up but you can never replicate the full experience of the discussion. The ideas from the conversations always seem to appear as a list that must be done when presented after the meeting.

AW: All the schools I have studied had teachers in them that it was difficult to include fully in the team and I feel that these teachers have impacted on the previously low attaining pupils in a greater way than on any other pupils. When thinking about the mathematics department there is a 'core team' and then there are others who teach mathematics.

TR: When I think about the department it is the people and forming them into a team that is one of the most difficult things. There is a significant group of people who will engage in the process of developing our ideas about teaching together. These people feel that they have an investment in the vision of the department and what we are trying to accomplish. When new people have arrived, they have generally been very keen to become part of that group and they seem to agree with the ideas that have been developed by the team. We try to ensure that our ideas are made very clear at interviews and I feel that if someone completely disagreed with the general philosophies, they would not accept a post or we would not offer it. However there is still that group who teach mathematics who remain on the fringes for various reasons. These people cause me a great deal of concern.

AB: I know that there are good conversations going on all the time between most members of the department but there are people who are not able to be involved. I try to involve these people in a way that makes them feel confident and comfortable and feel that their ideas are valued. For example a non-specialist teacher was at a department meeting and I heard her say she felt lost when listening to the mathematics being discussed. I have tried hard to make everyone feel comfortable, included and valued but it can be difficult. Just over half the team are really engaged with the process of developing the department but for various reasons it is difficult to fully include other people. I do not think there is anybody who chooses not to be part of the team but for different reasons they cannot be fully involved. Each of these teachers bring different experiences which can be very useful, however I am aware that they can still feel not 100% part of the whole vision.

Using teachers who come to the school during their initial training, and having a system of planning and reviewing lessons together, are effective catalysts for discussing what good teaching looks like, what good learning is and which approaches work in the classroom to develop pupils' mathematical learning. However, such discussions only reach those teachers who are part of the discussions. Those teachers who only work part-time or who have other responsibilities in the school often find that they cannot be part of the conversations and the more often they are not included the less they feel part of the team. There will be differences between being appointed a subject leader from a different school and being promoted internally when sometimes the previous subject leader is still in school. Either way there are likely to be people that were appointed before you had any influence who do not wholly agree with you and people who do not want to change. When you are appointed from outside you are expected to bring in different ideas. If you are promoted internally you know the school and its systems and you may know the changes that need to be made. It will make a difference when you have appointed many of the people in your team. Until then the role will require tact and diplomacy if you are to establish your vision in the department.

Working on mathematics

There will also be people who teach mathematics whose subject knowledge is not strong, either because of shortages of suitably qualified candidates or because they teach other subjects for most of their timetable. For example, there may be teachers who are very confident in themselves and confident about mathematics but have a different view of mathematics from the rest of the team. They may be trained in a subject discipline where mathematics is all about its applications. They may be good at making links to other subjects and have lots of interesting ideas. However, they may have never seen classroom teaching that focuses on mathematical thinking and enjoyment. If they have taught mathematics in the same way for many years, they may not appreciate being expected to change, hence they may not fit into the team. In the next section the heads of department discuss the effect that those teachers who are not fully included in the team have on the pupils that they teach.

> **TR**: I have to think carefully about which pupils people who are not fully part of the team are asked to teach. We work hard to balance any effect out and minimise any difference in the pupils' experience. I think that studying mathematics to a high level is important in an effective mathematics teacher alongside a teaching qualification, but it is not always possible to recruit teachers who are so well qualified.

> **AW**: I'll give you two specific examples of the effect that teachers can have on pupils, both of them from real classrooms. The first one is a teacher who is asking her pupils to draw a graph for some discrete data. She drew a graph on the board and then almost automatically joined up the points,

telling the pupils that they must use a ruler to draw a neat straight line. It is such a seductive error, and it is the kind of error that the pupils make. If she does not have a discussion about this kind of error with somebody, how will she be able to help the pupils recognise that kind of error themselves, and what might the pupils learn from her that they have to unlearn later? Another error I have seen is slightly different. A teacher was discussing the mathematical fact that an odd number added to another odd number will always give an even number. She said 'The algebra for that is $o + o = e'$. Algebraic understanding is an important issue at Key Stage 3. What should be done to make sure that all pupils fully understand the intricacies of algebra and are not confused by non-algebraic use of letters such as these?

TR: I think you could address the first example, which is an easily-made assumption, in a meeting by asking what are the misconceptions that pupils might make when drawing graphs and where those misconceptions might have come from and use the mistake as something to move everyone's ideas forward. The second example is a very fundamental misconception and perhaps could be dealt with in a similar way, but the discussion would have to be at a deep level. The discussion would be about what constitutes algebra and proof. It would be harder to discuss the idea without making it obvious where it came from and therefore potentially damaging someone's confidence. It would be important to make sure that the teacher is not exposed in front of the rest of the team. I know a teacher who feels that mathematics itself has changed because of changes in the way algebra is now taught. I would deal with the second issue by focusing on algebraic proof as a learning focus in a future faculty meeting. We would discuss 'How do we teach proof to Year 8?'

AW: There are some real subtleties about what is and what is not algebra. In the mnemonic 'sohcahtoa' (sine equals opposite over hypotenuse etc.) are those letters being used as labels or are they being used algebraically? Do they stand for particular numbers or general numbers? It is really, really, tough. If you have studied mathematics you know when to use letters and when letters are not appropriate and how to use them. You convey that implicitly to the pupils how to use letters. If someone has not had the experience then how do you explain that $o + o = e$ is not algebra?

AB: I know people who believe that you have to have a high degree in mathematics to be able to teach Year 7 and 8 pupils and a whole spectrum of people opposing that view as well. Personally I believe that mathematical subject knowledge is vital, but you have to be able to teach it as well and they do not always go hand in hand. The question was whether we address these things? Yes, the issues have to be addressed but you have to be so careful. It is easy to damage someone's confidence in themselves and their ability to teach the subject. Such conversations have to be behind closed doors not in a meeting with other people. Many people place a great emphasis on being able to be correct. I would like to think that my department supports and respects one another so that they can discuss anything they feel unsure about between themselves. In general what I do with my department models what I would like to see happen in the classrooms. We are happy for the pupils to make mistakes and see it as a point for learning but there is a difference with teachers and it takes care and tact but that does not mean that mistakes are ignored.

TR: It may be that the person who is likely to make mistakes values correct answers in their classrooms and therefore values being correct themselves. I think we should question the value we place on being right, being mathematically correct. In the classroom we value mistakes and misconceptions almost as much as right answers because of the learning opportunities they present. In the classroom we also explore the difference between a mathematical truth and a convention and such ideas. There will be some people in a meeting who will not see making mistakes as a problem. They will admit it, learn from it and be interested in exploring where the idea came from. However, there will be some people, possibly those people who have not studied mathematics themselves, who value only correct answers and will not necessarily be in a position to explore the reasons behind common mistakes. I would have to be very careful when talking with those people.

AB: This shows the importance of a department finding time to explore mathematics together. When you are leading a team you do not want to expose people or make them feel ridiculous. I try to develop a culture where it's OK to make mistakes, but as Tim says, there is a difference between the mistakes that people are happy to make and those they are not happy to make. The mistake we are discussing is a fundamental error rather than one where you have a guess and then explore to find out if it is correct or not. It is vital that teachers have the opportunity to learn from each other, ask questions and say if they are not really sure about something. I would say exploring mathematical ideas together is valuable in a whole range of different ways, people enjoy going through the experience. We teach mathematics because we enjoy going through a mathematical process and people enjoy getting into it. It is also valued because people remind themselves about how they want their pupils to behave and how they want their pupils to explore ideas within a lesson.

AW: When you introduce mathematics, is it a mathematical problem for everybody to get stuck into and have a good time with or is it curriculum related?

AB: Sometimes it is curriculum related but sometimes it is not. We never sit down and do mathematics for its own sake because we do not have the time. We do not meet regularly enough to give us time to socialise mathematically. When we meet and do mathematics I have an agenda; I intend the mathematics we do to demonstrate something but the teachers do engage in mathematical thinking in our meetings. There is no conflict in my mind that we are doing mathematics and I have another agenda as well. I ask the teachers to think about what they are doing, about the whys and how and the way that we structure what we do. The intention is to aid people in developing the way that they teach mathematics and doing mathematics together is a useful way to do this. If by doing mathematics together we learn how to teach better then that is fine.

TR: There always is an agenda even if it seems well hidden. I wanted to involve other people in leading the mathematics that we do in faculty meeting and I asked others in the team to take a lead, linking it to work that had been done together. The idea was that they introduce some mathematics related to what they had done and the rest of the team would be able to reflect on how the pupils would engage with the idea. However that has not worked this year. The team are not yet confident enough to ask the rest of the team to do mathematics; they have felt more confident in sharing what they think the pupils should be doing. It is not yet a common expectation that teachers do mathematics in faculty meetings. I think I need to spend more time making working on some mathematics a fundamental part of each meeting so that it seems the natural thing to do, before I start asking other people to share the lead.

AW: This is an example where it is not what you do, rather the context that you are working in and the way that you do it. Another school I know about has people working together in pairs doing curriculum development together. Each pair then introduces their particular tasks to the team and the team do it. The team spends an hour doing the task and talking about how the pupils would engage with the mathematics. This seems very similar to the model that you have talked about. It worked for them but it did not work in your context. It seems that it is not about whether this is something that we should do or could do, but rather what are the possibilities. Each different mix of people determine whether ideas are going to work or not, it is very like teaching really.

TR: I am determined to use faculty time to engage with mathematics and I will find the time to make this happen. Time is an issue for us as it is for many mathematics departments but this would be time well spent. It will have an agenda and that will be as Anthony said to improve and develop the teaching and learning of mathematics in our school.

AB: I see my role as somebody who helps teachers to develop in their ability to develop their pupils as mathematicians. I have chosen to do specific things to develop the specific areas of mathematics teaching that I believe needed to be addressed in my department. I choose tasks not necessarily to develop ideas that will be taken into a classroom but often to develop approaches which will be used to develop what is then taken into the classroom. Our work as a team is one stage removed from the classroom.

Approaching differentiation

It is not just resources and ways to approach teaching that concern mathematics departments; considerations such as differentiation and how pupils are grouped are constant sources of discussion for teachers. So how do these heads of department approach differentiation?

AB: Our approach to differentiation is to make sure that the tasks that we use are accessible to everyone and that they are capable of being taken wherever the pupils can take them. That's what we have tried to do but I am not sure how successful we have been. I know that at the beginning of the task some pupils already have a different understanding of the task from others so there are almost as many starting points as there are pupils in the class. If suitable tasks are used then very quickly everybody is working at a task that is meaningful to them. I think potentially there are many such tasks. We have worked on them as a department but it is a difficult area. We have the same discussions as other mathematics departments about whether pupils should be in sets or in mixed ability groups or balanced groups and so on. When you have people in sets you think you can teach the same thing to all of them in the same way but, of course, they are still individuals and that is never possible.

TR: This year we have focused on raising our expectations and the expectations of traditionally low attaining pupils by ensuring that they have access to the same curriculum as other pupils. We teach mixed ability in Year 7 and set in half year groups in Year 8. Within the faculty there are some people who do not mind teaching mixed ability groups, some people who positively want to teach pupils in mixed ability groups and some people who do not want to teach mixed ability groups. As I do not think I should drag the faculty along in my wake, we do have sets in Year 8 but we have focussed on developing a Year 8 curriculum that would be perfect for mixed ability groups but is equally useful for any kind of ability set. I think that there are a range of pupils in any set, but having ability groups changes the focus. If you are teaching a mixed ability group, some pupils will struggle to understand what is required. The same struggle will go on in a bottom set and as there are more pupils struggling, it may be tempting to assume that they are all stuck in the same way. In a top set, less pupils will struggle to understand at the start of a task, partly because there will be fewer literacy problems. However both sets can start from the same point but where the pupils get to may be different. I took on Set 3, the lowest of our groupings, so that the lower attaining pupils were not cut adrift and left to the unqualified teachers. Since we only have three sets, it is really important for the school that every set makes as much progress as possible. If a third of the year are not able to achieve a Level 5 in the National Key Stage Tests then the department will be in trouble. I want all the pupils to finish Key Stage 3 with a good basis for their GCSE. I chose to introduce a way of organising the curriculum that meant we could switch next year to mixed ability without having to re-organise the curriculum or the way that we teach.

Organising the way that pupils are grouped will continue to be a bone of contention in many departments, but these two heads of department are clear that all pupils are entitled to the same challenges and opportunities and that previous low attainment is not a reason to ask less of pupils although they may need more supporting experiences. Setting is commonplace in schools in England but we believe that it is not necessarily the best way to organise learning for pupils.

Developing thinking and problem-solving
However faced with making changes in the department we believe that changing to a task based pedagogy that asks pupils to problem solve for themselves, use appropriate mathematical tools and above all to think

mathematically seems more important than how the pupils are grouped. Often mathematics teachers emphasise 'getting through' the content in the curriculum. Clearly these heads of department see the role of the mathematics department as developing pupils as thinking, problem-solving mathematicians so how do they square that with the requirement to teach content knowledge and help their pupils to gain good results in examinations?

> **TR**: One of the things that tends to happen in mathematics lessons is to teach pupils in Year 11 the same things that they were taught in Year 7. It always seems to be prime factor decomposition at the beginning of every year. I remember vividly in my PGCE year teaching Year 8 straight line graphs. I did not have quite enough time to do everything and I was worried about this at the time. If I had looked forward in the medium term plans I would have seen that straight line graphs came up again in the summer term. It seemed that all the topics in the summer term plans were in the autumn term. I took a year or two to feel confident that there really was no benefit in rushing through any topic because the ideas came up again and again in the schemes of work. In time I gained enough influence to dictate how schemes of work would be used. I remember saying 'off the cuff' in a heads of faculty meeting that as long as the pupils could think and were prepared to learn to be able to do mathematics, I could teach the whole GCSE syllabus in Year 11. An assistant head picked the statement up and said, "That's a bit of a bold statement". I told him about a class I had taught who had had a very difficult year the year before I taught them. We started from scratch and they responded well and got good results. It was not anything amazing in my teaching, the reason for their good results was that they were prepared to learn and they were given that opportunity. The type of 'spiral systems' that are common in many schools are boring for teachers and I think they are boring for pupils. Developing the pupils mathematically is important, they need to think and process information and enjoy doing that. If they can think mathematically then they can learn the content they need for exams very quickly. It takes a lot of confidence to say this though. The pupils and their parents expect mathematics to be taught in a certain kind of way and many teachers cling to the simplification of ideas that teaching 'spiral systems' offer.

> **AB**: These are hard questions. GCSEs are important so Year 11 becomes examination preparation. Can they do this question? Can they do that type of question? So we do all these wonderful things in Years 7, 8 and 9 and it runs out in Years 10 & 11. We have concentrated our efforts on developing innovative approaches lower down the school. We have done all the playing around with and enjoying mathematics early on and then we say "right let's get ready for the exams." I suppose we have to question, why?

> **TR**: I remember reading Jo Boaler's (1997) work early in my teacher training. The two schools taught in very different ways. The one school offered a challenging, investigative way of learning mathematics and the other a conventional text book based approach. The results in each case were similar except that a much higher proportion of the first school's pupils persevered with harder questions. My mindset at the time was that I have

to teach all these things this week and those things next week. I became aware that Year 11 pupils cannot find the lowest common multiple of two numbers if you ask them to. If your language skills are OK and if you are thinking then 'lowest common multiple' tells you what it is. Pupils can appear to be relatively successful mathematicians but still not be able to use what they were taught in Key Stage 3. If they cannot use the ideas that they learned earlier then they have to be taught again later.

AW: I think good preparation for exams is about looking at what questions arise; thinking about 'how would I tackle this?' and learning some mathematics as you go along. It is also learning how to deal with questions that you have not seen before. One of the things in Boaler's book is that the two schools took the same exam and she got permission from the exam board to look at what they did. In one of the schools, if the question was not procedural or they did not recognise the procedure, they did not do anything. However, in the other school, if they did not know exactly how to proceed with the question they would have a go and start trying to do something. The sad thing was that the school which got the better results actually got worse results than it had got the previous year. Since the results were better than the other school, it was claimed as a positive result for the investigative school. The syllabus had been changed the year that these pupils took their examinations. Previously the balance had been something like 20% based on the exam and 80% coursework but it was changed that year to 50-50. The school did not change its approach and the outcome was lower results. Suddenly the exam was much more important and they did not change their approach; they probably should have done. So the story is a little bit mis-told because we know that there are skills to be learned in order to succeed in examinations.

TR: We know that there will be important changes to Key Stage 3 and GCSE examinations soon. The two papers at GCSE will be interesting and may well mean that mathematical thinking becomes important but it will be difficult to set the examination without the potential for the results to be as unreliable as the English results tend to be. The new National Curriculum makes it important to focus on the concepts and processes and therefore the assessments must be changed to reflect this.

Mathematics teachers are about enabling pupils to think and process mathematically, but they are also about enabling pupils to do well in examinations. These two foci are clearly not mutually exclusive but the balance has to be got right. As AB says it is very tempting to just concentrate on examinations in Years 10 and 11 but that is probably not best for the pupils. As TR reminded us, if the pupils are prepared to think and want to learn, they can learn to attain well at GCSE in a relatively short time, but all pupils will need to learn and practice examination technique as well as mathematical knowledge.

Leading beyond the department

Heads of department naturally focus on what goes on in their own faculty but they have a wider remit as well. It is not enough in most schools to take a lead on pedagogy within your own department – as a head of mathematics you will also have a leading role within the school.

AB: The head of faculty's most important role is to make sure that the department continues to develop and grow and just get better at helping the pupils learn mathematics. Teachers do not have the time to think about the issues to explore, they are too busy teaching. The crux of the role is to make sure that the department is focused on what is important. However I think that heads of faculty are the engine room for what happens school wide because they are the link between the senior management team and the classrooms. Essentially the heads of faculty drive what goes on in the classroom. Heads of faculty meetings are places where the different concerns and issues that affect every subject area can be shared and discussed and decisions made about whole school issues. It is important that the senior management team ensure these meetings happen.

TR: There has been some discussion about the function of the head of faculty meetings in the last few years because they have not necessarily provided productive discussion. At the moment the discussion tends to revolve around raising achievement which might be assumed to have something to do with teaching and learning. However the discussion is more to do with how to motivate the Year 11 and Year 9 pupils and what interventions will be needed and how to find the time for that. I really enjoyed a meeting where I had the opportunity to get people from other subjects engaged in doing mathematics and in talking about the learning involved and how that related to their subjects but that was unusual. I agree that the heads of faculty are the engine of the school but it needs a firm hand on the wheel if the focus is to be really useful. There are many different initiatives that the school can be involved in, creative partnerships, learning to learn and so on. If a school keeps toying with these ideas and not necessarily following them through then they are not useful. My mathematics department is often held up as a place where innovative things happen but so far, I have not had many opportunities to share these ideas within the school.

AB: It is my job to pick out what is important from the school wide discussions and talk those through in the department. Since the mathematics department does deliver and our results are good, we tend to get left alone. My role is to decide what fits best with the priorities within my faculty and how we can fit in with whole school priorities. Often there is a great deal of good practice going on in the school that has been built from the ground up and works for a specific reasons in a particular context. The initiatives that come from outside will need to be thought through and worked through before they will work in the same way. The head of faculty has to sort through these external ideas and maintains the big picture or vision of what is wanted in their department. I do not think that you can buy in ideas 'off the shelf'; there is a journey to go through in making lasting changes in any department. It will only work if the teachers properly engage with the ideas. The head of department has to guide this journey and has the opportunity to lead others.

TR: There is a school development plan and there is our department plan and I want to concentrate on our development plan but sometimes the school decides, for example, we should be focusing on homework when I want the department to focus on other things, but the school focus will be the one that takes precedence. Although I would like more attention paid to what we do; the department is appreciated. I have always been given the confidence that the senior management team see what we do as good and when asked I give well thought out and reasoned arguments so they know we are doing well by the pupils.

The responsibilities of head of department are wide ranging as we have seen, taking a lead within the department and contributing to whole school development.

Conclusion

In this conversation, the question we have addressed is 'What is important about taking a lead in teaching mathematics?' We believe that mathematical processes and thinking are important, and that is emphasised by the National Curriculum (QCA, 2007). However, most people who are teaching mathematics today were not taught to be mathematical thinkers and problem solvers themselves. Therefore, there will be a process of change and a feeling of risk taking and uncertainty as the skills required to teach mathematical thinking and problem-solving are developed.

We started by saying that leading a successful department is neither straightforward nor easy and in taking a lead on pedagogy there is much to think about and to decide both for yourself as subject leader and in discussion with the team of teachers in your department. It helps when you are clear yourself about your vision of a successful mathematics department, both how you think about the pedagogy that will enable pupils to learn well and why you think that. Engaging with other people who are interested in pedagogy will be a first important step in becoming sure yourself about your beliefs and values and setting out your own vision for the department. Branches of local mathematics associations and contacts through the NCETM may provide this connection or you may need to approach a local university and take masters level courses to find the right level of conversation for you. However you achieve it, the value of such conversations cannot be overstated.

In the next, related chapter, we will continue discussions with the two heads of department but in the next chapter the focus will be on the implications of taking a lead on developing the member of your departments' professional practice.

References

Boaler, J. (1997) *Experiencing School Mathematics: Teaching Styles, sex and setting*. Buckingham: Open University Press.

Burton, L. (2004) *Mathematicians as Enquirers: Learning About Learning Mathematics*. Dordrecht: Kluwer Academic Publishers.

Claxton, G. (2002) *Building Learning Power*. Bristol: TLO Ltd.

DCSF (2008) *The Framework for Teaching Secondary Mathematics.* http://www.standards.dcsf.gov.uk/secondary/framework/maths/fwsm/ accessed 07.07.2008.

QCA (2007) *The National Curriculum*. online http://curriculum.qca.org.uk/key-stages-3-and-4/subjects/index.aspx accessed on 07.07.08.

6
TAKING A LEAD ON DEVELOPING PROFESSIONAL PRACTICE:
Coaching and Mentoring

Clare Lee, Anthony Broadly, Tim Rattigan, Anne Watson

The previous chapter discussed many of the issues that you, as subject leader, have come across or will come across in taking a lead on the pedagogy of teaching mathematics. In this chapter, the same team will take a look at continuing professional development (CPD) in its widest terms. What do you do as a subject leader, day in day out, to develop the professional practice in your department? What are the mentoring issues involved in inducting new teachers to the department? What are the issues in developing teachers and meeting their entitlement for opportunities to increase their professional competence? What effective measures can be put in place to enable all teachers confidently to take their place in an innovative, effective department with vision and purpose? Where does coaching fit in? In the first section of the chapter, two heads of department discuss with two respected figures in mathematics education their role in developing the teachers in their department. The latter section of this chapter deals in more depth with the concepts of mentoring and coaching.

Using the Department Meeting to develop professional practice

Discussions on improving professional practice will often take place within department meetings. The meetings are vital in forming the department as a team and addressing the differences in experiences that teachers bring to the department. If the department wants to develop its pupils' mathematical thinking and learning, then there will be learning to be done by the teachers themselves, whatever their mathematics background.

In casting themselves as learners, the teachers can explore and consolidate their own learning and remember what it feels like to learn mathematics. Therefore the heads of department consider it vital that teachers 'do maths' in department meetings, not just exploring random ideas, but rather exploring the mathematical ideas in a given topic so that they are alert to the potential learning needs of their pupils or are ready to develop lesson approaches that will allow their pupils to learn. Department meetings are about becoming ready to go into the classroom and meet expectations. Are teachers ready with ideas and resources?

> **AB**: Four years ago when I became a new head of department I knew that I had a whole framework of ideas that I wanted the department to think

about. I started by trying to change the resources that were used in the department and spent a colossal amount of time changing and rehashing the schemes of work and the resources we used. I felt I had to make sure I could tick off all the areas of the National Curriculum so that an outside observer could not point a finger at me. What I really wanted to do was to enable the pupils to develop the three Rs that I spoke about earlier in Chapter 5. I started by developing a bank of ideas that might support teachers in using new ways that would help the pupils learn in those ways. As time went on, I realised that spending time giving people a bank of things to do was not the best use of my time. I wanted the teachers themselves to think through ideas and be able to create resources for themselves. Currently I actually resist any call to have a meeting to swap sheets and other resources because I think if somebody has developed something, they have developed it to suit themselves and their style of teaching with their classes. I feel that it is not possible to take something that someone else has written and simply transfer it to another class with another teacher. It is the thought processes behind the resource that is the useful thing. Therefore I am happy if people share those thought processes as they are ultimately going to be more use to others than the end product. If a conversation between teachers develops a common resource then that is fantastic, but just swapping the resource cannot be enough.

TR: I think that sometimes the resource can help provide the stimulus for the discussion to take place that helps share ideas and principles. Obviously this can happen without a resource, but some conversations happen just because someone has seen a resource that they want to share.

AB: I agree. We were talking earlier about teacher who were not involved in such conversations. Sometimes it is new teachers who are appointed to your department after the resources have been developed. I know that these teachers do not use the resources anywhere near as effectively as the teachers who were involved in their development. I had a team of teachers who had worked and grown together over three or four years. They had developed resources together and used them well. However when one or two left and were replaced it was as though a cog had been changed in a machine and it took a while before things began to run smoothly again. When someone has not been involved in the conversation, what to the rest of the team are resources that develop thinking and reflection are just a bank of resources and some of them look very sparse and even tatty to an outsider.

AW: I feel that there is something missing from this question. What is developed in a mathematics team is not just principles or just resources, although that is part of it. What is being developed is thinking about how pupils are going to learn. The thinking is about: 'what is it we want the pupils to learn and how are they going to learn it?' It might be that the pupils' learning is assisted by teachers thinking how to support the growth of mathematical thinking or by developing or using a particular resource, but what are the other things? If you watch teachers working you see all kinds of behaviour and patterns of language, structures of lessons and so many different decisions, only some of which are overt and can be talked about. I know departments who talk about the language you are going to use and how to include the pupils in its use. There are more subtle, less easy to identify, things that are done in lessons that are designed to get particular things to happen.

TR: We have produced a lot of resources and lots of ideas to support work on different parts of the curriculum. Some teachers use the ideas and some do not. The vehicle of the resources has helped some teachers to think about their own mathematical thinking. I know that teachers in my team are doing some work on triangles, Pythagoras and trigonometry with Year 9. These people are sharing resources, but they will not use a resource that they have not thought about or made some investment in. There was a conversation that I overheard yesterday and someone was talking about using a particular resource. They only wanted to use a small part of it because the rest did not suit the purpose that they wanted. The other teacher said that they had used it in the same way and could provide an altered copy. The thinking was there and I know that part of sharing resources is encouraging other members of the faculty to know about the thinking that has gone on. There was no expectation that the teaching had to be done in a particular way. I made some resources on multiplication and area and used them to teach one class but I had to make a whole set of new resources for another class because the first set were just not right. Every time I come to teach something I seem to need to re-think what exactly will work best with the new group. There are times when I wish I could use last year's resources. Anything to do with straight line graphs I find I have to start again, I have used so many different things and I wish I could stick with one, but it is a complicated concept and every time I teach it I feel that it could have been better. It is important to be engaged in that reflective process every day.

AB: Teachers are not presenters of facts to be gobbled up. I have friends outside of teaching who say 'After a few years don't you just have all your notes that you can use again?' If you were just presenting I suppose that could be the case, but each class is different and needs the same thought put into teaching just as Tim has described.

AW: There are things that are constant. One of the things that I am picking up in schools is a sense that there are tools that people use to help them to do mathematics. Pupils have to be able to think and make choices about which tool to use and how to use that tool. So for example, I watched a lesson for a research project.[1] The lesson required the pupils to measure a circumference. Rulers were provided and one pupil said he was stuck with measuring the circumference, the conversation went something like:

---

1. This observation, and some of the others in this and the previous chapter, were made as part of the Changes in Mathematics Teaching Project undertaken by Anne Watson & Els DeGeest, funded by Esmee Fairbairn Foundation, grant number 05-1838, but the views expressed here are Anne's and not of the Foundation.

Teacher, absolutely deadpan asks "Oh, why?"

The boy said "I can't do it with the ruler"

Teacher asked, "What do you need then?"

"Well, a piece of string"

"I'm afraid I haven't got any string, can you use a bendy ruler?"

"What a tape measure?"

"Yes, I have some tape measures you can borrow". The boy went away happy

At the heart of that conversation there is a problem solving approach which seems to be fundamental for many teachers. It is not problem solving as taught in a problem solving lesson, but problem solving as in "How to I do this?", "What do I need?" This is not just about mathematical thinking, it is not just about resources, it is about a mind set that the teachers have and that the pupils pick up.

Taking a lead on developing professional practice is about building a way of thinking about how mathematics is learned and then thinking about how approaches in the classroom enable pupils to learn in that way. Teachers in the department will discuss and share ways in which classrooms can be managed so that mathematical thinking may be developed. Some of that sharing will consist of seeing one another's lessons; planning together and sharing a mathematical experience in department meetings, which could be termed as co-coaching (see the last section of this chapter).

Other coaching will be enabled by resources that help teachers to act in the classroom to develop mathematical thinking and processing. However it is clear that it is not resources alone that enable the pupils to learn mathematics effectively, rather it will be the coaching discussions that prompt the creation of the resources or the conversations prompted by the resource. Without those conversations between teachers, the resource itself is will not prompt the mathematical thinking and learning that it otherwise might have done.

What counts as professional development?

As you appoint more teachers yourself, the issues in developing professional practice will become different. In your department, there will be opportunities to discuss with likeminded people the direction that you would like to lead the department and to choose the kinds of professional development that will relevant. There will be difficulties along the way; people who want to support the department but feel unsure about their ability to contribute and people who do not understand why they would want to change when they have taught in a particular way for many years. Each problem and issue will need careful handling but the heads of department are clear that the key is involving as many of the department as possible in discussion and negotiation.

Obviously, professional development will include courses outside the school to bring ideas and innovative practices to the department. These may be meetings of subject leaders or training courses provided within your local authority, the SSAT or similar organisations, or courses provided by commercial organisations. If they meet a perceived need and the knowledge acquired is used within the department, then such courses will be important to the department's development. The two heads of department consider that the greatest influence on their ideas came from being able to study and be reflective over time as a result of joining a masters level degree course.

AB: A lot of my ideas have formed through having the opportunity to read and to think and to discuss with people like Tim on the masters courses that we have taken at university. It has been important to me in developing what I stand for.

TR: Leadership courses can be useful but they vary in quality, I spent a lot of time thinking about my leadership, I want to influence people and get others to develop their thinking about how pupils learn and how they learn mathematics. I am not expecting them to believe what I believe but rather to develop their own beliefs and principles. That is important to me and how I see as my role as a leader.

AW: When I was a head of department that was true for me as well. Management training was about finding time for my personal thinking and how to put across that thinking but was not about doing that thinking. It is important that Heads of Department find time to talk to other Heads of Mathematics outside of the standard, statutory, formal meetings that are convened by the local authority or examination boards. This contact is really important but can be hard to set up. It could be through local meeting of subject associations, the ATM or MA. When I was head of department I used to go to Derby to ATM and spend weekends talking about what it meant to do mathematics as part of the 100% GCSE coursework pilot. I do not think I would have been as effective a Head of Department without these meetings. The TDA are funding a teaching and learning masters but to be effective this requires people to meet together to read, think discuss and learn

TR: In my department I would expect people to start a diploma course maybe the year after their NQT year so that there is the expectation that they continue their learning and development.

AB: The whole process of meeting together is so valuable, meeting together to consider mathematics and learning. The opportunity to read and to talk to other people about the processes and learning of mathematics is hugely beneficial.

As the conversations above demonstrate, the process of developing professional practice is complex. It must start within the department, growing teachers who may be at the start of their careers and nurturing ideas and skills as a team. Outside ideas are important as the department keeps in touch with current thinking and new ideas but those ideas will not take root in practice without purposeful encouragement within the department. Therefore the next section introduces coaching and mentoring as one of the most powerful ways of working in the department to nurture and disseminate ideas and practices.

Coaching and Mentoring

The effective department, as described by the two heads of department, has an ethos of exploration, risk taking and steady professional improvement. Such improvement has been shown to be the result of using mentoring and coaching. Hence, here we consider what coaching and mentoring are and how they can be used in a programme of professional development in your department. The section on mentoring is first as in our interpretation, mentoring requires less discussion than coaching.

Mentoring

There are many similarities between coaching and mentoring, the chief amongst them is that they are ways in which professionals work together to improve practice. However mentoring is specifically a process of "one person offering support to another through establishing a relationship and supporting their development, learning and growth" (Roberts & Constable, 2003 p.1)

Traditionally, mentoring is the long term passing on of support, guidance and advice. In schools, it has tended to describe a relationship in which more experienced colleagues use their greater knowledge and understanding of teaching to support the development of more junior or inexperienced members of staff. Using the term in this way reflects its origins from the Greek myth where Odysseus entrusts the education of his son to his friend Mentor.

It is common practice to appoint a mentor to help with the induction of staff new to the school or new to their role within school. So, if you are appointed as subject leader within the school where you already teach, you may still expect to have a mentor to help you with your new role. The experienced mentor will see their role as alerting their mentee to the systems within school, helping them settle in quickly and inducting the new member of staff into the ways of working within school. The word mentor is often used for the person who guides and supports trainee teachers within schools, using their experience and expertise to enable the beginning teacher to grasp quickly some of the intricacies of class management and pedagogy. A mentor should be ready to listen and also ready with ideas and advice to help with the problems that the less experienced mentee comes across as they start to get to grips with their new role.

A mentor may also work with pupils in school. Sometimes the mentor is appointed within school, a teacher or an older pupil, to give particular pupils a helping hand and an ear to listen and help them through a phase in their schooling, perhaps when pupils come to the school from another, or as the pupils approach their GCSE exams. Mentors may also be appointed for pupils from outside school, businesses often allow their employees to visit schools to act as mentor to raise pupils' expectations of what they can do and where their schooling could lead.

Coaching

Coaching is focused on developing skills and knowledge so that practice improves, hopefully leading to the achievement of departmental or school objectives. Coaching is intended to develop professional practice by improving performance. Coaching is often peer to peer where both parties are developing their practice in similar but perhaps subtly different ways. However, the term coach is also used to indicate someone who has a much more knowledge and status than the person being coached, for example an athletics coach. Therefore the term coach is often used alongside other terms such as a specialist coach who is much more like a mentor, or a co-coach where neither party in the coaching agreement takes precedence over the other.

Co-coaching is often used in a school setting as it allows people to take risks and develop expertise in a supported and non-threatening environment. The important point is that all parties taking part in a co-coaching agreement are intending to learn from their experience. The co-coaching agreement usually lasts for a set period of time and focuses on specific goals. For example:

- A head of department could work with another head of department from a different curriculum area in order to develop both parties' skills in delegation and distributed leadership.

- An experienced colleague could work with an NQT to develop the use of graphing software in school. The NQT may bring expertise in using the software and the experienced colleague may bring knowledge of the curriculum and classroom management skills. Both of the people in this co-coaching agreement want to learn from one another.

- A team of three or more teachers could work together in a coaching agreement. They could plan a series of lessons together, working on designing the best learning experience that they can. Once planned one teacher would teach the lesson watched by the others, or would video the lesson and watch it back with the other two. The positive aspects of the lesson would be brought out and where changes are needed, these are worked on together. The next teacher teaches the revised lesson and reports back to the team and so on until they have ironed out as many difficulties as they can. Teachers working in coaching teams are not limited to planning lessons, although much can be learned from this. They could also work together to, for example, improve behaviour of one class across curriculum areas or to consider how to challenge gifted mathematicians at all levels in the school. The National Strategy has produced some helpful guidance on this form of coaching which they term 'Learning Triads'. This coaching development programme is described in 'Leading in Learning for developing thinking skills in secondary schools'. This form of coaching closely mirrors Action Research as discussed in chapter 7 in that it goes through cycles in order to improve practice.

The principles of coaching and mentoring
There are many ways in which a coaching and mentoring programme can be instigated. However if someone is acting as a coach, whether as a specialist coach using their expertise to help someone else develop, or as a co-coach or in a learning triad, there are certain principles that should be followed. The following principles apply to all forms of coaching:

1. There must be is a genuine willingness to learn on the part of both the person who is coached and the coach.

2. It is essential to respect confidentiality.

3. It is important to allow the person being coached opportunity to make their own decisions. If either party is quick to make judgements, they could get in the way of progress.
4. The coach must be supportive and non-critical, helping the coachee to look beyond the obvious.
5. The coach must believe that the person who is coached has the answers to their problems within themselves.
6. Both parties must aim to be positive and seek solutions to any issues.
7. The coach must pay attention to recognising and pointing out strengths and to building and maintaining self-esteem.
8. The coach must challenge the coachee to move beyond their comfort zones.
9. The coach must help the person who is coached to break down big goals into manageable steps.
10. Both parties must be firm that self-knowledge improves performance; so the coach may help the coachee to know their strengths and where they need to focus their attention.

The best coaches believe in the ability of the individual to create the insights and ideas that are needed to move situations forward. Therefore the task of the coach is to use the advanced skills of listening, questioning and reflection in order to create conversations that enable the coachee to consider their own situation and see their own way forward. It is important that the person being coached sees the relationship as more like a partnership of equals than anything that seems to be parental or advisory. It can help to think of coaching as unlocking a person's potential to develop their own professional practice. Coaching and mentoring is helping another teacher to learn, it is not teaching them.

Coaching and mentoring for effective practice
Coaching and mentoring are particularly powerful tools for developing teaching for several reasons. Many teachers are unconsciously competent with regard to their current practice. They do not recognise the things they are expert in and therefore are not always able to articulate their practice in order to share it or to transfer their expertise from one teaching context to another. Coaching can help teachers to become more aware of what it is they do well, as well as what they are not doing so effectively. A coach can also help to identify the impact of specific aspects of professional practice on the quality of learning and standards. The link between developing pedagogy and its impact on standards is complex and difficult to pinpoint. A coach can analyse lessons to identify teacher actions and critical incidents which led to improved learning outcomes. Having another person to help collect evidence about the quality of the learning processes and outcomes can be vital when trying to learn what worked well and what was less successful.

Pupil learning is at the heart of effective practice. However evidence of learning is not always readily apparent to a teacher while they are busy teaching. Coaches can seek out evidence of learning and can help to identify how the teaching contributed to it. When a teacher is developing their teaching skills, for example, in questioning or oral feedback, it can be hard for them to reflect on their practice at the point of developing it. Coaching, particularly where supported by a video of the lesson observed, can help to facilitate such reflection. It is also true that some aspects of teaching are complex and difficult to refine, for example, the sharing of learning objects with pupils so they are clearly understood. The amount of time needed to develop an in-depth understanding of practice must not be underestimated. Time is needed in order to engage in collaborative action, thinking, reflection, discussion with trusted peers and reading what others have written in order to develop deep understanding.

Collaborative thinking helps move understanding forwards for both the coached teacher and the coach. Developing an operational understanding of innovative practice takes persistence. A teacher's practice and confidence may actually dip as they try to develop new skills and implement new approaches such as peer assessment. Coaching provides the supportive context that helps to nurture new practice through the initial tribulations and uncertainties. All effective teaching is rich in approaches that can be transferred from one teacher's classroom to another; for example, using no hands-up questioning and wait time. Specialist coaches can suggest approaches to inform future practice and support another teacher in developing them.

Developing effective practice in teaching mathematics takes time, but coaching or mentoring offers a powerful way of accelerating the process and generating real change in classrooms. In order to get started you will need to answer the following questions.

- What will be the focus of the coaching or mentoring? How will that focus be decided? What changes are needed?
- Who needs to be involved?
- Will we form co-coaching pairs or triads, or will we use specialist coaches?
- What do you need to do to make it happen?
- What do the people involved need to know?
- How do you decide on how and when to start?
- What will make it successful?
- How will you recognise that the coaching process has made a difference? What changes will you see?

Forming a coaching agreement

Within a coaching agreement, it is vital that both partners know exactly how you are working together. The initial conversations should be intended to create a sense of joint ownership and encouraging confidence and risk taking. At the start of the relationship an agreement should be reached about the purpose of the coaching so that both the coach and the person being coached know what is to be built or developed and where they are starting from. When anyone is trying to learn, the core of the activity lies in the sequence of two actions:

The first is the perception by the learner of a gap between a desired goal and his or her present state (of knowledge, and/or understanding, and/or skill). The second is the action taken by the learner to close that gap in order to attain the desired goal. The learner would first have to understand the evidence about this gap, and then take action on the basis of that evidence. Although the teacher could stimulate and guide this process, the learning has to be done by the student. (Black et al., 2003 page 14)

Questioning is an important skill for a coach and at the start questions should be designed to find out what really interests the person being coached, what their strengths are and where and how they want to develop their teaching. Questions will be an important part of the process throughout the coaching.

Questions could ask for:

- Meta-cognition – what was going through your mind when Jasmin gave that obscure answer?
- Analysis – how far do you think we met our goals for this coaching cycle?
- Synthesis – what do you think contributed to the penny finally dropping for those pupils?
- Evaluation – what do you feel worked well?

It will also be important from the start to ascertain the readiness of the person being coached for change. For some people any change can be a big step so a coach should be prepared to encourage starting with something small and manageable, whilst hoping both of you will be able to accelerate the change process as you learn within the coaching relationship. The coach should always allow the coachee to do most of the critical work as the relationship continues so that the rate of the process is controlled by the person being coached. The coach can be open about their own thought processes as this can help the coachee to be self-reflective by modelling the process of reflecting on and becoming aware of what you are doing and why you are doing it.

The whole coaching process should be designed to be supportive of change; sometimes this can take many forms and coaches must take their cue from the coachee. One of the many challenging skills in coaching is deciding on exactly what support will enable someone to move beyond their comfort zone and begin to enjoy taking risks and to experience the satisfaction of helping their pupils enjoy and achieve in mathematics. Be prepared to learn as a coach as well as facilitate learning, one of the joys of taking the role of coach is how much you can learn.

Recognising impact

Although this discussion of impact is at the end of this section, it is important to know from the start what you want to achieve from implementing a programme of coaching or mentoring and how you will know if that programme has been successful. If the programme has achieved its aims then something will have changed. Success can be measured in several ways but in the context of a mathematics department you might expect to be able to identify:

- What will teachers do differently as a result of the coaching or mentoring programme?
- How will those teachers know that they have made changes and how will they disseminate their practice?
- What will pupils be able to do differently as a result of the coaching or mentoring programme?
- How will you identify that difference in the pupils?

Discussing the changes the department wants to make or the differences that they would like to see in the way that the department works before starting a programme, means that all involved know what they are building towards and gives the process a sense of purpose. It will also be important to plan from the start how you will evaluate that you have reached your end point. If a teacher wants their pupils to behave better, how much better will represent success? Is that teacher looking for totally quiet and obedient pupils, or that they listen, cheerfully follow instructions and engage in the work that they are asked to do? Setting out what you will evaluate and how you will evaluate it is part of the start of the process, it is just that the evaluation is done at the end.

Coaching and mentoring are often seen as 'good things' of themselves and it is true that much is learned by the participants in a coaching programme but watching others' lessons 'just to see what happens' is not going to provide the influential results that are offered by a focused programme designed around a particular development. Once you have decided where you want to go, coaching or mentoring will provide an empowering process that will work for you as one of the tools to enable you to reach your ends.

Conclusion

The discussions in this chapter make clear that leading professional development is something that must run through all the activities, practices and decisions that a subject leader engages with in their role. The discussions with the heads of department make clear that the department meeting is an opportunity to develop their colleagues professionally, whether through exploring new ways to approach mathematics lessons or to address ideas that are of concern. A meeting that is purely administrative is a wasted opportunity.

Developing ideas and approaches for use in the classroom are necessarily at the forefront of teachers' thoughts and as this chapter demonstrates, can be vehicles for the kinds of conversation that lead to professional development. If a programme of coaching and mentoring is added into the mix of how the department works together then this can provide a more formal and focused opportunity for the staff to develop their professional practice together.

Outside providers must not be forgotten when thinking about meeting the professional development of the staff in the department. Clearly there is a lot to be gained from a one–off course that provides the information that the department is clear that it needs and is prepared to work to embed. However if teachers are to truly develop their professionalism, it may be that they need to look at higher level courses at universities and the conversations with the two heads of department make clear how powerful master's level study can be.

Continuing professional development (CPD) is the entitlement of all staff in school and it is each individual's responsibility to ensure that they receive appropriate CPD. However the department that learns together, grows together and therefore the subject leader will want to take a lead on this aspect to ensure the department keeps growing towards the vision it has set itself.

Further Reading

Using coaching to develop practice is part of two National Strategy folders, they are called:

Sustaining Improvement

http://nationalstrategies.standards.dcsf.gov.uk/node/175120

Leading in Learning – see particularly LearningTriads

http://nationalstrategies.standards.dcsf.gov.uk/node/95481?uc=force_uj

Brockbank, A., McGill, I. (2006) *Facilitating Reflective Learning Through Mentoring and Coaching.* London: Kogan Page.

Pask, R. and Joy, B. (2007) *Mentoring - Coaching: A Handbook for Education Professionals.* Maidenhead: Open University Press.

Starr, J. (2008) *The Coaching Manual: The Definitive Guide to the Process, Principles and Skills of Personal Coaching.* Harlow: Pearson Education.

Whitmore, J. (2002) *Coaching For Performance: Growing People, Performance and Purpose.* London: Nicholas Brealey Publishing.

References

Black, P. Harrison, C. Lee, C. Marshall, B. & Wiliam, D. (2003) *Assessment for Learning – putting it into practice.* Buckingham: Open University Press.

Roberts, M. & Constable, D. (2003) *Handbook for Learning Mentors in Primary and Secondary School.* London: David Fulton.

7
USING RESEARCH EVIDENCE TO INNOVATE, CHANGE AND IMPROVE LEARNING

Peter Johnston-Wilder

> It is teachers who, in the end, will change the world of the school by understanding it. (Stenhouse, 1984)

Part of your work as a subject leader involves innovation, change and thinking about how to improve the way your department works. This chapter is about action research. Action research is a systematic way to think about making changes within your department and evaluating the success of these changes. Many teachers have taken part in action research projects through various initiatives, for example the National College of School Leadership programme 'Leading from the Middle' (NCSL, 2005) or because they are engaged in a Masters course. This chapter will consider how you as subject leader can make use of action research in your quest to make your department as good as it can be.

In a sense, you do action research whenever you try out improvements to your practice. For example, with your department, you may look closely at a particular aspect of classroom practice to identify where change could or should be introduced. This may involve collecting data about what is happening currently in order to focus any proposed innovation upon actual needs within the department. When change is introduced, you may already monitor the implementation across the department and evaluate the impact upon learning. All of this can be seen as a form of action research. Starting from current practice and making the process more systematic has been found to be very effective in school and other professional contexts.

Stephen Corey (1953) was the first writer to see the potential of action research to help teachers develop their own practice. At the time he was writing, the tradition was that outsiders from universities carried out research on teachers and teaching and 'told' teachers what they should do in the light of that research. He advocated that teachers could carry out research themselves in a collaborative and systematic, even scientific, way. However, his ideas were too advanced for the time, and action research was not widely adopted until the mid 1970s when Lawrence Stenhouse (1984) began to advocate action research as process of emancipation from the externally imposed pressures on learners, teachers and schools. Carr and Kemmis (1986) recognised that action research was important for its own sake. They found that it was possible through systematic, critical, action research to understand the barriers to 'rational change': that is to reasoned and evidenced development of professional practice.

It is worth noting that although the origins of action research were in democratising change, it is now fostered by government agencies. Many people consider Kurt Lewin (1946) to be the founding father of action research. Lewin's particular focus was on social change and he discussed action research as a way to ensure democratic change by considering and comparing the effects of various forms of social action. Lewin's ideas advocated change decided by the people, for the benefit of the people. Action research requires the people instigating the change or affected by the change to be involved in the decision making process about the change. Hence many teachers also involve the pupils in the process of action research, as they are ultimately the ones who will benefit from good educational innovations. Nowadays, action research is endorsed as a methodology for reform in schools by government agencies in England such as the National Strategies and the DCSF.

In this chapter, you will explore the cyclical nature of the action research process and ways in which action research for improvement or change can be implemented within your mathematics department. You will also look at some of the different data collection tools that can contribute to your research and how your focus for change and development might evolve as you learn more about what is happening in your department and in your school. The chapter closes with a brief discussion of the potential costs and benefits of the action research approach to innovation and change.

Why action research?

The best argument for using action research is that teachers have found it improves their confidence in their professional skills. It also leads to practical improvements inside a department, improvements that carry conviction amongst teachers about why they are being introduced and how they work. Curriculum renewal resulting from action research is by necessity built around the needs and interests of practitioners. This is an important consideration when so much of school reform has been imposed 'top-down'. For example, mathematics departments may use action research to ascertain how and when to use the material provided under the APP (2008) initiative. Members of such departments will become surer about whether and how they want to use the material provided or whether they have a better way of assessing and monitoring the progress of their pupils. Much has been written about the way that lasting change occurs (for example Fullan, 2007) and experience tells us that the reforms which work best are the ones which teachers themselves have identified as relevant. People are generally more motivated and enthusiastic about changes when they consider the changes have genuine potential for improving their work in their own school.

Action research is thought to extend professionalism and lead to reflective practice (Schon 1983). Action research leads to teachers thinking about their professional practice in a systematic way; teachers who think about their practice in a systematic way are likely to extend their repertoire. As such they are more able to detect, respond and adjust to the shifting demands of the curriculum and the interests of the pupils. Action research also casts teachers as learners. In thinking about, and reflecting on their practice, teachers become learners themselves. In this sense, they share the joys and frustrations of the learning process with their pupils. This leads to a more effective role for the teacher and, hopefully, a more satisfying one too.

Therefore the arguments for using action research are compelling. As action research is based on educational principles, it allows teachers to come to a deeper understanding of a particular issue or barrier to progress in the department. The new understanding of the issue will in turn lead to solutions that have been developed by members of the department and fit the particular context of your department. In developing those solutions, members of the department will, in turn, collaboratively develop a reflective and systematic approach towards problem solving that increases the likelihood of future problems being tackled in a methodical and thoughtful manner.

What is action research?

Action research is concerned with a professional's perceived need to change practice more closely to meet their own vision of good practice and to implement such change in ways that are effective within their own particular circumstances. Contexts in which action research has been successfully applied include health care and legal practice, as well as a wide variety of educational settings. There is a wide and diverse literature on action research, some of which is listed in the bibliography for this chapter, and you will find different definitions of action research are used extensively. However, each of these has the following key aspects as central components:

- Action research is research carried out by individual practitioners, or by groups of practitioners, in their own setting to address a problem that they have identified as being of concern to them. In that sense, the research and its outcomes are particular to the setting in which the research was conducted, and to the practitioner whose practice was at the centre.

- Action research is a cyclical process of problem identification, design, implementation, evaluation and identification of new problems. The process of the research emerges and takes shape along with the early outcomes from the first explorations of the problem; the research process evolves as the researcher gathers more data and refines and develops their interpretation of the desired innovation in their practice.

- Action research is often, but not necessarily, undertaken as a collaborative exercise between small numbers of colleagues within a single setting or across a small number of related settings.

The last of these points – collaboration – is of particular significance to you as a subject leader in school. Collaboration adds to the research process; the discussion and dissection of the problem, the proposed solution and the nature of the evidence collected all add to the thoroughness of the research. Because of the essentially collaborative nature of the process, facilitated within a team of practitioners working together on action research, action research is of particular interest to subject leaders. A project in which the whole department works together to implement and gather data to evaluate an innovation within the department can do much to develop a team working ethos.

However, collaboration is not a necessary condition for successful action research. An alternative model would be for the subject leader to work alone to implement a new idea within their classroom, collecting data to evaluate the effect of the change on pupils' learning. If the innovation proves to be successful, then the evaluation can be used to help convince other members of the department to take up the new idea for themselves. Thus, subject leaders cast themselves as a people who are willing to take risks and show that they recommend to their team ideas that they have found to work. Whether you choose to use action research collaboratively or individually will depend on the nature of the innovation and the nature of your department team and, as usual, will be a matter of judgement.

Tensions within action research

One of the most important tensions in action research is also one of its strengths. The tension lies in the fact that the findings are in themselves not generalisable beyond the particular context within which the research was conducted. The solutions generated by action research are for specific problems in specific contexts; they are not intended to be general and their power lies in their specificity. However, this can result in a sceptical attitude towards the claims made as a result of action research projects. It is important to recognise that action research can generate genuinely new knowledge, but that this is essentially knowledge about 'our practice', and not about all practice. The insights gained into 'our practice' are often worth reporting to a wider audience as they may be 'of interest' to other practitioners and may stimulate others to view their own practice differently and to explore the consequences.

Action research is now seen by many as more efficient than 'top-down' initiatives, in changing the practices of professionals who are both used to acting autonomously and are required to do so. The DCSF is now an enthusiastic advocate of action research. However, action research is not intended to produce scientifically tested outcomes, but rather to produce good reasons for acting in the way that we do, expressed in a way that enables us clearly to articulate those reasons. Jean McNiff (2002) emphasises action research's personal nature when she says:

> A useful way to think about action research is that it is a strategy to help you live in a way that you feel is a good way. It helps you live out the things you believe in, and it enables you to give good reasons every step of the way.

Action research requires you to take a dual role as both teacher and researcher, developing the ability to watch and reflect on what you do. As a teacher, you mostly attend to the learners but as a researcher you are also paying attention to your own role. As a teacher, you plan a lesson with the needs of the learner as the main focus; as a researcher, you may plan the lesson with the change as the prime focus while not losing sight of learners' needs. This dual role takes time to master. From now on we will refer to the teacher undertaking this role as a teacher-researcher.

Representing the action research cycle

The essence of action research lies in its cyclical nature and there are many possible diagrams to represent this cycle. The iterative nature of the cycle may be represented as in figure 1, where the teacher-researcher might start at the top of the figure with an initial recognition that there is a need for change.

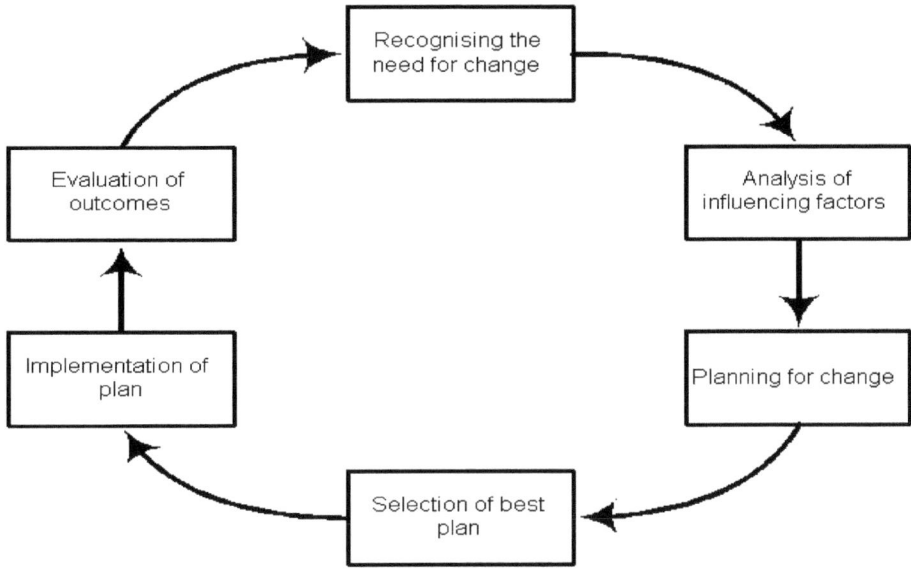

The teacher-researcher naturally begins by analysing a problem, looking at the situation in which it occurs to identify what factors might lie behind it, and seeking to identify possible solutions. As part of this analysis, the teacher-researcher usually needs to collect and examine data about the situation. For example, consider the following scenarios:

- A teacher is worried about a group of Year 11 pupils who appear to be under-achieving. How can you uncover their views and ideas? What have others done? How can you decide what to try?

- A member of the department has heard that interactive whiteboards can be used much more interactively than is current department practice. How can you find out how? How will you start? Who will be involved? Can you get some extra money for innovation from your school, the NCETM or from your local authority? (This might equally apply to other hardware such as graphic calculators.)

- There are increasing numbers of EAL pupils in the school. What is considered good practice? Where will you start? What are other schools doing in this area? How can you liaise with other departments?

The action research process always occurs in cycles and has four basic phases that recur; having completed phase 4 you always return to phase 1 and start to evaluate the result of your actions.

1. Look	2. Think	3. Act	4. Reflect
Form a picture and gather evidence about what is currently happening. Find out more about the problem. Define and describe the problem and its context and let the problem become a question. Talk to people and look in articles and books for ways that others have approached the problem and the solutions that they have found.	Use evidence about other people's approaches to think about the approach that might start to solve your problem. Discuss possible solutions and consider various plans. The thinking, discussion and consideration of this phase will result in a plan.	Put your plan into practice and collect data on your implementation.	Study your data to identify systematically and objectively what happened, what was surprising, what worked well, why some ideas worked and what could still be improved and document these findings.

During phase 1, teacher-researchers work towards identifying a list of potential solutions to the problem, usually involving some change or innovation in practice. Although none of the potential solutions might yet seem particularly strong at first, during phase 2, the teacher-researchers will identify one solution to be implemented in phase 3 and further evaluated in phase 4, then returning to phase 1 to begin considering a new cycle. It is only by acting to address a problem, and by carefully evaluating the outcome, that the teacher-researchers can learn about what works and begin systematically to refine and to improve practice.

Sometimes, in the process of evaluating the impact of a change, the teacher-researcher may become aware that the original problem is not quite what was believed and come to a new understanding of what constitutes the problem. In any case, it is extremely unlikely that a single iteration will on the first attempt address the problem completely. And so the researcher begins a second iteration and maybe a third and fourth iteration. Where and when the cycle stops involves pragmatic decisions such as 'how good is good enough?'; 'can we afford the time and emotional involvement required to carry on?' as well as 'have we solved that problem now?'

What can go wrong?

There are many things that can go awry when thinking about and using action research. The first has been mentioned before. Action research allows professionals to develop solutions within the context of their professional practice. The solutions that are derived from action research are not designed for other contexts, so that seemingly simplistic changes can negate the efficacy of a solution. If a new teacher joins the department, there may be an assumption that they will use the solution previously arrived at through action research, without any problem. Of course, this will be the case for many solutions but the in-depth knowledge of 'why we do what we do' arrived at through engagement with action research will not be present in the new teacher and a superficial use of a particular solution may result in some unexpected results. At the very least, a period of induction will be needed during which the new teacher begins to learn the meaning of what others in the department 'take as shared'.

A second problem that action research projects can encounter is that they 're-invent the wheel.' A problem in one department in a school is likely to be a problem in another part of the same school or in the mathematics department of a school nearby. If each department acts on its own, there will be a duplication of effort but also the outcomes will not have the robustness and rigour that they might have had when many people 'put their heads together'. Forming networks within and across schools can result in higher quality outcomes for all concerned, as can linking with higher education establishments and using action research as part of a masters course.

A further reason that action researchers sometimes seem to re-invent the wheel is that they go straight to the action rather than looking at what others have already found out about the particular problem in their department. Action research can be thought of as a balancing act between action and research, with neither one taking precedence over the other. The process is designed to find solutions to real problems in social situations. Professionals are supported to employ their time, effort and criticality to improve both their understanding of their practice and the results of their action within that practice. The outcomes of such research are context specific, although other people will have walked a similar path previously; in reading about their experiences and about other pertinent areas, solutions arrived at will be stronger than they might otherwise have been. Reading widely, at the start and during your research, will enable you to harness the ideas of many people in your quest for a solution to the problem you have identified. You will reach a more complete understanding of relevant issues and be able to imagine a robust solution in your context. Action research is most effective when the rest of the research community is harnessed in pursuit of the solution to your local problem; this often takes place through reading written reports. Because of your research, your resulting actions will be better focused and more effective; because of your actions, your research will gain a more complete understanding of the actual issues and solutions in professional practice.

Working on an example in your department

In order to see how you might use action research in practice within your department, you might find it helpful to consider a real problem that you and your colleagues face. There are many possibilities, but in order to illustrate how the process of analysing the problem can work in practice, you are invited to consider the following scenario of a departmental problem:

The mathematics department has been offering AS and A2 mathematics as options in Years 12 and 13 respectively for many years. Over the last five years, the grades achieved in AS mathematics in Year 12 have been declining. Furthermore, fewer than half of the pupils who opt to study mathematics at AS level have chosen to continue to study mathematics at A2. You have now decided that you want to improve A-level mathematics teaching.

In order to begin to address this problem, the teacher-researcher has available a variety of actions. Some possible actions are:

- Think about different ways you know of teaching A Level maths. Reflect on what seems to work.
- Try out new ways of teaching A Level maths. See what works best.
- Review the literature on teaching A Level maths. Decide what works best.
- Review the literature on teaching A Level maths. Take the ideas that you think are best practice.

In deciding how to proceed, the teacher-researcher is faced with the need to balance the imperative for action to address the problem against the challenge of knowing what to try and having a convincing reason for trying one action rather than another. In this sense, action research requires a balance of action against research. The best action research is done by teams that are a combination of doers and reflectors, practical problem solvers and analytic thinkers.

The action taken might initially be simply to try out something that has not been tried before, or experimenting to see what works. What you choose to try in any particular situation might be prompted by something that has been suggested to you or by an idea that you have come across incidentally. Research, on the other hand, offers a more systematic way of determining action: theorising about what might stimulate pupils' interest in mathematical topics in the AS course or seeking to conceptualise the reasons why pupils are not succeeding in mathematics at AS; systematically examining your own assumptions and prejudices about what has been happening. To engage in research, you need to connect with other researchers, to learn from their findings.

Professional knowledge is contextual; teachers will always have useful knowledge and the practice of action research rejects a view that there is 'good practice' that can be handed down from one generation of teachers to the next. Action research demands that knowledge is constructed, in the light of literature that fits the context in which it is used.

Doing Action Research

Getting started

Action research is time consuming and 'messy' and a lot of time must be spent on the identification of exactly what is the problem. For example: imagine a scenario in which, say, you want to develop your assessment practice. Consider the dimensions of this problem: Summative or formative? Questioning or giving written feedback? Assessing outcomes or processes? Better examination results or more secure learning? Which year group? And so on and so on. This is why it is important to take time over the initial stages so that you really do understand the issues involved in the problem that you are trying to tackle.

Examples of scenarios that you might choose to study are:

- Using interactive whiteboard to increase participation in whole class teaching;
- Using peer assessment to help pupils understand mark schemes;
- Developing a maths club to increase interest in advanced maths amongst GCSE pupils.

Collecting data

Generally, an action research project will include a small scale case study, making use of qualitative methods, and will be both reflective and reflexive. The data that you collect will help you describe what happened when you tried a change and what the pupils thought about the change and how you and other teachers reacted. By reflecting on this qualitative data, you will begin to understand the situation and think about ways to continue to achieve the good things that you see and mitigate the issues that have arisen. When you instigate the actions that you have thought of through the reflective process you are being reflexive and evaluating the data allows this reflexivity.

However, action research will sometimes include some quantitative methods. This is particularly important now that quantitative data is so much a part of all school experience. A school-based action research project will need to take account of the wealth of quantitative data that might be available and will need to make effective use of that data to take advantage of what insight it offers. On the other hand, there is much that the available quantitative data cannot tell us, and qualitative data will be needed to answer why something has happened. It is also true that small-scale studies in education often do not give a valid, quantifiable indication of whether one course of action is 'better' than another. The timescale is often such that differences are unlikely to show up in any data that tracks progress and a change in routine will often result in a stall in learning progress until pupils have learned the new way of working.

Remember in educational action research:

- you cannot control for variables, classes are always different from one another

- you cannot repeat the innovation, once it is done it is done, but you can review carefully kept notes or other recordings

- your involvement in the study and enthusiasm for the ideas will influence how pupils respond to change

- you are unlikely to find simple observable outcomes (in terms of attainment) as many factors will influence any attainment.

It is important to note that, at least in education, the use of control groups may be both unethical and impossible. If you, as the teacher, were convinced that a particular action or intervention will be effective, then you should use it for all your pupils and you should not be willing to set up a control group that would not receive this intervention that you believe to be effective. The other problem with control groups is that, much as you may think you are using your 'old way' of teaching with a control group, your thinking and therefore acting will have changed through your engagement in the research of your project and will be different. Sometimes you can use some data from a previous year group as control group data if you feel you really need to. Remember the most convincing evidence is what you did and the impact of that change on your pupils.

Tools for data collection

There is a variety of data collection tools available to the teacher-researcher engaged in action research. Consider what data collection tools would best help you assess the impact of your innovation.

- Interviews

- Surveys

- Documents

- Observations

- Field notes or Diaries and Journals

In the following sections, each of these is considered as a tool for data collection within action research. All that is offered here is the briefest indication of some of the issues that you need to think about in using these different methods of data collection. It is likely that you might need to read more widely about methods as your plans for your own research evolve.

Interviews

In your action research, you might find it useful to gather information from pupils, teachers or both. An interview can be a good way to do this. You might interview your subjects individually, or you might decide that there are advantages to interviewing them in pairs or in small groups. One possible advantage of interviewing pupils in pairs or small groups is that they are able to suggest to each other, ideas and answers to your questions. If your aim is to gather information about pupils' views generally and not to identify the views of individual pupils, then this can help to avoid a pupil being intimidated in an interview situation.

An interview is essentially a conversation in which you as the interviewer set the agenda. You can plan to structure the conversation to varying degrees according to the extent to which you need to ensure that each interview is identical. The table below offers an idea of how the different degrees of structure work in interviews.

If you want to interview a large number of people, each in the same way, then a structured interview in which you ask a list of questions in a predetermined order may look like the simplest solution. It will ensure that the interviews are easily compared with one another. However, if you see an interview as being like a conversation, then a structured interview can impose unrealistic constraints; when a pupil gives an answer to your standard question that indicates that they have an unusual view about what makes a good maths teacher, you might really need to pursue the idea further in order to understand more clearly.

In contrast, in an unstructured interview you and the interviewee have the freedom to pursue interesting insights as they arise. However, an unstructured interview can have all the complexity of free conversation. The interviewee may produce complex responses, with frequent hesitation and false starts. In unstructured interviews, each interview may take a completely different path, and the result can make it very difficult to compare the outcomes of different interviews.

Because of such difficulties, semi-structured interviews will often be the preferred approach.

- Structured interviews
    - Have uniform questions in predetermined sequence
    - Analysis is generally easy, (this is an especially important factor in the event that you decide to interview large numbers of people)
    - Constrained, you cannot pursue an interesting point or view.
- Semi-structured interviews
    - Have predetermined topics but interesting ideas can be followed up.
    - The form and sequence of the questions may vary
    - Analysis can be hard for more than a small number of interviews
- Unstructured interviews
    - These allow interviewee to speak with minimal intervention
    - They enable the pursuit of unanticipated insights and discoveries
    - There is a possibility of awkward silences and forced answers
    - Analysis can be very complex

Now imagine that you want to interview a pupil about what makes 'a good maths teacher'. It is worth taking time now to consider which type of interview would be appropriate and what questions you would ask. Just as important as identifying the questions to be asked are the decisions about the precise wording of each question and how to sequence the questions. As in any research in a real educational context, there are some serious ethical issues to be considered when asking a pupil to identify the characteristics of a good mathematics teacher and it is important to spend some time identifying these and considering how you might address them.

Surveys

Survey methods can provide a time efficient method of gathering large amounts of data. Occasionally in an action research project you might decide that you need to have a snapshot of the views of a large number of people, such as all pupils in a year group and for this you might use a questionnaire.

Your questionnaire will usually consist of standardised questions which, if well designed, can lead to relatively easy analysis and can enable direct comparisons between individual responses or between subgroups. It is often helpful to make your questionnaire responses anonymous, as respondents may find this less intrusive and they may be more willing to respond more honestly. However, the disadvantage is that the responses may be rather superficial and may lack the depth that can help you as the teacher-researcher to build meaningful explanations.

Sometimes it is helpful to include some open-response questions in a questionnaire to enable your respondents to give you more information. However, the analysis of such responses is much more difficult and the information gained is often less informative than would be obtained from a few interviews. It can also be difficult to persuade respondents to answer open-response questions as they require a much higher level of commitment from the person completing the questionnaire.

Closed questions can be presented in various formats requiring different kinds of response, ranging from a simple yes or no to more complex multiple-choice responses. Sometimes it can be particularly helpful to use a scaled response, such as five-point Likert scale, as this can facilitate more sophisticated analyses comparing response patterns to different questions. Alternatively, you as the researcher might prepare a list of possible responses to your question and invite respondents to indicate a rank order according to which of your suggested responses fits best. Such rank order questions can be relatively easy to process and analyse, but there may be problems interpreting the results, especially if you have not succeeded in listing all the possible responses that your respondents might want to make.

A well-designed survey questionnaire can provide the means to gather a large number of responses to a set of standard questions quickly. In a project to identify 'what makes a good mathematics teacher', you might have identified a list of possible factors that might characterise the good teacher. Incorporating such a list into a questionnaire could be achieved in many different ways. For example, the list might be presented as just that – a list – and the respondents could be invited to rank the items in the list from most important to least important as characteristics of a good teacher. Alternatively, each item in the list might be placed in a statement about a 'good mathematics teacher' and respondents could be invited to indicate on a 5 or 6 point Likert scale the degree to which they agree with the statement.

What kinds of survey could you use to collect evidence on the issue you have in mind?

Documentary evidence

In a school setting documentary evidence can be found in:

- Registers
- Minutes of meetings
- Schemes of work
- School development plans
- Lesson plans
- Pupil work
- Work trawls
- Etc

Documentary evidence is often freely available and it is not intrusive to examine this evidence. However it is often not very richly informative as it will be in note form and very brief. Also it may not always be objective as it will be written from a particular point of view for a particular audience and therefore the evidence may be misleading

Pupil work is a particular type of documentary evidence. This evidence will be familiar to all teachers and will show certain things. Work trawls will give insight into the quantity and quality of work done by the pupils and the level of written feedback that they receive. It may provide insight into the sense made by a learner of the learning work they engaged in when it was produced. Certainly, pupils' work will be useful alongside other data.

Observations

Observations, usually of lessons, can be useful at many stages of the study. They can help define or refine the research focus and research questions and provide evidence for the effects of the innovation. Observations are generally a rich source of data that can take some considerable time to analyse.

There are several ways of classifying observations according to who is the observer and the nature of the observations that they make:

- Fly on the wall or non-participant observation
- Participant observation by:
  - Teacher
  - Assistant

– Pupil

- Structured observation: for example, the kinds of lesson observations that are made as part of your work as a subject leader monitoring the work of the department.
- Audio, video, photographs

Non-participant observation is in some ways the most objective, in that the observer sets out to have as little impact as possible upon the setting that is being observed. However, this is extremely difficult in practice. Consider what happens when you, as head of the mathematics department, go to observe a lesson that is being taught by a member of your department; simply by your presence in the room, the pupils' behaviour is altered and the situation is changed.

It is often therefore helpful to acknowledge that truly non-participant observation is impossible and to consider carefully the extent to which the participation of the observer is appropriate, both professionally for the benefit of the learning situation that is being observed and in research terms for the trustworthiness of the observations made. The extent of the impact of the observation upon the situation can sometimes be minimised by using an observer who is ordinarily a part of the setting that is to be observed; this might be for example a pupil in the lesson, or a teaching assistant who is a frequent visitor to the class.

Sometimes it is desirable to make a recording of the situation to be observed using video or audio. Such a recording can be very useful if you wish to review particular incidents and to study closely the surrounding events. However, it is often difficult to obtain a good recording without distorting the behaviour of the actors in the situation, especially the pupils. A recording, especially video, can provide extraordinarily rich data for later analysis, but the process of analysis can be extremely time-consuming.

Field notes and diaries
Field notes are taken in situ, during observations, unstructured or semi-structured interviews. They can be less intrusive than video or audio recording and certainly raise fewer legal and ethical issues. Field notes allow for contextual information and interpretations that cannot be captured by recordings; indeed field notes are often made from video recordings in discussion with the participants, and this is a process of 'triangulation' (see below). However it is important to recognise that note-taking may distract the researcher from noticing! Overly zealous note-taking may lead the researcher to notice only those actions or features in the episode that were pre-determined by the researcher before entering the field, rather than maintaining an open mind. However, it is important to remember that it is impossible to notice and make notes on everything that goes on, so you may need to decide and agree upon a focus before observing a lesson or a teaching episode.

A diary or journal entry will typically consist of notes and reflections recorded by the researcher after the event. These notes will record the immediate thoughts and reactions of the participants and therefore are often reflexive. They are not objective; the person making the notes was involved and almost certainly wanted the innovation to work but they will be interesting and provide important data when reviewed after the event.

You are strongly recommended to keep a diary or journal during your project and to use the journal to record your thoughts and reflections as the project unfolds. Such a record about the evolution of your own thinking can be invaluable in highlighting to you the insights that you have absorbed into your practice during the study. It can also help you not to overlook those fleeting insights that flash past you at the end of a busy day.

Each method of data collection has its own strengths and weaknesses and the value of each lies in its fitness for purpose. You cannot individually interview all members of the school to find out what they think about the way that mathematics has been taught, but you could interview a small group and encourage them to express their views. You cannot go to each pupil's home to interview their parents to find out how they would like to be involved in their child's mathematics, but you could send home questionnaires or conduct some telephone interviews.

Triangulation
Triangulation helps make your results more convincing and believable. It involves trying to see the same outcome from different perspectives, for example looking at the video of a lesson, reviewing your journal entry for that date and comparing that to what some pupils said in a small group interview. When multiple sources of data testify to the same result, it is reasonable to believe that that was the outcome. Triangulation can also be achieved by looking at the observations of multiple observers or when the same result is seen on different occasions in different settings.

Try it out:

Typically, a useful action research project for you as a subject leader in mathematics will be based on an aspect of teaching and learning Mathematics in your school. For example, you might decide to focus upon:

- the use of specific pedagogic techniques;
- cognitive or social/cultural issues that impact on learning;
- the use of particular resources such as digital technology;
- a new method for teaching a topic.

The following list provides some suggested research questions that you might consider as starting points while you think about the implications and possibilities for action research in your own school setting.

- How does an investigative approach to teaching a topic affect the teaching-learning process?
- How might a teacher design practical work within a mathematics teaching programme?
- What is the relationship between the design of tasks and pupil thinking when engaged in modelling tasks?

- How does teaching style impact upon gender-related learning styles in Mathematics?
- How does the teacher plan for differing abilities within a mathematics class?
- How can the availability of portable personal technology, such as graphic calculators, be incorporated into the teaching of a topic in mathematics?
- What strategies can the teacher use in teaching to build pupils' confidence in and enjoyment of mathematics?
- How do PLTS impact upon mathematics teaching?

As you focus upon a specific question or issue for your own research, you will need to think about the following questions. The answers to these questions will help you to plan your actions in a systematic way to address this focus.

- What are possible ways of addressing the problem?
- Who might you ask to get a wider perspective on this issue?
- What innovation might you make?
- What possible problems are there?
- What evaluative tools might best assess the impact?
- If interviews, what type of interview might be appropriate? Why?
- For other methods, what are the advantages and disadvantages for your own project?
- Which methods might be appropriate? Why?
- Is there potential for 'triangulation' in your study? If not, then why not?

Writing up your research
The most effective way to share your findings is often to write the research up for colleagues to read. Action research projects are often sketchily written up and, as can be seen from the previous discussion, this can lead to the findings not informing the wider research and teaching communities in the way that they might. Also the findings of such studies can remain sketchy and not well explained or understood. Stenhouse (1984) said that it was in making the findings public that an enquiry becomes research. Writing a report on your enquiry can have several good effects. By writing a clear description of the problem or issue to which you sought a solution, and by providing a full account of the way in which you went about solving it, you will force yourself to reflect on and clearly appraise your actions and the reasons behind the justification for what you believe you have found out. However, a description by itself is the action without the research. It is when you carefully evaluate what you did, what the background was to the decisions you made and what exactly is indicated by the evidence you have gathered, that the results of your research become both more convincing and more lasting. The act of writing up consolidates the learning that will have resulted from your investigations and helps the department, the school, and the wider community really to know and understand what they have found out.

When writing up your project it will be important to set out the initial focus of your study, making sure that you explain what you did and why you did it that way. Then you will move onto describe the data you collected and how you went about collecting it; be sure to explain why you collected the data in this way. The next section will explain how you analysed your data before moving on to the exciting part which will tell about your interpretation of the data, that is, what you found out. Be sure to set out how your focus has evolved over the time of the project. What did you think you would find out and what did you find out? Most action research reports end with a discussion of what needs to happen next as there are always ways to continue to develop and improve.

If your project has relevance to a wider audience and the report communicates this clearly, then your report can be shared more widely than your department. Such reports can be made available to the wider mathematics community through a professional journal such as 'Mathematics Teaching' published by the ATM, or 'Mathematics in School' published by the MA; instructions for submitting material for publication are available on their websites. Alternatively, such reports are sometimes published by the NCETM on their website portal.

Conclusion

Why should you, a busy teacher, or a subject leader, with so many calls upon your time, choose to spend such a significant time and effort on action research? What benefits might you find if you do?

Essentially, the process of action research is a formalisation of something that all good teachers and subject leaders will do as a matter of course in order to improve and develop practice. It provides an approach to questioning and monitoring practice, identifying aspects of local practice for improvement, and bringing new insights and understanding to enhance teaching and learning. When built into the practice of a department, action research can become an integral part of the professional development of the teachers in the department; the shared focus and goals and the sharing of new insights can help to build a team spirit and a shared purpose among the members of the department. Above all, the sharing of innovation can energise the professional practice of the participating teachers and can be immensely satisfying.

Having said all this it is important to consider whether you really want to spend the time and effort required to engage in action research. Engagement in action research is a personal choice and some teachers will prefer to discover from others what is effective and implement ideas developed elsewhere. Some people might suggest that teachers do not have the time, opportunity or expertise to carry out effective action research. However, teachers are professionals and therefore, if they want to, they can acquire the skills they need to research their own practice. Teachers who carry out action research also testify to the fact that they become more aware of their own skills and better teachers overall and that it is a good use of their time. In the end, any new innovation within your own department, even if the idea has been tried and developed elsewhere, will benefit from the critical and systematic evaluation and improvement implied within an action research approach.

Further Reading

Bell, J. (2005) Doing Your Research Project: A Guide for First-Time Researchers in *Education, Health and Social Science* (4th Edition). Maidenhead: Open University Press.

Cohen, L., Manion, L. & Morrison, K. (2000) *Research Methods in Education* (5th Edition). London: RoutledgeFalmer.

Elliott, J. (1991) *Action Research for Educational Change*. Buckingham: Open University Press.

Hopkins, D. (1993) *A Teacher's Guide to Classroom Research* (2nd Edition). Buckingham: Open University Press.

McNiff, J. (2002) *Action research for professional development.* http://www.jeanmcniff.com/booklet1.html accessed on 5th Feb 2009.

References

APP (2008) http://nationalstrategies.standards.dcsf.gov.uk/node/132204 accessed on 25th July 2009.

Carr, W. and Kemmis, S. (1986) *Becoming Critical. Education, knowledge and action research*. Lewes: Falmer.

Corey, S. M. (1953) *Action research to improve school practices*. New York: Columbia.

Fullan, M. (2007) *Leading in a Culture of Change*. San Francisco: Jossey-Bass.

Gore, J. and Gitlin, A. (2004) [Re]Visioning the academic-teacher divide: power and knowledge in the educational community. *Teachers and Teaching: Theory and Practice*, 10, 1.

Lewin, K. (1946) *Resolving social conflicts*. New York: Harper & Brothers.

NCSL (2005) *Leading from the Middle*. http://www.ncsl.org.uk/programmes-index/lftm-index.htm accessed on 12th June 2009.

Schon, D. (1983) *The Reflective Practitioner: How Professionals Think in Action*. New York: Basic Books.

Stenhouse, L. (1984) Artistry and teaching: the teacher as focus of research and development in: D. Hoskins & M. Wideen (Eds.), *Alternative perspectives on school improvement*. London: The Falmer Press.

Winter, R. (1989) *Learning from experience: Principles and practice in action-research*. New York: Falmer.

8
USING ASSESSMENT DATA TO ENHANCE PROFESSIONAL PRACTICE

Mick Marks and Clare Lee

> Not everything that counts can be counted and not everything that can be counted counts! (Einstein)

Data is everywhere and in recent years IT systems have developed to the point where large amounts of data can be recorded and made available to everyone. In schools, mathematics subject leaders are encouraged to use data by their local authorities, by secondary National Strategy advisors and by their school senior leadership teams. Mathematics subject leaders are told that using data is essential to an effective, improving mathematics department. This is true, but only if useful data is collected or accessed and that data is analysed carefully. In this chapter, we will look at the data that is available and how to use it in an efficient and manageable way to make a difference to the quality of teaching and learning in a mathematics department. We will also look at how data can be used to answer questions beyond the straightforward and to look at the effectiveness of the initiatives, experiments and interventions that may be undertaken by the department.

Data analysis, done well, enables subject leaders to gain an understanding of the strengths and weaknesses in their department, to raise questions about the relative performance of individuals and groups within the school and to look for issues. However, once the analysis has been completed, action must still be taken to celebrate strengths, to address issues and weaknesses that have been identified and to answer the questions raised. It is in reflecting on the analysis and deciding what actions must be taken that a subject leader's professional knowledge is vital and, by taking action, the subject leader will be able to improve the outcome of their pupils' mathematics education.

Firstly it is important that we clarify some terminology that will be used throughout the chapter:

Attainment is raw scores in national Key Stage tests (commonly known as SATs) or exams. "Standards" usually means attainment.

Achievement is the attainment and progress that pupils make over a period of time. Progress is usually measured by Contextual Value Added or CVA i.e. the improvements in attainment made over a period of time or from one Key Stage to another.

The above definitions will be used throughout this chapter. Attainment refers to scores in tests or exam results that are compared against a national average. The phrase 'Standards of Attainment' is commonly used in schools and by local authority or Ofsted staff when referring to attainment measured against the nationally standardised criteria for levels at Key Stages 1, 2 and 3 or grades at GCSE and A Level. Achievement refers to the progress that pupils make over time and in the main data sources is known as 'value added' or 'contextual value added'. Of course, achievement can be used informally in a school setting; a teacher may say 'you have achieved well over this half term' which means, compared to where you started, your knowledge skills and understanding have improved more than I might have expected. Improvement at a rate that is much faster than is predicted by national data could be referred to as 'good' achievement. Achievement can be looked at formally in data sources as value added and also informally using teachers' knowledge and experience. To assess good achievement, a teacher must know what constitutes good achievement from one point to another and some of the ideas discussed in this chapter will help to develop this knowledge. Surprisingly many people, who should know better, local authority personnel and even Ofsted, can sometimes use these terms in different ways. There are references to attainment and achievement that do not meet the above definitions in many widely available documents.

What use is data?

Data is available from many sources, for example:

- national Key Stage 2 tests;
- teacher assessment, informally or using the Assessing Pupil's Progress Materials (DCSF, 2007);
- internal examinations
- GCSE and A Level results.

Data can be used to identify where pupils are performing well and where they may be underachieving. Data can be used to raise issues and questions about provision for certain groups of pupils. Therefore subject leaders can be led by data analysis to focus resources, be that teaching assistants, teachers with particular strengths, technology and so on, where they can make a difference to pupil learning and check that those changes do make a difference. Data does not offer solutions or take account of what is happening around the school e.g. significant refurbishment, staff absences or resignations. Data is there to be analysed, to provide evidence about what is going well and where things can be improved.

Internal data is used most effectively when:

- mathematics teachers meet regularly to moderate work so that they have a good understanding of standards;
- pupils are involved in discussing and understanding their own standards and in setting their own targets for improvement;
- clear lines of accountability exist so that subject leaders regularly talk to teachers about how well their pupils are learning, and members of

the leadership team talk to subject leaders about the pupils. When these conversations are held regularly in a supportive way, all concerned feel part of the move to raise attainment;

- subject leaders and leadership team members are trained in the use, interpretation and the limitations of data;
- the data identifies weaknesses in the pupils' grasp of aspects of mathematics so that teachers can remedy the situation. The item level analysis option in RAISEonline (DCSF and Ofsted) or the Assessing Pupil's Progress (DCSF 2007) materials are examples of how this can be done.

All activities within a school have an impact on standards and achievements, some more than others. It is important that subject leaders understand the impact of innovations brought in and changes that are made. Understanding impact is an important aspect of using data, but in many schools this it is not well used. For example, if a group of 15 boys in Year 11 perform better than expected, is it because of the learning mentor, the extra revision classes, the day to day teaching, the support of parents, the involvement of the Local Authority subject consultant working with the group or a combination of all of these activities? Which activity or combination of activities works best? If records of who takes part in various initiatives are kept, sometimes it is possible to untangle this web. Did all the boys take part in all the initiatives? Have results gone up overall, indicating developments in teaching and learning are making a difference throughout? When was an improvement first suspected? Had the revision classes taken place then? By keeping records alongside a well established tracking system, some conclusions can be reached about the efficacy of certain initiatives.

What data is available both locally and nationally?

There are two main, nationally available, sources of data on the performance of pupils in school, RAISEonline and Fisher Family Trust (FFT). There are also other sources of data available to schools and colleges who have pupils who study beyond 16 years old: the Learning Achievement Tracker (LAT) and data sources that local authorities can make available to schools. The important aspects of each of these data sources will be detailed in the next few sections of this chapter. There are also commercial packages available that schools use but discussing the advantages and disadvantages of these is beyond the scope of this chapter.

RAISEonline data contains attainment and achievement information at subject and pupil level. It provides many graphs, tables and charts on the attainment and achievement of pupils in mathematics departments at all Key Stages up to Key Stage 4. It can be accessed through the website at *www.raiseonline.org* but a password is needed to enter the site. Individual passwords can be obtained from the school RAISEonline Administrator. RAISEonline will be the first stop and the prime source of data for schools and mathematics departments and is the source that is used by Ofsted when planning an inspection. It has a full report that is the equivalent of the previously available Panda Reports (Performance and Assessment Reports jointly produced by DCSF, Ofsted and QCA) and has various other reports. For example, the Exceptions Report in

RAISEonline summarises achievements in the current year. This one page summary of achievements is the one that many Ofsted inspectors use to get a feel for a school. It gives an overall summary of the progress that all the pupils are making, boys and girls, ethnic minorities, looked after children and so on.

Table 1 below is taken from RAISEonline and shows the relative performance of mathematics compared to all other subjects taken by pupils.

Table 1

Relative Performance Indicator

This analysis shows the relative performance in 2007 of subjects in your school at Key Stage 4 for all pupils. For information about how this indicator is calculated, please see the Help article.

Subject	Entries	School Average	Average In All Other Subjects	School Difference	National Difference	Relative Performance Indicator
Art and Design	130	36.7	34.4	2.4	2.6	-0.3
Business Studies	59	31.5	33.6	-2.0	-1.7	-0.3
Combined Science - Double Award	174	34.3	36.8	-2.5	-1.0	-1.5
Combined Science - Single Award	24	21.0	21.3	-0.3	-2.2	1.9
Design and Technology	61	30.7	33.6	-2.9	0.3	-3.2
Drama	36	39.8	36.2	3.6	2.2	1.4
Economics	13	32.8	34.6	-1.8	-6.7	4.9
English / English Language	200	36.5	34.0	2.4	1.7	0.7
English Literature	167	37.0	36.9	0.1	0.9	-0.7
French	11	32.9	34.0	-1.1	-3.3	2.2
Geography	48	36.4	39.0	-2.6	-1.3	-1.3
History	58	33.9	38.1	-4.3	-1.7	-2.6
Home Economics	40	31.6	32.2	-0.6	0.7	-1.3
Information Technology	37	25.6	34.3	-8.6	-1.8	-6.9
Mathematics	201	36.3	34.0	2.5	-0.1	2.6
Music	10	42.4	40.5	1.9	-0.9	2.8
Other Languages	2	28.0	41.8	-13.8	5.7	-19.5
Other Sciences	5	44.8	46.2	-1.4	-3.8	2.3
Physical Education/Sports Studies	36	38.0	37.7	0.3	2.2	-1.9
Religious Studies / Education	58	39.9	38.6	1.2	0.4	0.8
Spanish	14	39.1	41.2	-2.0	-2.8	0.8
Statistics	6	46.0	44.0	2.0	-2.5	4.5
Vocational Studies	18	40.0	37.7	2.3	0.3	1.9

The second major source of data available to most schools is from the Fisher Family Trust (FFT). Most, if not all, Local Authorities have chosen to buy into this highly informative data source. The FFT only contracts with Local Authorities and does not contract directly with schools.

8. USING ASSESSMENT DATA

Fischer Family Trust data is available in three parts:

a) A pupil-level database provided to the Local Authority by FFT. The Local Authority usually forward this data to the school, either electronically or, more commonly, on a DVD or CD. Since 2008, Fischer Family Trust data is available online (see below). The school's data manager or a senior member of staff is likely to have access to this database. The Local Authority is provided with a pupil-level database and that is broken down into databases for individual schools. The database contains information about estimates for children for the future and information about value added for those children who have recently completed the tests.

b) FFTlive is a new online development and is constantly under review. This currently provides subject value-added information at KS3, GCSE and post 16. It can be accessed at *www.FFTlive.org*: a password is required to enter this site. Passwords are given to schools by the Local Authority. A member of the school's senior management team is likely to have this password.

c) FFT provide a Self Review Document that greatly assists schools with judging their achievements in mathematics.

Local Authorities buy into Fisher Family Trust because it gives more detailed information than RAISEonline. FFT data will almost certainly be very familiar at senior leadership team level in schools, however in our experience many subject leaders have not been introduced to this data. Mathematics subject leaders may have to ask their senior management team about this data source and how to access it in their school.

FFTlive is potentially accessible to everybody interested in school performance. It can be accessed anywhere over the internet, unlike the main FFT data source. At the time of writing it is very new; it first went online in 2007. It provides subject-level value-added at KS3, GCSE and post 16. RAISEonline only provides data up to Key Stage 4. FFTlive provides colour-coded guidance at all Key Stages up to A Level and allows schools to know whether they have done well, not so well or just about average in mathematics compared with national results data. FFTlive does not have any pupil level data at the moment, although, at the time of writing, the latest update says that they are providing new and more secure passwords to enable schools to access pupil-level data online.

The self-review document provided by FFT is very helpful in completing the School Evaluation Form (SEF). The self-review document contains a great deal of information; it gives important details about the relative performance of groups of pupils, more detailed information than is available in RAISEonline. Many schools now ask their subject leaders to complete a SEF every year and collate the department SEFs into the school SEF. If this is the case in your school, make sure you have access to the FFT self-review document to help you make judgements about the strengths and weaknesses of your department and decide where you need to make improvements. Local Authorities usually provide this self-review document on a CD or online.

Table 2 is taken from the Fischer Family Trust Self Evaluation Form and identifies those groups of pupils at GCSE whose progress is significantly improving in mathematics.

Table 2

Indicator: Mathematics Mean GCSE Grade
Significance - Over 3 Years Combined: Within expected range

Value-added - Trend	Category	Pup (3 Yr)	Actual 2005	2006	2007	Est/Act Difference 2005	2006	2007
Improving	Girls - Lower	136	2.16	2.51	3.17	-0.27	0.15	0.36
Improving	Boys - Lower	132	2.59	2.84	2.95	-0.08	0.31	0.36
Improving	With FSM	76	2.61	3.26	3.63	-0.27	0.25	0.35
Improving	SEN Action	101	2.25	2.13	3.08	-0.10	0.05	0.61
Improving	Black Caribbean	76	3.16	4.35	4.50	-0.15	0.38	0.21
Improving	Indian	137	4.15	4.50	4.92	-0.14	0.34	0.22

This report highlights areas where pupil progress is significantly different to 'expected'. The analysis is based upon a Contextual Value-Added approach which takes into account each pupil's prior-attainment and a range of pupil and school context factors. In effect, the analysis compares the progress made by each pupil with that made by 'similar pupils in similar schools'.

In this analysis the term SIGNIFICANT is used to mean those aspects where we can be 95% confident that the difference is larger than would be expected. The report shows, for a range of indicators and for a range of pupil categories, areas where performance (over the last 3 years) was significantly high or low or where value-added has changed to a significant degree. In the data shown for individual years.

Significantly higher than 'expected'   Significantly lower than 'expected'   Uses FFT SX Model

RAISEonline and FFT provide similar data; both refer to the attainment and achievement levels at department and pupil level. RAISEonline will produce estimates for pupils but before schools can use RAISEonline to set targets they have to enter the pupil-level prior-attainment data. For that reason, many schools have not used RAISEonline for target setting at pupil level. FFT automatically produce estimates for individual pupils.

The RAISEonline Contextual Value Added reports use a range of data, as does FFT, and most of the criteria used are broadly the same for each data source. The measures used for deprivation in FFT and RAISEonline are different; RAISEonline uses IDAC (Income Deprivation Affecting Children – for more information see *www.odpm.gov.uk*), and FFT uses ACORN types (for more information see *www.caci.co.uk/acorn/pclookup.asp*) for identifying deprivation. Both identifiers use data at near postcode level but they calculate it slightly differently and therefore there are a few anomalies or differences between the two.

Using RAISEonline and Fisher Family Trust data

Colour coding is used to identify significant changes from previous results in both RAISEonline and FFT. Every result shaded green is above expectations, blue shaded results are below expectations and white indicates that the result is as expected. So in general, green is good and blue is bad on both data sources.

As this chapter goes to press the national tests at Key Stage 3 have been abolished and schools are able to make their own arrangements for assessing and recording their pupils' progress during Key Stage 3. Therefore RAISEonline will no longer report on progress at Key Stage 3. At this time we do not know whether teacher assessment data will be collected nationally. Schools can enter their own data into RAISEonline and therefore can make use of most of its facilities for analysing data at Key Stage 3 but will be unable to compare with national data.

Both data sources also need passwords. Some local authorities are providing generic passwords for FFTlive as it currently does not have pupil-level data so there are no data protection issues. A generic password enables schools to access the data from all other schools in their Local Authority and compare their results to those of other schools. Other Local Authorities generate passwords for individual schools so that they can only see their own data.

Many Local Authorities group schools in families or clusters of schools. Such groups enable subject leaders to identify schools in similar positions to themselves whose results are different, especially those whose results are better. Visiting such a school can be very informative. If the school is in a similar position why, for example, do their EAL pupils seem to perform better overall than those at your school? Good results generally mean good practice although this is not always the case. For example, the other school may be better at training their pupils to take the tests whilst you consider interest and enjoyment is important and this shows in your A Level take up. Finding out about other schools' practice is not straightforward but visiting other schools in similar circumstances can be a good starting point for developing your own department's practice and, where Local Authorities share it, data can indicate where you might want to go and what you might want to investigate.

Subject leaders must be aware of data protection issues when thinking about passwords. Where the password gives access to pupil-level data, it is important to think carefully about who has the password. If a teacher has a password and they leave the school, that password must be cancelled. If the whole department uses a generic password to access pupil-level data, it would have to be changed if one teacher leaves and this can lead to confusion and aggravation. RAISEonline provides a headteacher password and a school administrator password and the administrator can generate individual passwords. The standard school FFT data and the SEF document are usually provided by the Local Authority electronically so whether or not you need a password to access that information will be an internal matter for the school.

Other sources of data

There is a third main source of information for a subject leader and that is Local Authority data and analysis. Most Local Authorities have data teams which provide schools with data to support school improvement, whether it is through electronic information or a virtual office, or, more commonly, a hard copy of a school profile, which may be sent on a CD. The Local Authority school profiles may be very detailed and contain lots of information. The headteacher or member of the senior management team will know how to access this school profile. It will normally include details about attainment and achievement in mathematics because mathematics is a core subject.

The Local Authority will also have access to the school's mathematics KS2 to GCSE national, value-added graphs. This will have all pupils plotted, both overall and by gender. However schools or subject leaders may have to specifically ask for this information if they want to see it. Teachers should ask their Local Authority for the "NCER report VA34A for maths". This will be a national value-added graph for mathematics where Local Authorities plot pupils at GCSE and A Level but not at KS3. If a Local Authority does not subscribe to FFT then this pack of data will provide value added information at GCSE. The information is from the National Consortium for Examination Results and is available to all Local Authorities and through them, to schools. The Local Authority has to input data so that schools can use it, but it is there if schools ask for it. Every pupil who has taken mathematics GCSE in each year will be plotted on the same graph, which shows where they are in relation to the top 25% of pupils, the bottom 25%, middle 50% and so on. This graph used to be in the Pupil Achievement Tracker report but it is not now available in RAISEonline.

There is a fourth source of information which is only for post 16 pupils and it is relatively new. It is produced by the Learning and Skills Council (LSC) and called the Learning Achievement Tracker. The Learner Achievement Tracker (LAT) contains value-added graphs and tables for each school for every post 16 subject including mathematics. Since March 2007, the LAT software has replaced the value-added section contained within the post 16 e-Panda report. The LAT can be accessed through a website at *https://gateway.lsc.gov.uk/ ProviderGateway* but a password will be needed to enter the site. Schools have to contact the local LSC to receive a password. The LAT is the only source of value-added data that is available to Ofsted at post 16 before an inspection. It has been produced so that sixth form colleges and other providers of post 16 education have a way to track their pupils' progress. The post 16 e-Panda is still available, provided by Ofsted, and downloadable by schools with a password. It is published in April each year and contains attainment-level data but no pupil-level data.

There are other data packages available for schools from commercial companies. Some commonly used examples are those provided by NfER; CATS, reading assessments and marking the optional tests in Year 7 and 8. Other data sources commonly used in schools are MIDYIS, YELLIS and ALIS. These packages provide more information on pupils but whether it is better information than that available from RAISEonline or FFT causes a great deal of debate. Some schools buy into these packages and others do not and there is no clear evidence that there is any difference. If your school does use these packages then this will be another source of data to use in analysing the strengths and weaknesses of the mathematics department.

Why use these data sources?

FFT, RAISEonline, Local Authority data, LAT and commercial schemes all have the same purpose. That is to provide data that enables subject leaders to identify which pupil or groups of pupils are underachieving or performing in a way that is better or worse than expected. Schools can then use the data to:

- firstly, identify which groups of pupils need additional support in order to catch up;

- secondly, identify whether or not strategies that are in place are effective i.e. by monitoring the progress of pupils who are receiving additional support. In other words, data can measure the impact of what the department is doing in order to raise achievement.;

- thirdly, to hold schools and subject departments accountable to external agencies including Governors, Ofsted, LA, parents and pupils.

Table 3 below is taken from RAISEonline and shows the overall attainment in mathematics at GCSE by different groups of pupils.

Table 3

	Average Points per Pupil in mathematics, Key Stage 4 2007			
	Entries	School	National	Sig
Special Educational Needs				
No Identified SEN	174	37.5	39.0	Sig-
SEN without a statement				
School Action	28	25.9	28.3	
School Action Plus	3	9.3	25.5	
SEN with a statement	2	14.0	24.2	
Ethnic Group				
White				
British	113	34.9	37.0	
Irish	0	-	38.0	-
Traveller of Irish Heritage	0	-	22.4	-
Gypsy/Roma	0	-	21.6	-
Any Other White Background	0	-	37.6	-
Mixed				
White and Black Caribbean	11	35.3	33.4	
White and Black African	0	-	36.0	-
White and Asian	4	27.0	40.2	
Any other Mixed Background	2	31.0	37.4	
Asian or Asian British				
Indian	38	39.5	41.7	
Pakistani	8	32.5	34.9	
Bangladeshi	2	34.0	35.8	
Any other Asian Background	0	-	40.5	-
Black or Black British				
Caribbean	13	33.7	33.2	
African	2	37.0	35.7	
Any Other Black Background	5	30.4	34.0	
Chinese	0	-	47.3	-

In the vast majority of schools, RAISEonline and FFT identify similar strengths and weaknesses within mathematics. Sometimes additional important information can be extracted from FFT. For example, FFT provides data and information about value added in mathematics using a combined figure from the last three years, whereas RAISEonline separates each of the last three years.

Sometimes it is important to show information about the progress of pupils over a period of time. FFT compares the school's results against the national figures but uses the results of pupils from the last three years. So if the school has 200 pupils in each year, this year's results would be compared against a cohort of 600. Sometimes that helps to give you an indication of what the department is like overall. So, for example, RAISEonline could indicate a mathematics department's performance over three years at GCSE as green, green and blue. If this year the performance is coded blue that indicates poor performance against national figures. The view formed by the senior management and by Ofsted will be that the standard of achievement is significantly below average. However if they looked at the equivalent FFT report the performance could be shaded green, because for two out of the three years progress has been good. It would depend on just how poor the performance was in the third year and the reasons for that poor performance.

FFT have different criteria for calculating value added; they have 'prior attainment value added' which is the equivalent to the 'contextual value added' in RAISEonline but using subtly different criteria. FFT also provides more detailed information about the value added of different groups of children by gender and prior attainment group. Looking carefully at the performance of different groups may well reveal which group of pupils caused the significant drop in performance of the department discussed above.

RAISEonline currently provides detailed information about the proportion of pupils making progress through two levels in mathematics at both KS3 and GCSE, data which is not available in FFT. These relatively new indicators are used mainly by the Secondary National Strategy and are likely to become part of the DCSF performance tables in 2009 or later. These graphs show the number of levels of progress that pupils make from KS2 to KS3 and from KS3 to KS4 and because of the style of graph used, they are often referred to as 'stickmen graphs'. At the time of going to press we do not know if these graphs will continue to be made available. However, if they are this indicator of progress must be treated with care as it is possible for this data to obscure what is really going on. For example, consider a newly arrived pupil, whose progress has been assessed as having just gained a Level 4, commonly referred to as 4c; suppose during Key Stage 3 the pupil progresses well and achieves a high mark in Level 5, referred to as 5a, then that pupil has nearly made two levels of progress but would be shown on these charts as having made only one. Whereas a pupil having just missed a 5 so assessed as 4a, and then at Key Stage 3 just attaining a Level 6c, has really made just more than one Level of progress but is assessed as making two. The data in these 'stickmen graphs' provide no more information than that contained in the other RAISEonline reports. The RAISEonline CVA report clearly indicates whether the department is making good progress or not.

The secondary National Strategy uses 'two levels of progress' to make judgements about departments and for their own accountability systems. They set attainment floor targets, for example that a mathematics department has to enable 50% of its pupils to attain Level 5 or above at Key Stage 3. If

48% of the pupils at the school attain Level 5 or above and that constitutes good progress as indicated by CVA, the department may be judged 'good' by Ofsted. However National Strategy consultants may well view the department in a different light. This can cause confusion. However the National Strategy and Ofsted are not really measuring the same thing. Ofsted are looking for progress and attainment; the National Strategy consultants are simply looking at a target figure. However a subject leader may have to be prepared to explain this carefully to a confused department.

RAISEonline now looks at the "expected" rate of progress from KS2 to GCSE mathematics. This assumes a level 4 pupil will progress to a "C" grade at GCSE and a level 3 pupil to a "D" grade etc.

You can download any report in RAISEonline into an Excel spreadsheet. It can be a really good exercise to use an Excel spreadsheet and insert a column so that you can subtract the national results from those of the school. If all the negatives are highlighted in red and all the positives are not highlighted then it can be seen at a glance how high or low the standards are in the department and where there are relative weaknesses. RAISEonline can be transferred straightforwardly into other programmes such as Excel or SIMS. FFT data does not transfer so straightforwardly.

SEF, Ofsted and all that
The guidance for inspectors, and for schools when doing self evaluation, is that the full range of data should be used. Therefore mathematics departments need to use all the data that is available to them when identifying which groups of pupils are doing well and which ones are falling behind. Making judgements on the performance of the mathematics department is a bit like baking a cake. All the ingredients are gathered and mixed to get the finished product. That finished product is the overall summary judgements but to get the full flavour of the department, all the ingredients have to be included. Sometimes the FFT analysis will give most guidance on what to say about individual groups of children; sometimes it will be other data that provides the important information. Overall, subject leaders need to be looking at the full range of data available to them.

RAISEonline data, performance tables, together with the LAT and the school's own Self Evaluation Form(SEF) form the basis of the initial judgements made by an Ofsted inspection team prior to an inspection visit. FFT and Local Authority data is not available to Ofsted inspectors, other than where the school has chosen to mention it in the SEF. Ofsted will look at all the available information and form judgements which they combine into a Pre-Inspection Briefing (PIB) report which is given to the school before an inspection. In the PIB, both attainment and value-added data are considered and judgements are formed. At this stage, areas for further investigation during the inspection are identified. If there is a judgement in the PIB based on external data that the mathematics department considers is wrong or misleading, then the subject leader will need to prepare evidence for the inspection team when they are come in. The data that is collected may well have been mentioned in the SEF but the subject leader will need to have the evidence ready for the inspectors.

Increasingly subject leaders are being asked by the senior management team to complete the achievements and standards section of a SEF for their department. When completing the SEF, there is no need to repeat, for example, any data about Level 5s and above or Level 6s and above because that is all available from RAISEonline or the school's own data system. The subject leader should analyse the data and include their judgements and evaluations about the progress and attainment in the department. For example, a subject leader might say 'at GCSE boys achieve very well (FFT page 7) but SEN girls are only making average progress (ibid)'. An Ofsted inspector visiting the school would then look at page 7 of the FFT documentation expecting to see green shading for GCSE boys in mathematics. If the school believes FFT or in school analysis provides a more accurate reflection of the strengths and weaknesses of the department than RAISEonline then this should be referred to and made clear in the school or departmental SEF. If there are anomalies between RAISEonline and FFT, the department should attempt to identify why this has happened. If a figure in FFT was green, but the same group of pupils in RAISEonline had no shading, then there would be an investigation and discussion within the school as part of the inspection. However 95% of FFT and RAISEonline reports contain no significant differences between the two. In the vast majority of cases, they raise the same issues.

More commonly, departments will have a different picture to the judgements that Ofsted make using RAISEonline because circumstances have changed. So for example, differences could occur because of issues in matching pupils at Key Stage 2 and 3; RAISEonline might have 85% matched pupils and FFT might have matched 93%, or the school might have done their own matching and raised the percentage even further. The new figures might make a difference to the overall judgements about a department. Another reason for differences might be that attainment and progress in school is different to that seen in the previous year. This may be especially true if the inspection is in the summer term. The two terms since the last exam results could have seen significant changes and the picture could have become completely different. Often a mathematics department can have weak achievement because there is a recruitment issue. Many areas of the country have difficulties recruiting qualified mathematics teachers and many people teaching mathematics are not fully qualified. In those circumstances, whoever is holding the mathematics department accountable has to make a judgement about whether or not best efforts have been made to improve recruitment. Normally the judgements made on leadership and management and achievement are the same. However, if the circumstance is that there is a genuine recruitment difficulty and the subject leader has made best efforts to resolve it but has been unsuccessful, then Ofsted will take this into account.

When completing the SEF, schools can place the school in context within local conditions. Many Local Authorities are involved in Building Schools for the Future. If a school has been knocked down and a new one built, then that is likely to have an effect on standards. This has to be included in the SEF as part of the context within which the department is operating. There are other contexts that should be mentioned in the SEF, for example, if your local

8. USING ASSESSMENT DATA

authority or if many of your feeder schools are in special measures. If the Local Authority is itself in special measures, then the support that subject leaders receive is unlikely to be as good as schools in other Local Authorities. If many of the secondary school's primary feeder schools are in special measures, that is also likely to have an effect on pupils' progress at secondary school and can be mentioned in the SEF. Neither of these issues, or other similar issues will be obvious to Ofsted inspectors looking at the school's results on RAISEonline and therefore have to be mentioned in the SEF.

Target Setting
Both RAISEonline and FFT are useful in helping teachers set challenging targets for their pupils. They currently provide estimates at subject and pupil level for future performance at both KS3 and GCSE. RAISEonline provides estimates at different levels, the top 75% of schools, top 50%, top 25% and top 10%. FFT also provides estimates at different levels; FFT B estimates are based on the previous performance of schools similar to your own, whereas FFT D estimates are based on the performance of the top 25% of similar schools. Very broadly speaking, FFT D estimates of performance are similar to RAISEonline top 50% estimates. The DCSF has instructed all Local Authorities to encourage schools to use FFT D estimates as a minimum aspiration.

If a school is constantly achieving rates of progress that are less than those estimated by FFT B, then expecting them to set targets at FFT D may not be realistic, as they may be unachievable. When setting targets, it is important to apply common sense as well as challenge. There have to be good reasons to use FFT B to set targets. On the other hand, those schools that are regularly performing above FFT D will not be challenged by using FFT D to set targets and in this case schools can turn to RAISEonline. RAISEonline provide several estimates at school level for mathematics departments. If a school historically performs well above the FFT D targets, then RAISEonline top 25% or top 10% estimates will enable them to set challenging targets in discussion within school and with their Local Authority. A subject leader may investigate all the different estimates in order to set targets that will challenge their pupils. Using FFT D targets will be time saving, but if a subject leader wishes to challenge their department to achieve more, there are currently estimates for attainment at Key Stage 3 and GCSE available from RAISEonline that will support this.

Table 4 is taken from RAISEonline and identifies past trends and estimates for the school's future performance. This information can be used to support the mathematics department in setting challenging targets for the future.

Indicative school targets

School targets based on historic transition probabilities. Similar schools are those with similar prior attainment. The average prior attainment for the school is: 27 <= school prior attainment < 28

	Historic results						2009 based on current school progression rates		2009 Proportions based on probabilities							
	Percentage Level 5+			Percentage making 2 levels progress					Top 75% of similar schools		Top 50% of similar schools		Top 25% of similar schools		Top 10% of similar schools	
	2005	2006	2007	2005	2006	2007	Level 5+	2 Levels progress	Level 5+	2 Levels progress	Level 5+	2 Levels progress	Level 5+	2 Levels progress	Level 5+	2 Levels progress
English	74%	65%	73%	25%	14%	19%	74%	15%	84%	33%	85%	37%	87%	41%	89%	46%
Maths	64%	73%	72%	35%	42%	39%	74%	45%	82%	67%	83%	70%	84%	73%	85%	77%
English and Maths	61%	61%	64%	-	-	-	66%	-	76%	-	77%	-	79%	-	81%	-

The process of setting targets should always include scrutinising the estimates for each pupil and using what teachers know about individual pupils to decide which estimates look about right and which ones need to be adjusted. Adjustment may be up or down. Once the targets have been set, the subject leader should hold teachers accountable for enabling their pupils to make progress towards attaining those targets. When subject leaders monitor the grades by teaching group, they may find one teacher has lowered many target grades by one level or grade. This will be where their management skills are needed. They will enquire why the changes in targets have been made and seek to support the teacher in overcoming any problems that are uncovered. Rigorous, challenging targets can raise everyone's expectations and thus results, but they must be appropriate for the context of the school and the pupils within it. Subject leaders in consultation with the senior management team may decide to set aspirational targets that are unlikely to be met but may be inspirational for the department, or to set realistic targets that the pupils are likely to meet. There are no hard and fast rules about this but everyone must be aware of the status of the targets so that if they are met or not the correct judgement can be made.

Tracking data

Internal tracking data is becoming more sophisticated as IT systems improve and could become more important now that there are no longer national tests at Key Stage 3. Typically this will be a pupil tracking system which uses the school's management information system or a spreadsheet. Tracking usually monitors the progress of pupils towards their targets. Targets are typically set annually or by Key Stage. Teachers generally identify current levels of attainment, predicted levels of attainment or identify whether or not a target will be met. In any event, the software into which the data is entered usually produces a list of pupils identified as underachieving.

Depending on school policy, two, three, four or six times a year, data about the current attainment of pupils is collected and their progress towards the targets that have been set is monitored. Schools usually ask subject leaders to answer two questions:

a. What is the current level of attainment of a pupil? The response needed is often subdivided 4a, 5c and so on.

b. What grade or level is the pupil going to reach at the end of the Key Stage? Are they on track to achieve their target?

The purpose of tracking is to identify underachievement. Externally verified data estimates, such as FFT or RAISEonline should be used to inform the targets against which the progress of pupils is monitored. Some schools seek to set their own targets without reference to external sources, but this can be a problem. For example, a grammar school used a target-setting process based on what they thought was right for them. When they compared their outcomes at the end of the year, they had not reached national expectations for grammar schools. Their own expectations were less than they should have been for high-attaining pupils. If targets are set using appropriately challenging external data, you can be sure that pupils are making good progress if they are moving at an appropriate rate towards those targets. All school information managements systems have a facility built in to set up tracking systems to allow pupils progress to be monitored. Subject leaders will get to know the school tracking system so that they are in a position to guide other teachers about what to assess and how to record current levels of attainment.

The result of tracking progress will be a list of pupils who are not on track to reach their targets. If pupils are found to be underachieving, then something different must happen for these pupils to help them achieve more. Teachers spend a lot of time and take a lot of trouble with assessing pupils and recording the data but the outcomes are often not used to help the pupils improve. Some mathematics teachers explain underachievement in terms of the pupils; they do not do homework or they do not attend extra lessons at lunchtime. A more appropriate response may be to take a look at teaching in, for example, Sets 2 and 3 and reflect with the teachers of these classes on how teaching could be improved so that the pupils are able to learn better. Underperformance will always be linked to the quality of teaching and learning. It may be that improving rates of homework or making extra revision classes more appealing will help; but thinking about underachievement must include an investigation of the quality of teaching and learning and ways to improve in this area.

Tracking data measures something different from exam or test data, if the data used is a good indicator of pupils' progress. In some departments, the data used are the results of tests which have been constructed by teachers in the department. It is unlikely that even a well-constructed test will test effectively all the areas in which pupils may have made progress. On the other hand, it is often very difficult for teachers to make good judgements of the level attained by their pupils, especially if the teachers do not have much experience of making these judgements or the department does not use moderation. Day-to-day assessment information could be aggregated to form a reliable teacher assessed level, if the department supports one another in making accurate judgements. The APP (Assessing Pupil Performance *www.standards.dfes.gov. uk/secondary/keystage3/subjects/maths/focus/asses_maths/*) could help teachers to focus on specific criteria in more detail but teachers must be careful not to return to the days of 107 tick boxes to record attainment. The APP is designed as a best fit, or holistic, moderated judgement so that teachers can show that genuine progress has been made between assessment points. However, it is easy to make this a chore that has no impact on the pupils' learning. It is possible to include the pupils themselves in the process of assessing exactly where they are, what progress they have made and where they want to be. Including the pupils could make the process more useful and help the pupils know where they have to improve. The process will be even more powerful if the pupils are also helped to know how to make that improvement.

There are statements within educational literature that equate tracking with assessment for learning. These two concepts are not the same. Assessment for Learning (see Chapter 9, this volume) involves day-to-day, in-class assessment that is acted on with a very short timeframe and generally involves the pupils. Tracking data is about gains over a period of time. The tracking system does provide important information if you analyse it, but it is repeated summative assessment and not assessment for learning. Assessment for Learning in day-to-day lessons is the single most important skill for a teacher to use to enable pupils to make good progress.

What data is it sensible for a head of department to collect and store?
The data that subject leaders collect and store should be enough for them to answer the following four questions about their pupils

- What is the current level of attainment for each pupil?
- What is their current level of progress?
- What is the target grade?
- Are pupils performing above or below expectations?

If the department's systems allow you to answer these questions then the systems are adequate. However there is a little more data that may be useful. The longest that subject leaders can be required to keep data is 5 years and any data more than five years old should be cleared, remaining aware of data protection. If the data is electronic, it must be completely deleted; if it is on paper it must be shredded. Every school keeps a central record of examination results, and this is likely to be kept for much longer than five years as there are often queries from old pupils about their results.

Through research, the education system is starting to learn more about what has an impact on teaching and learning. Schools can use their data systems to begin to understand what really works in their context, however, currently, this course of action is rarely undertaken. Schools try things out, bring in this initiative or that, but often forget to evaluate the impact of what they are trying. The data tracking system is ideally placed to provide data that will measure the impact of a new approach or something that has been introduced to try to combat underachievement. If there is a facility to record on the tracking system whether a Year 11 pupil is part of the new evening club or the Easter revision classes, or if a Year 9 pupil has been involved in catch up lessons, the impact of these ideas on pupil performance can easily be tracked and measured. If there appears to be no difference in the attainment or progress of the pupils involved in an innovation on the tracking system, then its efficacy must be questioned.

Everything that everybody does in a school will have an impact on a pupil but it can be hard to know to what extent. Subject leaders are in a position to start to investigate what happens if teachers take part in a different approach to teaching or offer some extra provision. If pupils in an experimental group do make significant progress, it is important to recognise that it may be due to other factors as well as the new initiative, but if the data shows improvement then that is a good argument for continuing with the initiative and possibly including more pupils. Data can be a powerful tool to use in action research but care must be taken about which groups to use as control groups. If the department is convinced that a change in the way that they teach will bring real benefits, then it could be considered unethical to deny some pupils a chance to experience the new teaching just so that the department has a control group. However, it is usually possible to use last years' data as a 'control'; alternatively a teacher who is sceptical about the efficacy of the change could volunteer to be the control group. Comparing the results of an innovation against a control group can help to convince even the most doubtful teacher.

If a number of pupils have been identified as underachieving, and strategies have been put in place to remedy the situation, the pupils themselves will have a view on how effective the changes have been. It is worth asking the pupils if they have noticed any difference to their learning experiences as this may help you decide the impact you are having on improving progress

Conclusion

Data analysis is important, although we would be the first to say that it can take on an importance that it does not deserve. Data recording and analysis should not take up too much time, it must be streamlined and focussed on continuing improvements in the real business of the department, high quality teaching and learning. When a subject leader becomes adept at using the various data sources, including the school tracking systems, they can be sure that they know their department's strengths and weaknesses. Sometimes surprising things can be uncovered. Teachers and pupils can be shown to be underperforming when they thought they were doing as well as could be expected. Their expectations of themselves can be raised and they can be supported in making changes, improving the outcomes for those pupils. How those expectations are raised, whose ideas are sought and used and what decisions are made about using teaching and learning approaches or what innovations are introduced; now that is the job and skill of a good subject leader.

It may be that, as a new subject leader you take over a department that has seen itself as performing poorly. Perhaps the school has had recruitment problems for a few years and the existing teachers despair of improving. If such a department is to improve, the teachers have to begin to see themselves as successful. Tracking data can be used to provide this positive impact. The minute that any progress is apparent, improvements can be celebrated, which will help to overcome any psychological barriers that may have developed.

If the question raised by the data is 'Why is that group underachieving?' then the answer is available by scrutinising pupils' work, through lesson observations and by asking the pupils themselves. Information on standards can be gained from scrutiny of the work produced within the department, from for example, a topic that was identified as not done well in item level analysis on RAISEonline. Work scrutiny was part of all Ofsted inspections but is not part of the new shorter inspections, except as a part of lesson observations. However, there is every reason for departments to continue with work scrutiny as it provides useful data and helps share expectations and standards of work. A work scrutiny could take place during half an hour of a departmental meeting and it is best done regularly so that everyone is used to the process. It could be done just once a year but is probably more useful twice or three times a year. If possible, include a member of the senior leadership team, the head of department and all the teachers in the group that looks at the books and other artefacts produced by the pupils. The point is to look at the progress that pupils are making. What were they doing five weeks ago or last term? Are all the pupils doing something different and at a higher level now? This process is very effective in raising expectations within the department; it aids everyone's understanding of how judgements of 'good work' are reached and also helps all department members take ownership of the next steps for improvement.

Generally, most weaknesses that are seen in the data can be identified by what happens in lessons, so lesson observation data is important. Many schools' lesson observation schedules lack the flexibility to customise them for the particular focus of your department. It is important to make sure that when observations are done they collect data on the areas that the department has agreed to develop even if it has to be an attached note. If achievement and standards are weak over a period of time or at a Key Stage or with a particular group, say boys, then lesson observation monitoring should be flexible enough to accommodate observations that will help the department know how to improve their practice in the areas identified.

Remember that data can be collected from the pupils themselves. Such data collection has to be structured and the department has to be sure what they want to find out. Pupil data can be gained through structured interviews or discussions with a group of pupils or through surveys. If the questions asked are worded suitably then pupils can contribute valuable data to help the department know how and where to improve. If pupils are asked, they can make available data on all the strengths and weaknesses of the department and, in particular, the different learning experiences they encounter. Pupils can often pinpoint the problems associated with their learning very accurately. A number of commercial surveys are available to use that provide analysis of pupil feedback.

Communication will always be the key to finding answers. In our experience, people often know only too well what is going wrong but they are not asked, so they do not say. As a subject leader your job will be to set up a culture where communication is considered vitally important. If an issue is raised by the data, all concerned should be specifically asked about solutions and effective listening can often be the key skill in leading a successful department.

References

DCSF, (2007) Assessing Pupil's Progress. The Standards Site *www.standards.dcsf. gov.uk/secondary/keystage3/subjects/maths/focus/asses_maths/ma_app_implement/* Accessed on 29.12.08.

9
LEADING ASSESSMENT FOR LEARNING MATHEMATICS

Clare Lee

'Assessment for Learning' is a term that seems to have picked up some negative connotations recently but here it is used as it was when first coined (Black et al 2003) to denote the process of making day by day, hour by hour, minute by minute adjustments to what is going on in the classroom so that the activities better meet the learning needs of the pupils. When assessment is used in this way to gain evidence in order to modify the immediately subsequent learning activities that pupils engage in, it can also be called formative assessment. Only formative assessment has been shown to be a powerful way to raise standards in the classroom (Black et al, 2003) because it enables teachers to synchronise learning activities to the pupils' needs more closely and it enables pupils to take greater charge of their own learning. If formative assessment is going make the difference that it could, it has to permeate every classroom in every school and that, of course, includes mathematics classrooms.

It is important to remember that Assessment for Learning or formative assessment is not about grades and testing. Data collection and analysis are considered in Chapter 8 of this volume and they have their value in a well managed mathematics department, providing evidence of the difference that the department is making for the pupils in its care. However the summative assessments that provide such data are about checking up on learning that has happened, not about enabling that learning to happen. Assessment for Learning, or formative assessment, is about enabling learning and enabling pupils to learn more and in a better way. Therefore it is Assessment for Learning that has been shown to make a difference to attainment and standards (Black et al. 2003).

If Assessment for Learning is so important, and there is already information available about it, why is it not used in every classroom already? There are many reasons for this, but the chief reason is that it is not easy to make the changes that are required. Teachers have a vision of what good teaching is and that has often been built during their own school experiences. Making changes to that vision feels risky and is actually difficult to do, in the way that changing any ingrained habit is difficult. If teachers are to make the changes needed to fully incorporate Assessment for Learning, they must be offered support and motivation over time without expecting everything to be easy and straightforward. Departments may well decide to use Action Research (see Chapter 7, this volume) as a tool to support one another in beginning to embed Assessment for Learning in their day to day practice.

So what does a mathematics department do to embed Assessment for Learning in its practice? In a recent interview, Dylan Wiliam (2008) said that there are five characteristics of effective Assessment for Learning. Teachers should:

1. find out systematically where the pupils are in their learning;
2. provide feedback that moves the pupil's learning forward;
3. make sure that pupils understand what success looks like;
4. activate pupils as learning resources for one another – using not just peer-assessment but also collaborative learning and reciprocal teaching;
5. activate pupils as owners of their own learning – not just using self-assessment but also developing their ability to manage their emotional response to feedback and their resilience and to use meta cognition.

In this chapter, I set out in some detail what it means to incorporate these characteristics into mathematics lessons day to day, hour to hour, minute by minute. Subject leaders often find it best to lead by example, so their first step will be to ensure the characteristics of Assessment for Learning are present in their own practice. The next step will be to explore which of the characteristics are currently used within the department and which need to be worked on. Subject leaders can then make a plan to ensure that the teachers, and therefore the pupils, in a mathematics department can make use of Assessment for Learning to improve attainment and to improve the pupils' ability to learn mathematics. Indeed in working this way the subject leader will be modelling the use of Assessment for Learning with their department, finding out exactly where the teachers are in their knowledge and providing experiences that will help increase that knowledge.

Systematically finding out where the pupils are in their learning

The first characteristic is very important. How can teachers systematically collect high quality evidence on every pupil in the classroom at some point in every lesson, in such a way that they can act on the information gained?

The quality of the evidence collected is affected by the activity that produces that evidence. If teachers ask questions, leave thinking time and ask for answers from randomly picked pupils, they may obtain high quality evidence if the thinking time was sufficient but it will only be from the pupils who answer the questions. Trying to collect answers from everyone would destroy the pace of the lesson. This is not to say that asking questions in this way is undesirable in a lesson, in fact it is a very useful approach. It ensures that everyone is thinking and engaged and enables the teacher to gauge what the class knows, understands and can do in a general way. Where the class ethos is focused on everybody learning effectively, pupils can use such sessions to gauge their own learning by comparing it with others' answers and can ask for any help they need to move their own learning forward. However, it does not collect evidence from everyone or even nearly everyone.

So do we need to do short quizzes every lesson and collect in the marks? Definitely not. An approach that might be considered is to ask a challenging question as this enables learning at the same time as providing good evidence. Teachers could ask pairs to discuss the question and to reach agreement on the mathematical ideas or processes that they consider should be used to answer it and any problems they can foresee in working on an answer. After a short time, they could ask the pairs to move into fours and discuss the ideas and problems. It may be that in these discussions some of the ideas are discounted or some of the problems removed. Again teachers could ask the groups of four to agree on the ideas and processes that they think will be used and the problems that they can foresee. These can be written on a sheet of paper and either collected by the teacher or displayed, depending on the timing of the activity. If they are displayed, they can be grouped and then discussed. As there will only be eight or so papers, it is possible to consider each one and to group the pupils and assign work in a way that will move each pupil's learning forward.

The quality of the evidence will partly depend on the question asked; a simple question will reveal very little and may not be worth the lesson time spent on it. However a question that is too challenging will simply reveal that no-one in the class can begin to attack it and tell the teacher and the pupils themselves very little. Many teachers use mini whiteboards to collect evidence from all pupils but there are often problems both in the questions that the pupils are asked to think about and how the teacher uses the answers that are displayed to adapt subsequent learning. The problems arise, for example, when the questions asked are quick fire questions with very little thinking time. Some boards may go up a second or two after the others enabling the slower pupils to write down the same answer as those around him or her. Although teachers may spot wrong answers, there is rarely enough time allowed in these sessions for the pupils to explore the reasoning behind their answers or to tackle misconceptions. If the pupils are always giving right answers then the work they are being given is too easy for them. Work that moves learning forward is often difficult, at least to begin with, and therefore mistakes are often made and will need to be explored.

High quality evidence will be gained when the teacher and the pupils themselves explore their thinking and reasoning, checking where they are confident and where they have a lack of knowledge or misconceptions. Such evidence will build the pupils' image of themselves as competent mathematicians and show clearly where they must make their next learning effort to continue moving forward. This level of exploration is rarely seen in traditional mathematics lessons. The pupils rarely struggle with a problem and therefore are rarely rewarded by the satisfaction that comes from successfully achieving a difficult goal. They consider that if they cannot immediately see how to tackle a problem they 'can't do it'. Mistakes and difficulties simply indicate that learning could be about to happen and learning will happen if the teacher and pupil are alert to these problems and flexible enough to facilitate that learning. An exploration of the ATM, MA, NRICH or NCETM websites will reveal many ideas for questions and activities (e.g. Watson & Mason 1998) that are well worth exploring and that will reveal the kinds of high quality evidence needed to show where pupils are in their mathematical learning.

The timing of the evidence collection is also important because, when the teacher knows where the pupils are in their learning, they must act to modify subsequent learning activities to take account of the evidence if they are effectively using Assessment for Learning. Experienced teachers may find it easy to change their plans mid lesson to meet the learning needs they have uncovered and therefore can collect evidence at any time during a lesson. However less confident members of staff will find this more difficult and therefore may wish to collect evidence at the end of the lesson, at a time when they have an opportunity to think about the next learning activity.

As someone thinking about or already leading a department, you are likely to be aware of the difficulties of encouraging teachers in a mathematics department to change their classroom practice; acting in this way in the classroom may be a big change for some teachers. The traditional view of a mathematics classroom (see, for example, Ofsted 2008) is of a quiet place where pupils work individually through a series of graded exercises that they find fairly straightforward until they get 'stuck.' If they get 'stuck', they ask the teacher who explains how to do the particular question they are 'stuck' on and off they go again. These are 'ingrained habits' that teachers have to work hard at changing. The teacher in an Assessment for Learning classroom views mathematics as a series of interconnected ideas and processes. The pupils are asked to think and reason, struggle and talk to one another. Being 'stuck' may mean that they have not thought enough about the problem or that they have not researched enough in books or by asking other people specific questions that they need to answer on their way to solving a problem. Being 'stuck' may also mean that they need to learn something new and their teacher will know this because they use activities that allow such evidence to come to light. 'Being stuck' will certainly be seen as an honourable state (Mason 1985) which pupils can learn to see as affording opportunities to move forward The teacher responds by teaching what the pupils need to learn, not what they know already or what is next in the medium term plans or the scheme of work.

In order to assess if the first characteristic is embedded in department practice, a subject leader has several points to explore: the quality of the evidence collected, the timing and how the teacher or the pupils themselves act to modify subsequent learning activities in the light of the evidence. It will also be important to look at the way that mathematics is presented and the way that lessons are conducted. Do the teachers support one another in providing activities that allow evidence of learning to be revealed by all pupils? Is the scheme of work sufficiently flexible to allow time for teachers to teach their classes in a way that responds to the pupils' needs and experiences? And, of course, how exactly will the department begin to develop ways to address any issues that are found?

Provide feedback that moves learning forward
The second characteristic for using Assessment for Learning effectively is giving feedback that moves learning forward. It does not matter whether the feedback is written or given orally; what matters is that the pupils can act on it to learn more. Therefore this is not about giving pupils grades or levels or writing 'good' against certain parts of pupils' work, a practice that can

appear to pupils as a random scattering. Neither of these common practices can be shown to affect pupils' learning positively. Feedback that affects pupils' learning shows clearly what they have done well and indicates how to continue to improve their learning.

> External rewards (stickers, merit marks, etc) act like grades – treating every piece of work as a test freezes children into complacency or demoralisation. Children need feedback which is linked to the learning criteria of the task. The reward should be celebration of the learning achieved or the effort expended.
> Clarke, S. (2003, p13)

The most important aspect in terms of learning is that the feedback is acted on. Therefore any feedback must be given at a time when it can be acted on, not at the end of a learning episode. Teachers often advise pupils about what to do 'next time'. However for most pupils there never is a next time. They may well study the topic again in mathematics lessons, but by then they will probably be using a new exercise book and even if they are not, it is unlikely that they will remember to look back at the advice given. It is likely that the pupils will tackle similar problems to the one that they were given the feedback on but not the same problem. It is unlikely that most pupils will recognise that the similar problem is the 'next time' that the teacher was advising about. If a teacher spends time giving advice to a pupil then the pupil should use that advice otherwise teachers are giving a hidden message that it is alright to ignore what they say, which it is not. Therefore any feedback should be:

- clear about what has been completed well;
- clear about what improvements should be made or what to do in the immediate future to continue to learn;
- at a time when the improvements can be made or the advice acted on;
- part of overall lesson plans, giving time for pupils to read, ask questions and act on the feedback.

Again as subject leader you will recognise the difficulties in acting in this way. The habitual ways of giving summative feedback, eighteen out of twenty, Level 5 and so on, will not make a difference to learning and therefore a subject leader will need to decide whether it should be taking up teachers' precious time. However the type of feedback that does make a difference will take more time to complete. Therefore teachers are reluctant to give that type of feedback and cannot be expected to provide it as often as the more traditional forms. As subject leader, you will need to support teachers by suggesting the type of work that is worth giving detailed feedback on and work that can be assessed in other ways, for example self or peer-assessment, possibly including this in schemes of work. Teachers must know that they have the time to give good feedback and that they are not overloaded. Discussing the way feedback can be given in department meetings can be very helpful as can asking staff to monitor the subject leaders marking and comment on it. It may also be important as a subject leader, to monitor pupils' books in order to provide the motivation to teachers to try this way of working and allow the pupils to experience how good feedback will help their learning move forward.

Make sure that the pupils know what success looks like

The third characteristic of effective Assessment for Learning is that of making sure that pupils know what successful work looks like. Many pupils go through their school career thinking that successful work in mathematics is the completion of several pages of short questions requiring use of an algorithm in progressively more complex ways. I am not advocating that they never complete such exercises, as pupils do need to develop fluency in applying certain mathematical ideas. However I am saying that if this is their only experience of what successful mathematics looks like then it is an impoverished view. If you ask mathematics teachers what they understand mathematics to be, they talk about exploring, being able to model real-life situations, thinking mathematically and enjoying the satisfaction of a positive outcome to solving a problem they had to struggle to complete. If it is agreed that this is mathematics, then how can we show the pupils what it looks like to succeed in exploring a piece of mathematics, in thinking mathematically or in struggling to solve a problem?

There is no 'right' way. Many teachers model the process of problem solving for their pupils, including them in gathering ideas, trying out the ones that look likely and taking wrong turns. Actually watching their teacher trying out ideas and sometimes not succeeding can be very revealing for the pupils but...

- the best modelling will come from a problem that the teacher has not tackled before, because the pupils will see through any subterfuge;
- the pupils must know the point of the exercise otherwise why would they want to be part of potentially getting things wrong?
- pupils must be involved in discussions and decisions about what ideas to pursue and what mathematics to use. The teacher may have an idea of what would work but for the pupils to 'see' the process they must be truly part of that process;
- teachers often make small mistakes and even make deliberate mistakes but modelling successful problem solving can involve making time consuming mistakes. It is important to prepare your pupils for this. If they are to see what a struggle to find a way through the problem and the satisfaction of an eventual solution 'looks like' then it must be a true struggle and real satisfaction when the problem is solved.

Teachers usually know an efficient way to tackle a problem and almost always know 'the right answer', which may make modelling the process of problem solving seem to them like taking a big risk. What if the pupils make no suggestions? What if it takes more than the lesson allocated? Can I really spend time exploring ideas that I know will not work, just because the pupils are sure that they will? What if the pupils' think less of me because it looks like I do not know the answer? Pupils will make suggestions if you give them enough thinking time and possibly time to talk to a partner to try out their ideas first.

The time issues are complex; if mathematical thinking and problem solving are important, and if the department feels that pupils should take part in the mathematical process and enjoy mathematics, then time will have to be allocated. Possibly time could be more easily found in Year 7 as part of addressing the requirements of the new National Curriculum (QCA, 2007), then if it is found to extend the pupils' mathematical learning the approaches could be spread to other years. The pupils will need to know that they are going to be part of a process that involves thinking like a mathematician so that they can learn what thinking like a mathematician is like. Teachers can clearly explain that if they already knew the right way and the right answer then they would not be showing the real process.

There are of course other ways for pupils to see successful mathematical thinking and processing. Every time that they truly listen to one another talking through their mathematical ideas they are presented with a model of thinking. Some examples will be successful, some will not. Every time a pupil comes to the board and explains their thinking or pupils work together in twos and threes to work through a complex problem and report back on how they solved it, pupils are presented with models of mathematical thinking. Asking the pupils to look out for and note down other pupils' successful mathematical thinking during a lesson and using the plenary at the end of the lesson for them to report back on the thinking that they saw and heard happening can be a useful way of both drawing the pupils' attention to others' thinking and encouraging pupils to assess for themselves thinking that is helpful and successful.

Each of these examples is about making mathematical thinking public, something that is often neglected in the rush through the content to formal assessments. It is important to know that the act of making thinking public is part of effective mathematical learning. Vygotsky expressed what happens when pupils are involved in discussing ideas together like this:

> It is necessary that everything internal in higher forms was external, that is, for others it was what it now is for oneself. Any higher mental function necessarily goes through an external stage in its development because it is initially a social function…Any higher mental function was external because it was social at some point before becoming an internal, truly mental function. (Vygotsky, 1981, p. 162)

For Vygotsky, the more pupils are involved in expressing mathematical ideas, the more they can internalise those higher mental functions that they need in order to understand and use mathematics. However there are more prosaic reasons for making sure that pupils use language themselves in the classroom.

> …mathematics education begins and proceeds in language, it advances and stumbles because of language and its outcomes are often assessed in language. (Durkin and Shire, 1991, p. 1)

Mathematical language and expression is often specific and different from the pupils' more usual forms of expression. It is often demanding and in some cases can be ambiguous e.g. the word 'square' has several meanings. Pupils need to use mathematical language themselves in order to come to terms with these problems and not 'stumble' because of unknown vocabulary or ways of expression when they are taking part in external assessments.

> ...Children need to learn how to mean mathematically, how to use mathematical language to create, control and express their own mathematical meanings as well as to interpret the mathematical language of others.
> (Pimm, 1995, p. 179)

When pupils are used to expressing their mathematical thinking they know how to create mathematical meanings and they know how to control mathematical ideas so that they can work through ideas and solve problems. In order to encourage more thinking, exploring and articulation of ideas in mathematics classes Subject Leaders may have to convince people in their department that this is a good idea. It may help to explore the idea that pupils who are used to exploring ideas together and making their thinking public are better at spotting gaps in their own knowledge and making such gaps obvious to their teachers. Once their teachers know about those gaps, learning tasks can be better synchronised with what the pupils need to know which is at the heart of Assessment for Learning. Pupils who know that they are encouraged to explore their mathematical knowledge, and talk it through with both their teacher and their peers, are consequently more secure with what they know, are better at thinking through ideas themselves and therefore evidence shows (Black et al 2003) tend to achieve better results in examinations.

Enabling a department to allow its pupils to know what success looks like may need quite a lot of discussion between teachers. The teachers themselves need to be confident about what constitutes successful mathematical thinking and processing. Teachers may need the support of watching a lesson where another teacher models the process of problem solving for their pupils in order to feel confident about acting in this way in their own classrooms. It will not be enough to provide resources, although these will be important. Introducing activities that clearly show the pupils what it means to think and process mathematically will be a problem solving activity for the whole department. A subject leader may well link up with another department that routinely uses discussion and thinking in order to provide models of good practice and to ensure that 'rules of engagement' are common across the school, or decide to try approaches with one class so that expectations can be clarified. The Ofsted report (2008) recognises the importance of using approaches that require pupils to think and discuss their ideas but recognises that the way this is done will be different in every department.

Activate the pupils as learning resources for one another

The fourth essential characteristic of effective Assessment for Learning is that in the classroom the pupils are consistently helping each other to improve their learning. In a classroom that has Assessment for Learning embedded, everyone's focus is on learning and on moving that learning forward. If the pupils have to wait for the teacher every time that they are stuck or need help, then time will not be used effectively to learn. That is not to say that the teacher just sits back and lets learning happen. It is the teachers' role to set up contexts and resources that support learning. Teachers offer experiences that may result in learning, but learning is a personal and complex activity that depends on many factors which includes the teacher and much more. It may be that an intervention will be needed, a point could be raised that all the pupils need to consider so the teacher asks for everyone's attention and talks through the concept or misconception. It may be that some pupils have huge gaps in their knowledge and therefore need in-depth discussion with the teacher to help them learn or alternatively some pupils are much further forward and need some specific challenge to allow them to move forward.

However there is usually only one teacher in the classroom; there may be teaching assistants but there are many more pupils. If the work is appropriately challenging and the pupils rely only on the teacher for help then no matter how hard the teacher or teaching assistant is working there will be pupils waiting for help and possibly becoming frustrated. Pupils should therefore help one another as and when they can in order to make sure that everyone learns as much as possible during the lesson. The teacher will monitor carefully to ensure all learners are being challenged to think and are not for example developing incorrect methods.

There are more reasons than economies of scale for pupils to see helping one another as an important aspect of their role in the classroom. As discussed above, the more discussion is entered into, the more that each pupil strives to make their thinking public, the more they will sort out their own misconceptions and gaps in their knowledge and the more they will gain in confidence about what they know and can do (see for example Alexander, 2006 & Mercer, 2007). Teaching someone else is an excellent learning and consolidation exercise. Pupils who teach others become more secure in what they know and come to understand their own competence in mathematics. Indeed it can be said that in taking on the role of teacher, they take on the identity of one who knows about mathematics (see for example Wenger 1998). So encouraging the pupils to help each other in their learning is valuable for all the pupils.

Those who need help obtain help quickly and the pupils are likely to use language in a way that is more understandable for their peers than their teacher's explanation. The pupil who is helping may understand more readily where stumbling blocks may be and the pupil who needs help may feel more able to ask question after question of their peer until they understand. Those pupils that are giving help consolidate what they know by explaining to others and gain confidence in their own knowledge. They are also likely to have that understanding challenged and quite possibly extended by those they are helping.

From an Assessment for Learning point of view, as the pupils work together to move their learning forward, their learning needs are exposed clearly. If the pupils can easily grasp and use a particular concept, this will be obvious to them and to the teacher and more challenging ideas can be introduced. If the pupils find difficulties in coping with the work, the exact nature of those difficulties can be ascertained and the teacher and pupils together can search for ways to overcome them.

In a mathematics department, activating pupils as learning resources for one another will be easy for some teachers and harder for others. Most teachers will be convinced by the 'economies of scale' argument. Often the pupil voice will also be convincing. A short interview with pupils who have had the opportunity to support one another will show just how much pupils appreciate and learn from this way of working. However, if the department is going to be effective in using Assessment for Learning, finding appropriate tasks where peer-assessment and collaborative learning and reciprocal teaching are a necessary part of the mix will be important.

Activate pupils as owners of their own learning

The fifth and last essential for embedding Assessment for Learning is to ensure that pupils have the emotional resources to help each other in the classroom. Many teachers say that it is their job to teach mathematics not to get involved in 'psychological mumbo jumbo'. However, unless the emotional aspects of learning mathematics are considered, pupils will neither achieve what they could nor enjoy mathematics in the way that they might. So what emotional aspects do mathematics teachers need to pay attention to?

Many pupils get locked into the idea that in mathematics they must always be correct and never make a mistake. In society at large, many people talk about mathematics as having one correct answer and often only one way of reaching that answer, or at least only one correct way. Although many teachers that I talk to are trying to overcome this, by stressing that there are many ways to tackle problems and reach an answer, there are still teachers who lack confidence in using anything other than the algorithm in their favourite textbook or who are so concerned with speed and efficiency that they will not let pupils explore and try other ways. This concentration on the 'right answer' and the 'right way' leads to many common but undesirable ways of pupils working in the classroom. For example they may:

- refuse to answer any questions;
- laugh at other pupils who answer a question wrongly (possibly relieved that it was not them);
- want to copy from the board into their books rather than make their own notes;
- rip pages that contain errors out of their exercise books and re-do the work;
- sit at the back of the class and slide under the desk in the hope that they will not be noticed;
- prepare their exercise books in order to write in the answers when the teacher reads them out
- refuse to do any work at all.

Assessment for Learning is about focusing upon learning and learning is about making mistakes. A recent survey I helped to conduct (Birmingham 2008) showed that almost 98% of the pupils who responded considered that they learned from their mistakes. So how can pupils become more comfortable with making mistakes in mathematics?

It is important to make sure that pupils know teachers expect them to make mistakes and expect them to develop strategies to help them correct their mistakes. If pupils never make mistakes then they are almost certainly not being challenged enough and the work that they are doing is probably too easy for them. Obviously some pupils will take to some ideas 'like a duck to water' and not make mistakes while learning a great deal, however this will not always be the case. Often, while pupils are exploring, trying out ideas, seeing the full implications of an idea or concept, how much they can accomplish and how unfamiliar and complex the situations can be in which they apply ideas, that is, when the pupils are learning mathematics, they will make mistakes. As pupils discuss their ideas with one another and their teacher, as they challenge themselves to try out ideas in more unfamiliar and complex settings, they will begin to iron out their misconceptions and grow in confidence. Teachers will watch out for mistakes and misconceptions. They will ask questions that require thought and complex processing, and allow time for the pupils to answer, intervene and help the pupils learn from any mistakes. Teachers will use phrases like "You have made a mistake there, now you can learn how to do that!" or "I need to know that you can do these, have a go at the first and the last one and let me know if you find any problems, then we can get on with something you really need to learn". Teachers can show that they are interested in what the pupils need to learn, after all that is what teachers are in the classroom for. Instead of asking "who got all the questions right" they might ask "Were there any interesting problems that we need to discuss that you couldn't sort out between yourselves?" It is important that pupils know that they can and do get answers and processes right, but it is the problems that need sorting out. Instead of hiding problems and issues and making them seem shameful, they can form the basis of valuable learning if everyone takes an interest in sorting out problems and talking about ways to overcome them.

The above ideas lead on to the second emotional aspect of learning relevant to this chapter, that of fixed learning theory versus growth learning theory. These ideas were developed by Dweck (2000 and 2006). Many pupils come to secondary school but especially to mathematics classrooms, with a fixed theory of learning. That is to say, pupils believe themselves to have only a limited capacity to learn mathematics and that there is a ceiling beyond which their learning is unable to go. They are often concerned that this ceiling is very low, leading to similar behaviours as those listed as a result of feeling that everything has to be 'right' in a classroom. If you believe that you cannot learn mathematics, why try? You will only look stupid and some pupils make a conscious decision that they would rather look lazy than stupid. This belief is commonplace in society, reinforced by statements that I have heard from parents such as 'I couldn't do maths at school so he won't be able to' or 'she couldn't do it at primary school either'. There are more subtle indications of a belief in a fixed theory of learning; phrases like 'work hard to reach your potential' may reinforce the idea that pupils have a fixed potential and many grading and target setting systems can reinforce the idea that there is a fixed ceiling to what can be achieved. The common practice of setting according to some measure of ability can also result in reinforcing a fixed theory of learning. Setting can result in many pupils having limited access to the programme of study (which is their entitlement) because of the set they are placed in. This means they never have the opportunity to 'be as good as they can be'. Boaler (1997, 2009) explains further about the self-fulfilling prophecy of setting.

Pupils with a fixed theory of learning are always concerned to demonstrate that their ability is better than other people, as this shows that their fixed ceiling is not low. Their energy therefore tends to go into demonstrating that they are better than others rather than into learning more. They are also helpless when faced by difficulties as they have no strategies to overcome any barriers. Difficulties, making mistakes or not achieving in public tests, confirm to people believing in this theory that they have reached the limit of their ability and that they cannot do anything to change this.

In contrast if a pupil believes in the growth theory of learning they believe that the more effort they put in, the more questions they ask, the more they will learn. They are not afraid of making mistakes because that simply indicates where they need to apply their learning effort and they know that it feels good to struggle through difficult tasks and succeed. They know that they have the ability to improve in any area that they want to. This is not to say that everyone will reach the same end point or that everyone will read mathematics at university. Rather, the growth theory of learning indicates that everyone can learn more than they know at present. They may learn in different ways, they may respond differently to different approaches to ideas but they are willing to try different ways because they believe that they are able succeed in learning more.

People with a Fixed Theory of Learning…	People with a Growth (or incremental) Theory of Learning…
believe that ability leads to success	believe that effort leads to success
are concerned to be judged as able to perform	believe in their ability to improve and learn
gain satisfaction from doing things better than others or succeeding with little effort. They emphasise interpersonal competition and public evaluation	derive satisfaction from personal success at difficult tasks
experience helplessness, as when difficulties are encountered they have no strategies to overcome them	apply problem solving techniques and self instructions when engaged in tasks

Teachers working to establish a growth theory of learning in their pupils will seldom use such things as competitions or quizzes because such teachers focus on the process of reaching the outcome rather than the outcome alone. For the same reason they will only rarely attribute a numerical mark or level to pupils' work. They will ask pupils to consider how well they have applied learning strategies and approaches, such as problem solving strategies or approaches such as, 'think for one minute, ask a friend, ask another friend and only then ask the teacher'. Teachers will show clearly that they value the effort that was put into solving a problem rather than a simple right answer. Consequently they will concentrate lessons on those processes. They may ask pupils to make a mind map of all the ideas that they think may be relevant to solving a problem before going on to try and solve it. Another way would be to ask pupils to write out the solution to a problem that they have worked on in pairs and display their working. The whole class would look to see how many different ways there were of approaching the problem, which seemed most understandable to them, which the most efficient and so on. One teacher I know emphasises her interest in and the value she places on the pupils' process of learning mathematics by asking them to fill in a journal at intervals. She asks them to reflect on what they found straightforward and easy to learn, what they found hard to learn and what helped them to overcome their difficulties. She then reads these journals so that she knows what difficulties they found and can help them more in future lessons.

Working to establish the growth theory of learning in a classroom builds self esteem in pupils:

> Self-esteem ... is a positive way of experiencing yourself when you are fully engaged and are using your abilities to the utmost in pursuit of something you value. It is not something we give people by telling them about their high intelligence. It is something we equip them to get for themselves – by teaching them to value learning ... to relish challenge and effort and to use errors as routes to mastery. (Dweck, 2000 p. 4)

When we ask pupils to explore mathematics, make mistakes and think about ways to overcome them, express their mathematical ideas and support one another in learning, we are building their self-esteem. The pupils use their abilities in something that is valued and that makes them feel good. They do not get the fleeting feel-good factor of achieving a higher mark than other people but the sustained good feeling of knowing that they can learn and that they can succeed.

> Self esteem is an appreciation of your own worth and importance and having the character to be accountable for yourself and responsible for others. (White, 1994)

As pupils help one another and take responsibility for each others' learning, they also build their confidence in being a valuable member of their community which is a further boost to their self esteem. They build their emotional resources to be able to overcome difficulties, to persist and try other ideas when problems seem hard to solve. Pupils do not feel demeaned by admitting to problems as they see that they will be able to help others at another time.

They recruit others to work together as they understand that the more views they have on a problem the more likely they all are to find a way through any difficulties. All these are good working practices for beyond school. Pupils who think in the 'growth' mindset do well beyond school (for example at university or in employment) as when they encounter challenges they know what to do. Pupils with a 'fixed' mindset can drop out, as they consider the first difficulty that they encounter to indicate that they cannot cope with these challenges.

Activating pupils as owners of their own learning, means allowing them to develop the emotional resources to be able to take that ownership. It means that throughout the department pupils must know for certain that mistakes are part and parcel of learning as effectively as possible. Mistakes are paid attention to, explored in order to ensure that everyone feels secure in their understanding of mathematical concepts and processes. Mistakes can be considered in this way because the department is developing a growth mindset where it is learning that is valued and not performance alone.

Conclusion

So there is a great deal to think about when embedding Assessment for Learning in the classroom. The notions of objective led lessons, questioning, effective feedback and peer and self-assessment are part of Assessment for Learning but they are not the heart of it. If you want to think about introducing these ideas there are books and publications that will support your thinking (Black et al, 2003, Clarke 2005, Lee, 2006, DfES 2004 and many more).

At the heart of an Assessment for Learning classroom is a focus on learning and on supporting that learning effectively. This means that teachers systematically find out where the pupils are in their learning and enable the pupils themselves to know how well they are learning. Teachers also provide feedback that moves the pupil's learning forward. They may provide such feedback themselves or set up systems, possibly peer-assessment systems, that allow the pupils to establish for themselves where they are and crucially how to continue to learn more. Teachers will also ensure that pupils understand where they are meant to be going and what success looks like. This may well be about setting clear learning objectives but will also be about making sure that the pupils really know what it means to explore mathematical ideas, use mathematical processes and think mathematically.

Teachers will also encourage pupils to be learning resources for one another as that will make the classroom an effective and efficient learning environment. They will use peer-assessment but also learn collaboratively and act as teachers for one another when appropriate. Most importantly teachers will make sure that pupils take ownership of and responsibility for their own learning. This will mean using self-assessment but, perhaps more importantly, developing the pupils' emotional resources to manage their own learning. This will require times when the pupils think about and reflect on their own learning and take part in the evaluation of that learning. Pupils will need to learn to develop a growth theory of learning so that they see mistakes as part of the process and not as an indication that they have reached the limits of their ability and develop resilience and persistence in overcoming difficulties.

Assessment for Learning can be the catalyst for important changes in a mathematics department as there are some ways of working that are common in mathematics departments that work against embedding Assessment for Learning. Assessment for Learning requires a classroom where there is a great deal of discourse, where pupils talk about their mathematical learning and make their mathematical ideas public so that they can be explored and analysed by teacher and other pupils alike. In an Assessment for Learning classroom, ideas must be explored and pupils will work together to ensure everyone understands and learns successfully. As a consequence there is less repetition, so it is unlikely that the teacher will use a cyclical scheme of work. The level of challenge is high as the teacher knows the level of challenge that the pupils can cope with and that support will be there so that everyone can successfully meet the challenge. The pupils know what success looks like and how to work towards being successful, they know what it means to think, explore and communicate mathematically.

There are risks in moving away from traditional ways and reconstituting a mathematics department in this way. Teachers will feel that they do not know what is expected of them and pupils will want to return to the old ways where they knew where they were and they did not have to do so much thinking. Because of these considerations it is hard to use Assessment for Learning effectively, hard but not impossible. The rewards are great. Teachers know they are doing the very best they can for their pupils and pupils that are involved in the process and taking responsibility for their learning know they are successful pupils - and just as a by-product the pupils seem to do really well at examinations as well.

Further reading

Alexander, R. (2006) *Towards Dialogic Teaching*. Cambridge: Dialogos UK.

Black, P. Harrison. C. Lee, C. Marshall, B. & Wiliam, D. (2003) *Assessment for Learning – putting it into practice*. Buckingham: Open University Press.

Boaler, J. (2009) *The Elephant in the Classroom: Helping Children Survive, Achieve and Enjoy School Maths*. London: Souvenir Press.

Dweck, C. (2006) *Mindset: The New Psychology of Success*. New York: Random House.

Mason, J. Burton, L. & Stacey, K. (1985) *Thinking Mathematically*. London: Addison Wesley.

Mason, J. and Johnston-Wilder, S. (2006) *Designing and Using Mathematical Tasks*. St Albans: QED Press.

Mercer, N. and Littleton, K. (2007) *Dialogue and the Development of Children's Thinking*. London: Routledge.

Watson, A. and Mason, J. (1998) *Questions and Prompts for Mathematical Thinking*. Derby: Association of Teachers of Mathematics.

Wenger, E. (1999) *Communities of Practice, learning, meaning and identity*. Cambridge: Cambridge University Press.

References

Boaler, J. (1997). *Experiencing School Mathematics: Teaching Styles, sex and setting.* Buckingham: Open University Press.

Clarke, S. (2003) *Enriching Feedback.* London: Hodder & Stoughton.

Clarke, S. (2005) *Formative Assessment in the Secondary Classroom.* London: Hodder Murray.

DfES (2004) *Assessment for Learning Whole School Training Materials.* www.standards.dfes.gov.uk/secondary/keystage3/all/respub/afl_ws accessed 22nd August 2009.

Durkin, K., and Shire, B. (1991) *Language in Mathematical Education Research and Practice.* Buckingham: Open University Press.

Dweck, C. (2000) *Self-theories: Their Role in Motivation, Personality, and Development.* Hove, E Sussex: Psychology Press.

Lee, C. (2006) *Language for Learning Mathematics – Assessment for Learning in Practice,* Buckingham: Open University Press.

Ofsted. (2008) *Mathematics: Understanding the score.* London: HMSO. Available at: *www.ofsted.gov.uk/content/download/7137/73098/file/Mathematics%20-%20understanding%20the%20score.pdf*

Pimm, D. (1995) *Symbols and Meanings in School Mathematics.* London: Routledge.

Vygotsky, L. S. (1981) The Genesis of Higher Mental Functions. In *The Concept of Activity in Soviet Psychology,* edited by Wertsch. M.,Armonk, N.Y: Sharpe,

White, M. (1994) *Self Esteem, Its Meaning and Value in School.* Cambridge: Daniels Publishing.

10
ORGANISING THE TEACHING OF MATHEMATICS FOR CHILDREN AND YOUNG PEOPLE WHO HAVE ADDITIONAL TO TYPICAL NEEDS

Melissa Rodd

In this chapter, children and young people are understood to have 'additional to typical needs' when they have developmental, emotional or social challenges, disabilities or Special Educational Needs (SEN).

This chapter is aimed at subject leaders of mathematics, but could also be useful for mentors, teachers in training, experienced teachers and mathematics advisors/consultants who have some responsibility for organising the mathematics learning of pupils with additional to typical needs.

Though, overall, children and young people who have additional to typical needs achieve a very wide range of attainment in mathematics, the majority of them do not achieve age-related expected levels. Indeed, for many, of these pupils, 'age-related expectation' is an inappropriate measure. The central theme to the chapter is addressed to teachers' thinking about the mathematics learning of such pupils. The central aim of the chapter is to support a leading teacher in guiding, encouraging and supporting the mathematics teaching team in their teaching of pupils with additional to typical needs.

In order to support thinking and discussion the chapter is divided into two main sections: *Disability and Difference* and *Beliefs and Practices*. Resources are given in the final section in the form of web-links.

Disability and difference
How is it helpful to think about children and young people with, in the phrase used here, 'additional to typical needs'? Indeed, why this cumbersome phrase has been used, instead of 'special needs', is to prompt reflection concerning who is, or might be, a pupil for whom some different provision would be helpful. Central to this chapter is the intention to encourage subject leaders who have responsibility for leading a department of teachers to *develop ways of thinking* about the sort of pupils' needs that are additional to typical in such a manner that the educational opportunities of these and other pupils are enhanced.

Historical snapshots
A short review of the history of how pupils with 'special needs' have been viewed in the English education system will help practitioners to see where current attitudes and provision have come from by presenting some historical

snapshots of educating pupils with 'special needs' in England.

Going back to before the Second World War, few young people anywhere in the UK had opportunities to be educated beyond the age of 14; a minority of young people were educated in grammar schools or public schools, which educated some pupils up to 18, but did not cater for pupils with 'special needs'. Schooling for the majority was a basic education, not dissimilar to primary education today. Children with sense, severe motor or mental impairment were often institutionalised; these pupils were clearly classified as different: they started off with a difference and this difference could be said to be exaggerated by separation and specialised attention, which is not to say that the care and education they received was not considered in these children's best interests nor that the care was not delivered with compassion.

In 1944, R. A. Butler's Education Act fundamentally changed the structure of education by organising schooling into primary and secondary sectors and entitling every child to secondary education. Children in the school year they turned eleven took an exam that was to determine their educational path: academic grammar school (for about 20%) or practical/technical secondary school often called 'Secondary Modern'. The position of the children with sense, severe motor or mental impairment was unchanged: some went to specialist institutions otherwise there was minimal acknowledgement of need. Comprehensive education was introduced throughout most of England by the early 1970s because having academic and vocational pathways at separate schools, and sorting children for an academic or vocational education respectively, was considered too absolute a decision to make at eleven years old. Today, despite the advent of many 'specialist schools', most children and young people are educated in a 'comprehensive' environment where the pupil population is intended to have a significant variation on such normally distributed measures as IQ and to have a range of social backgrounds.

Some of the ways in which people think today about education, and by implication about pupils with additional to typical needs, can be traced back to 1960s' demands for equality, respect for difference and for 'social justice' in the wave of the Civil Rights Movement and other liberation struggles. Some of these demands resulted in legislation like the 1975 Race Relations Act and the 1976 Sex Discrimination Act that forced society to act differently when it came to race and gender. The Disability Discrimination Act was passed in 1995. Ways of thinking, in our case thinking about education of children with additional to typical needs, are influenced by society's structures (for example, laws) and the introduction of language that supports thinking in certain ways and the social activities that reinforce that language. For example consider the word 'entitlement', where does the word come from and how does the notion of 'entitlement' influence what you do? Up until the 1970s the dominant way of thinking about children with disabilities was that these children were special cases, not like ordinary children and other arrangements had to be made for them.

And then came the Warnock Report.

The Warnock Report

The key assertion that has had a profound effect on the notion of 'special needs' is the Warnock report's finding that one in five children had a special need at some time during their schooling. That is 20% of the population! These days teachers are so used to tracking special or additional needs that it is difficult to enter the mind-set that conceptualised 'special needs' as in some sense alien rather than just a variation of difference as it tends to be viewed today, but that was what it was like. The Warnock Report was a bombshell – if 20% of the population had some 'special need' and only 5% of the population were in designated Special Schools then the mainstream schools contained children with needs, hitherto unrecognised. This Report was central in changing the way people think about additional to typical needs. The notions of inclusion and the practice of making arrangements for children with additional needs to participate in mainstream education are consequences of the Warnock Report.

These historical snapshots are intended to provoke reflection on how teachers think about the education of children and young people who are, with respect to some parameter, on a tail of a normal distribution. The position, prevalent up to the mid-twentieth century, that such young people were a distinct category and required 'different' treatment has changed dramatically since the Warnock report to that of recognising that needs are on various continua and may come and go, in terms of urgency or severity, over periods of time (webref under 'Warnock Report' in references).

I now turn to the designation of needs: who has additional to typical needs and issues concerning acquiring a designation of additional to typical needs.

Diagnoses and needs

> The term 'special educational needs' (SEN) has a legal definition, referring to children who have learning difficulties or disabilities that make it harder for them to learn or access education than most children of the same age. (*dcsf.gov.uk*)

A pupil who has a certified diagnosis of a condition, a consequence of which is that they have additional to typical needs, is likely to be given more resources than a comparable child without a diagnosis. The resources on offer may be anything from an assistant in the classroom, to being supplied with some enabling technology, or being allowed extra time in an exam. Some schools or departments may see this resource-enablement as a positive incentive for a pupil to get a diagnosis.

Conditions giving rise to needs

Additional to typical needs arise from disability, SEN or extraordinary circumstances for an individual. In the short subsections below, some ways of thinking about specific conditions are offered. It is important to recognise that these needs are experienced differently by each child or young person. Furthermore, each teacher has their own personal responses arising from their experiences that may not be known to the subject leader. For example, the teacher may have a disabled relative or might have had a childhood trauma, and this will influence the relationships that teacher has with pupils. It is a life-long process for a teacher to develop personal qualities like compassion, emotional responses like lack of embarrassment, together with culturally sensitive behaviours like appropriate eye and body contact. Motivation for a teacher to want to develop such personal qualities is supported by good leadership in the mathematics department. The subject leader who can engender a common sense of purpose within an atmosphere of mutual support, respect and shared values is likely to be able to support other teachers to lower their personal defences so that they can be more responsive to these pupils with additional to typical needs.

Specific learning difficulties: dyslexia, dyspraxia and dyscalculia
Teachers trained in the UK will be familiar with 'dyslexia', 'dyspraxia' and 'dyscalculia'. These are SEN (and are not classified as disabilities) that are related to words, motor regulation and numbers respectively. The 'dys' prefix means abnormal, difficult or impaired and each of these conditions may be mild to severe. Pupils with these conditions diagnosed will be receiving some support on account of their designated SEN. Whether or not there is a diagnosis, these pupils are at risk of being frustrated and 'turned off' from learning mathematics.

Dyslexia: Although there are many different 'definitions' of dyslexia, it is now generally recognised as a frequently-occurring condition that makes reading, writing and spelling difficult. Because pupils with this condition have difficulties in symbolic processing, and short-term memory, dyslexia tends to affect a pupil's mathematical learning. A lot of pupils have challenges with reading and word processing generally that places them on the dyslexic continuum. In Further Education Level 2 post-compulsory courses in areas like art and design, for example, college tutors have reported to me that typically over half a cohort's students have dyslexic profiles. This suggests that many school pupils will have undiagnosed dyslexia. Dyslexia training programmes routinely explain that it is helpful to the learning process if information is presented visually and schematically with intelligent use of colours to code ideas and represent categories. Such pedagogical approaches are essential in helping someone with dyslexia organise and structure their short term memory, and it is also a good approach to take for the majority of pupils that include those with dyslexia undiagnosed.

Dyspraxia: This condition is due to the immaturity or the impairment of the brain's capacity to organise bodily movement. Poor motor coordination due to dyspraxia often – but by no means always - goes together with dyslexia and other developmental conditions; for example, 'attention deficit' (ADD) or autistic spectrum. Again, there may not be a diagnosis of dyspraxia and the pupil may not be aware that his/her frustration arising from performing badly on motor-coordination tasks is due to such a condition. When pupils find motor-coordination difficult, it is important that the teacher tries to find another motor-coordination task that is possible – for example by using larger, easier to manipulate equipment or by physically guiding the pupil – thus helping the coordination to improve. Motor-coordination is part of self-regulation which in turn is part of the ability to focus attention.

Without focused attention, deliberate, self-constructing, learning cannot be achieved. Pupils delayed in motor-organisation capacities due to dyspraxia, but not otherwise delayed developmentally, are likely to experience, probably subconscious, emotional conflict concerning what they are aiming for and what they achieve, so consistent and realistic encouragement is particularly important.

Dyscalculia: This label is used less consistently than 'dyslexia' or 'dyspraxia'. For some dyscalculia is a rare condition caused by brain damage, resulting in the person having no sense of number. For other people, 'dyscalculia' is to do with low attainment in mathematics, relative to standardised levels of achievement. There are tests for dyscalculia available commercially, though the results of these tests do not diagnose 'the dyscalculic condition'. For pupils who have been designated as having non-brain damaged dyscalculia, it is helpful to provide personalised, catch-up teaching and to treat their mathematical development as delayed, rather than permanently impaired.

Autistic spectra

Autism is an impairment of social-connectedness. People who are diagnosed as having Autistic Spectrum Conditions have a different way of being within the social context. This difference in social instinct results in poor social-awareness, communication problems and anxiety. Not everyone sees autism as a disability but rather a psychological evolutionary pathway that can be favourable under certain conditions (Baron-Cohen,1997). 'The autistic spectrum' is a term that has been used for some years now to capture the sense of a range of conditions related to autism. At one end of this spectrum are severely disabled people, often referred to nowadays as having 'classic' or Kanner's' autism, who do not speak, have poor coordination and exhibit behaviours that are very different from those of people not on the autistic spectrum. Children and young people with this severe condition are unlikely to be educated in mainstream schools. On the other end of 'the autistic spectrum' are people having what is often referred to as Asperger's syndrome or 'high functioning autism', who are intellectually able while still having social communication impairments; children and young people on this end of the spectrum will generally be in mainstream schools.

This section has been named 'autistic spectra' in order to highlight the multidimensionality of conditions related to autism, for referring to 'the autistic spectrum' (which is the term in common parlance and which will be used below) might *mistakenly* lead teachers to think 'if Kanner-autism is severe, then Asperger's syndrome is mild'; but this is not the case. Distinguishing a spectrum related to intellectual functioning from a spectrum related to interpersonal functioning is helpful in understanding this condition: pupils with Asperger's syndrome may have some exceptional intellectual talents, but they may have severe inability to understand another's point of view. Some less intellectually successful pupils who are assessed as on the autistic spectrum, may be able to form strong emotional bonds with teachers or teaching assistants with whom they can predict and communicate feelings though their cognitive skills are weak.

Though the self-orientation characteristic of autism leads to behaviours that can be 'difficult', in many cases, self-orientation leads to behaviours that are obsessional, detail-focussed and repetitive. These behaviours can develop learning, often in areas like music or mathematics, to such an extent that the person with autism is seen as 'gifted' with exceptional talent. Although such a pupil's capacity to imagine other peoples' feelings is impaired, which is sometimes expressed as 'people with autism don't mind-read', the 'mind-reading' capacity can be developed. Mathematics is a particularly good area of the curriculum for this; the predictability of number in, for example, think-of-a-number tasks, can be used as a non-threatening vehicle to show the pupil that s/he can work out what is in the teacher's head!

Attention deficit hyperactivity disorder
The cluster of behavioural disorders known as ADHD (or ADD, if there is no hyperactivity) is medically diagnosed (see nhs.uk/conditions) and is the most common behavioural disorder of school pupils in the UK (up to 9%). Teachers have the problem that the criteria for having AD(H)D include: having a very short attention span, being very easily distracted and being unable to stick at tasks that are tedious or time consuming, being unable to respond to instructions and being unable to concentrate. Yet this sort of inattentiveness is found in many classrooms as are hyperactive behaviours like being unable to sit still, constantly fidgeting, being unable to settle to tasks, and exhibiting excessive physical movement. Teachers will also be used to pupils being impulsive and not waiting for their turn, breaking rules and acting without thinking. From a medical point of view, ADHD is a condition children often grow out of. From a teacher's point of view, something has to be done immediately to help the individual learn, as well as not jeopardising the education of the other pupils in the class. Of course, some pupils that cannot take in a teacher's instruction or do not wait their turn may have autism and those that exhibit excessive movement may have dyspraxia. In other words, there is not a one-size-fits-all advice for teaching ADHD pupils. Mathematics can be a helpful discipline for these pupils, if they are given mathematics work that is non-threatening and helps develops mental and social structures.

Conditions needing on-going medical attention
Medical conditions such as cerebral palsy, MS, ME, epilepsy, diabetes as well as sensory impairments and Down's syndrome will need a teacher's sympathy and some specific training (which is outside the scope of this chapter). Specialist advice is needed to deal with on-going issues like access to supportive technology and, particularly for epilepsy, emergency action. Mathematics can be a helpful way in to learning and achievement because helping these pupils to understand structures as part of mathematics may help them embody structure more generally. For example, a pupil with cerebral palsy may not be able to coordinate making a three dimensional model, but suitable technology is available for the pupil to have a virtual three dimensional experience within the context of the mathematics curriculum.

Low overall prior attainment
Children and young people who are positioned as having 'low prior attainment' are of many different backgrounds. This brief section considers pupils who

have no other obvious condition but whose attainment is low relative to other pupils in the cohort. The stimulus for organising the learning of these pupils is to offer some questions a subject leader might use to orientate teachers in the mathematics team to think specifically about these pupils whose attainment is low, but who have the capacity to increase their achievement.

1. Have they been given the opportunity of one-to-one tutoring? Ann Dowker's research showed that targeted support on specific difficulties was effective. (*www.dcsf.gov.uk/research/data/uploadfiles/RB554.pdf*)

2. Are they a member of a group all of whom have low attainment? Can this group be reconstituted, so that these pupils habituated into low attaining modes can experience other role models?

3. Are they being offered 'junk mathematics' or 'real mathematics'? Azfal Ahmed's work with low attainers found that they were not being given rich tasks to work on (Ahmed 1987).

4. If they say they don't care about their low attainment, or they say they are confident (without being competent), can you intuit their 'state of mind' (see discussion of performance versus mastery below) and understand why they are saying this?

5. Can you help them make an effort (see discussion of effort below)?

With groups of pupils who have got into the habit of underachieving, relationships with individual pupils are of central importance. If teachers who have the responsibility of organising timetables for staff recognise this, then these groups should be assigned the most reliable teachers who are enthusiastic about mathematics and interested in their needs.

Disability and SEN

Not all disabled pupils have SEN and not all pupils with SEN are disabled! The respective legal definitions are given as:

> A disabled person is someone who has: a physical or mental impairment which has a substantial and long-term adverse effect on his or her ability to carry out normal day-to-day activities.
>
> Disability Discrimination Act 1995

> A child has special educational needs if he or she has a learning difficulty which calls for special educational provision to be made for him or her. Special educational provision is provision that is additional to or otherwise different from that normally available in the area to children of the same age.
>
> Education Act 1996

A example of a pupil who is disabled, but does not have SEN, is someone with a medical condition that is considered from the medical point of view as a disability but does not affect the pupil's learning in the school environment. A pupil with dyslexia, and no other condition, exemplifies SEN without disability. In 2005 a Cabinet Office report estimated that 24% of the adult UK population was disabled and 7% of the child population. The current estimate for pupils with SEN in England in 2008 is 18%.

I have discussed specific (e.g. dyslexia) and overarching labels (disability and SEN) to which teachers need to adapt their teaching. All of the specific conditions mentioned have advocate groups that post advice for teachers, as well as families, friends and carers, on internet sites that are easy to access from an internet search on the name of the condition. What is also important for teachers to have in mind is that many pupils with additional to typical needs will not have a helpful label, specifying a condition that elicits sympathy and resources. Teachers will probably be familiar with the situation where some pupils have parents who demand special help for their child and other pupils do not have such personal advocates. Indeed, some pupils might not even have their additional to typical needs noticed until their mathematics teacher notices their barriers to learning. Such barriers include, for example, discrepancies (he says answers, but does not write them), resistances (she searches for a nice colour pen, rather than writing with an available one) and avoidance (he disputes the importance of mathematics, rather than engaging with it). Part of developing as a teacher is to develop beliefs about how pupils learn and when behaviours as exemplified above are noted, a teacher may start to articulate what conditions s/he believes are essential, desirable and ideal for learning. Such a process is enhanced by a subject leader interested in the ways his/her team think about learning.

Beliefs and Practices

In this section, I take three issues that are central to a mathematics subject leader who is responsible for a team of mathematics teachers:

- How do the teachers in the team think pupils learn? Will pupils with additional to typical needs be served well under these belief systems?

- How do teachers think they can motivate and engage pupils? In particular, what do the teachers believe pupils with additional to typical needs are able to sustain?

- How can my classroom observations of teachers in the team be used to develop teachers' practices that are sensitive to unusual or unpredictable ways of thinking and being, such as those of pupils with additional to typical needs?

These three bullet points each cover a vast range of material. I have chosen one issue to focus on in each so that a subject leader has a practical entry to thinking about them. These issues are respectively:

- Concerning beliefs about learning:

    - Performance vs. mastery

- Concerning pupil motivation:

    - What is 'effort'?

- Concerning observing colleagues classrooms:

    - Capturing 'what', distinguishing 'why' and considering 'states of mind'.

Thinking about pupil learning

Some beliefs about learning are articulatable. The following express different, distinguishable beliefs:

'Pupils learn when they feel safe and are loved'; 'pupils learn when they follow their own interests' – these are beliefs about conditions for learning.

'Pupils learn when they construct their own knowledge'; 'pupils learn when they have a clear explanation' – these are beliefs about the nature of learning.

What beliefs about learning do teachers in the mathematics teaching team talk about? It is worthwhile discussing differences (rather than allow the tendency to merge different beliefs). The examples presented above, could be a starting point for teachers to recognise how beliefs differ, the aim being to understand distinctions and how beliefs are applied in practice. It may be team-building to ask teachers to explain their point of view and to listen and come to understand other teachers' alternative views. There is no grand learning theory that is 'correct', but different theories that help people to think in different ways.

In this section, a way of thinking about what learning is, that was developed by Carol Dweck and presented in Chapter 9 is considered for the context of additional needs. This theoretical take on the nature of learning is helpful for those charged with leading the education of pupils with additional needs as it helps focus on the difference between 'what there is evidence for' and 'what yet may emerge' and foregrounds attitude to learning rather than purely cognitive factors.

Performance versus mastery

Everyone has to perform sometimes: making an important phone call, putting on a 'brave face' in difficult circumstances, having to speak to a group, or producing written work in an exam. With assessment of mathematical attainment resting so frequently with exam performance, despite the scrapping of KS3 SATs (in the Autumn of 2008), the notion of performance is very relevant to pupils' experience. Do pupils gauge their alignment to mathematics in terms of how they perform in tests? As one young person said to me "I'll see if maths is for me when the results come out".

Not everyone is so guided by the external light of others' assessment of their performance. Another young person remarked to me that it was more important for him to understand than to get a top mark; he was orientated to towards getting to grips with understanding new branches of knowledge rather than being concerned with how his performance appeared to others. Carol Dweck, a psychologist interested in how people adapt and learn, coins the term 'mastery orientation' for these getting-to-grips people and 'performance orientation' for those "how did I do?" people who identify with others' assessment of their performance. This section uses as reference and recommended reading, her book "Self Theories: their role in personality, motivation and development" (Dweck 2000).

There are inevitable value judgements that people associate with these orientations. As teachers, many of us would say that we would like the pupils to have a mastery orientation until it came to high stakes public exams and then we'd be happy with a (short term) performance goal. The 2008 mathematics Ofsted report confirms that the extent of test orientation is a problem in schools in England (ofsted.gov.uk). Dweck's (2000) research shows that it is not generally possible to switch easily from one learning orientation to the other, as these learning orientations are linked with beliefs about the nature of intelligence, which has built up over some time. People with performance orientations generally view intelligence as 'an entity' that can be found by testing, whereas those with mastery orientations consider intelligence 'adaptive and malleable' and that it develops with use. It makes sense to develop mastery orientations to learning, for all pupils, but how can this be done?

In order to address how to promote a mastery orientation to learning, I am using ideas adapted from Carol Dweck's work (Dweck, 2000). Dweck presents four commonly held beliefs (below). Please respond to these statements yourself before reading on. Make a brief note of which you consider true and why; also consider how other members of your department would respond?

1. "Students with high ability are more likely to display mastery-oriented qualities."

2. "Success in school directly fosters mastery-oriented qualities."

3. "Praise, particularly praising a student's intelligence, encourages mastery-oriented qualities."

4. "Students' confidence in their intelligence is the key to mastery-oriented qualities."

None of these are true! To précis Dweck's explanation: High ability students are most worried about failure and question their abilities when they hit obstacles (1) success in school does not boost students' desire for challenge, it makes them vulnerable to failure (2) praising students for their cleverness does not give them confidence in themselves but can lead them to fear failure and to not cope well with setbacks (3) many confident people do not want their intelligence tested and they are shaken when confronted with difficulties (4).

Here are some pointers that teachers can use to help students develop mastery orientations for learning, whatever their attainment profile by:

- acknowledging, as well as demonstrating, that everyone gets stuck and praising a student's perseverance when stuck;

- recognising that self-esteem can only come from within as a result of achievement, judging carefully which tasks are difficult but not impossible for a student so that the student can struggle and achieve;

- promoting tasks that *cannot* be completed quickly (these can include small-group games, projects, as well as more traditional mathematical investigations). [Mathematical investigations often give opportunity for pupils to work through many cases/examples that are short, generated by the pupil and do not produce anxiety]. In these ways, the pattern of engagement, immersion and reflection can be experienced without fear of failure or over-eagerness of completion-reward.

It is all very well to say that teachers want pupils with additional needs to develop a mastery orientation to learning, and the tips listed above might help, but shifting the responsibility for learning from teacher to pupil is no easy thing. To delve into what might be needed for pupils to shift to a more mastery-orientation, I discuss next what is involved in a person making an effort and how a pupil might be channelled by a teacher to make an effort in some way that would help them to learn mathematics.

If teachers want to enable pupils with additional to typical needs to develop mastery orientations to learning, what needs to be developed? No matter how enthusiastic the teacher, how well thought-out the task or how well-set up the discussion the putative learner's mind must be receptive to changes that constitute learning. The next section looks at types of effort as part of the developing receptivity of mind. 'Effort' is a term that refers explicitly to conscious action, rather than unconscious response, and is used in a more or less colloquial sense. The word 'attention' is much more complicated as it can refer to both conscious and unconscious attention of different processing pathways and has a technical and colloquial usage. (The colloquial usage of 'attention' is closely related to 'effort' and the technical usage is outside the scope of this chapter).

Thinking about motivation and engagement
Teachers are familiar with needing to motivate their students and contemporary discourse (e.g., the DCSF website referenced) refers to teacher enthusiasm, relevant tasks and opportunities for the learners to make meaning through discussion. Teacher attitude, well-designed tasks and carefully-planned talking-points are aspects of planning for learning that come from or are initiated by teachers; in this section, I want to consider how teachers can develop pupils' mental orientation and initiative so that they, the putative learners, are able to make an effort to learn the intellectually challenging discipline of mathematics.

What is effort?
I would like to distinguish two kinds of effort for the purposes of this chapter: straining and training. Starting with 'straining effort', consider these situations: lifting up a particularly heavy weight, getting past an unexpectedly unpleasant smell, making yourself swallow something that tastes disgusting. These scenarios illustrate situations in which the individual is straining to make an effort because, for example, the need to put a suitcase on a luggage rack, the desire to make oneself more comfortable out of the range of the smell, or the pressure to be polite in a social situation.

These are examples of a person's effortful responses to situations that do not happen very often. The situations may be endurable but they are not what the person does day-in-day-out. In making an effort in these situations the person is straining to do a one-off act and this straining may well restrict the breath and be tiring. However, not all effortful behaviours are like these straining efforts, another class of effortful behaviours, can be characterised roughly as: efforts to stay on track, or training. Consider this image of keeping on track: the toy made of a curvy vertical wire with a ring, loosely linked around the wire, that is to be moved from beginning to end without touching the wire. Trying to move the ring round the curvy wire takes concentration; it is an effort. It might cause great strain to someone with Parkinson's disease or with motor coordination disabilities, but the ring can be enlarged so that anxiety can be reduced. Keeping the ring on track is a self-actuated activity, a choice of task requiring some effort.

This sort of effort is akin to that of a dancer practising their dance, a musician concentrating on their piece, or a mathematician occupied by their problem. The person still exerts 'effort' if it is an activity they want to do. Take the dancer for example: the muscles must be primed and active, the gaze needs to be focussed and the sequence of steps internalised through many repetitions and in the forefront of movement memory. How could these intentional activities not be effortful? Such effortful behaviour is training: the behaviours are done frequently, are criticised (by self and/or coach) and are part of the life of the person.

Straining and training in the mathematics classroom
In the mathematics learning situation, in particular at school where there is no choice, teachers and pupils can discern effortful behaviour of these two types: straining and training. There may be other types of effort that you can characterise too. What education professionals can ask is: what sort of effort should reasonably be expected from pupils (a) everyday, (b) occasionally (planned and unplanned), (c) for rare 'performance' occasions such as exams? We could also ask what sort of effort could reasonably be expected from teachers in our team every day, occasionally, and for a one-off event. [Aside: as a student teacher I was told to plan a splendid lesson for every class once a week (i.e. one out of three lessons) as a custom-splendid lesson every time was not considered sustainable.]

What could teachers do to facilitate children and young people with additional to typical needs to develop the capacity to make a sustained, but not strained, effort in most lessons for most of the lesson? In my experience, many such pupils are in the habit of not-focussing on one thing for more than a few minutes. They do not expect to make a training effort to keep on track and their teachers do not expect them to keep on track. Clearly 'encouragement' is needed, but what should encouragement consist of? Consider the consequences of 'encouraging' a pupil by rewarding him/her for making an effort: such action will tend to reinforce a performance-orientation to learning. Threats, punishment or temptation of prizes are tactics that evoke a performance orientation and straining efforts. Straining is associated with vulnerability and anxiety which, particularly for pupils with poor self-regulation, can often lead to difficult-to-deal-with behaviours.

However, it can be possible to change pupils' unfocussed minds and start to establish pupils' 'training' effort. One idea is to do with helping the pupil to establish relationships – for some pupils the relationships with the teacher will be the most important. For some other pupils, establishing a relationship with a place – his special seat, for example – or a tool – like her own laptop - may be a way to support a child or young person, especially those pupils with needs associated with ADHD or autistic spectrum, to find a way to self regulate around the doing of mathematical tasks. Even for pupils who are centred by having their own seat or laptop, the relationship with the teacher is always going to be important; for example, a teacher of a pupil on the autistic spectrum will be able gauge through his/her relationship with the young person how much eye contact s/he can tolerate and under what circumstances.

In some sense, the more that the relationship is important for the pupil and the teacher, the greater the effort, in the sense of strain, that can be evoked by that teacher. This is unlike a client learning an IT skill, say, from a practitioner with whom there is no strong personal feeling; we would not expect a great straining effort to take place in that situation. The strain-ful effort puts the student in a vulnerable situation with respect to the power of the teacher. This vulnerability is experienced in different ways, for example, in failure when the child feels that s/he has tried hard but not done well enough. A child can strain sometimes, that's okay. And relationships with profound emotions position us to strain, like that of being a pupil to a teacher that one respects. How do teachers of mathematics develop their relationships with their pupils so that they establish a willingness to try, to have a go, whether the teacher is alongside or not? This requires imagination of other minds, not only by the teacher but by the pupil too; for some SEN and disabilities this imaginative capacity is impaired, so progress is likely to be slow.

When children and young people have additional to typical needs, issues of entitlement and of personalisation become more visible. Using Dweck's theory, I hope you can see how the principles of developing a mastery orientation to learning and a belief that intelligence develops with use (rather than is a 'given entity') is particularly useful approach to those with additional to typical needs who may be well below standard achievement levels. Nevertheless, trying to develop another person's sustainable effort is easier said than done, especially when teachers are dealing with certain SEN and disability conditions! Indeed, should teachers reflect on whether it is possible to require this sort effort of another person?

One part of a subject leader's job is to appraise members of the mathematics teaching team. Appraisal invariably includes observation of teaching. This next section, *Observing in the Context of Additional to Typical Needs*, aims to help observers, like subject leaders in their appraisal capacity, to recognise and to respond to complexities in the teaching-learning process associated with additional to typical needs. The help, offered to such observers, is in the form of outlines of two 'ways of thinking' about the people being observed (this inevitably includes pupils as well as teachers given the classroom context). One way of thinking is concerned with minds and the other with bodies.

Thinking about observing colleagues teach pupils with additional to typical needs

This section is to help subject leaders prepare to observe their colleagues teaching classes that may include pupils with additional to typical needs. As any class may include pupils with additional needs, this section refers to observation generally but exemplifies issues with pupils with, for example, dyspraxia, autism, ADHD.

The key idea in this section is that humans observe bodies with their senses and they imagine minds with their minds; mathematics teachers observe pupils' writing, discussions and questioning and they imagine pupils have (mentally) understood/misunderstood the topic. While it would be too big a digression to ask the very general question "What is a mind?" or to consider the different natures of various human and non-human minds, it is worth noting at this stage that all cultures cultivate the minds of their populations. For example, members of communities acquire skills (e.g. navigation) and develop shared values (e.g. discovery is good) and these are both aspects of cultures' influence in developing minds.

Capturing 'what', distinguishing 'why' and considering 'states of mind'
Although there is a point of view that considers that the human mind is in some sense separable from that person's body - this view is epitomised in Descartes' famous aphorism "cogito ergo sum" ("I think therefore I am") – this is in distinction to the current scientific view that has built up over the past 150 years. From William James's work in the late 19th century to contemporary neuroscientists, the contemporary view of mind is that mind is embodied: what we do physically affects how we are able to think. This embodied view of mind is particularly pertinent in the context of working with pupils with additional to typical needs, for example:

- a pupil who is impaired in their fine motor co-ordination (e.g. with dyspraxia) and who does not represent visual detail in their drawings and sketches, may have difficulties attending to certain types of detail in mathematical contexts. For example, a pupil is not able to discriminate fine gradations on a measuring instrument (even though her eyesight is adequate). Without a physical capacity for suitable experience, the mind may not be able to represent a particular feature.

- a pupil on the autistic spectrum who is impaired in their ability to judge the social context of words' meanings may act 'inappropriately' even while trying to conform. For example, teacher says "go back to your seat", pupil then walks backwards to his seat arousing the mirth of the other pupils and being (in effect) disruptive. (What is going on in this pupil's mind? A hunch that someone familiar with autism might posit is that the words "go back" are already processed when he starts his backwards step and the need to process the whole phrase holistically is not appreciated).

- a pupil who exhibits the diagnostic criteria for ADHD (having a very short attention span, being very easily distracted and being unable to stick at tasks that are tedious or time consuming, being unable to respond to instructions and being unable to concentrate) might seem like a much younger child who, in order to defend him/herself, presents as omnipotent (e.g. talking too much) or fearful (e.g. moving around too much as if fleeing) or denying a problem (e.g. overconfidence in their mathematical work) (see the section on states of mind, below).

This last example, in which a pupil "seems like a much younger child", (after all, children 'normally' grow out of ADHD-like behaviours), the focus is not on the specific behaviours or their lack, but on the sort of behaviours that are being exhibited. Thinking about 'what are they like' in such a way, leads to the notion of 'states of mind' which will be addressed further below.

The two ways of thinking that enhance a teacher's observational capacity are:

First. Capturing 'what' and distinguishing 'why'.

Second. Considering the other person's 'state(s) of mind'.

These two 'ways' are not alternatives, nor are they metaphorical 'lenses' or frameworks. Together they constitute an approach to observation that is sensitive and provides good-quality evidence. The first way of thinking draws on techniques from social science research as well as advice from contemplative traditions. It is focussed on detail. A reference consonant with this way of thinking and orientated to the mathematics learning-teaching environment is John Mason's *The Discipline of Noticing* (Mason 2002). The second way of thinking comes from the field of psychoanalysis as part of a theory of development of the mind and personality. It is holistic. The work I have used, and recommend as a reference, is Margot Waddell's *Inside Lives: psychoanalysis and the growth of personality* (Waddell 2002).

Capturing 'what' and distinguishing 'why'
A central teaching in social science research methods is to record (as) accurately (as possible) events in the field of interest. This is why objective recording devices like video or audio-recorders, are routinely used to capture what it was that happened in terms of (what to a human observer are) sense-data like sounds and visual stimuli. Nevertheless, the recording does not speak for itself, people interpret the data recorded for the purposes in which they are interested; they give accounts, or stories, of why something happened.

In order to support teachers working with pupils with additional to typical needs, subject leaders will need to do some classroom observations to find out as directly as possible how individual teachers cope with these special pupils. And while a recording device, a dispassionate machine, can capture data, its presence may put the teacher being observed on the defensive. It is, therefore, preferable for the observer him/herself to capture what is happening through fieldnotes or memory, yet be accurate and thorough. In order to be able to do this, the observer has to take the stance of the dispassionate machine, though, naturally s/he is emotionally involved in the scene about to take place. It is not an easy task to record events dispassionately yet be emotionally engaged and it is difficult to give general advice.

Application to classroom observation:

Here are two classroom observation notes:

First. Jack was swinging his right leg back and forth. The direction of Jill's gaze was towards the window.

Second. Jack was fidgeting, Jill was distracted.

In the first case, what is recorded is close to a description of behaviour. In the second case, what is noted is an attribution and is an interpretation of the evidence. With children and young people with additional to typical needs, there are (by definition!) lots of behaviours that are not typical: a child with motor coordination problems or dyspraxia may not be 'messing about' with her protractor, but, because she is unable to control the positioning of the instrument, she is moving it about on the page of her book. A young person with autism or Asperger's syndrome may not be 'lost in his own world', but, because he is listening, has turned an ear towards the speaker rather than looking in the speaker's direction.

In adopting these ways of thinking there are paradoxical demands on the observer: to intuit the state of mind of another and to be able to sit outside attribution and to faithfully record what happened. The observing teacher needs the self-discipline to resist responding him/herself to classroom events (though, in extreme situations, the observer will need to act) and to be able to articulate what was the observed evidence for attribution of pupil or teacher state of mind. This is not a skill that can be learned abstractly and will be part of the team building if done with an attitude of receptivity and openness within collaborative partnership with the teacher.

Considering a person's 'State of Mind'

Psychoanalytic theory offers ways of understanding people's minds and personalities through naming and classifying how life is felt, or experienced, by individual people. In the tradition emanating from Melanie Klein, (1882-1960), a central way of understanding people is to recognise their 'state of mind'. In this psychoanalytic tradition, 'states of mind' are named in terms of age-related developmental categories: infancy, childhood, latency (from about six or seven years old to pre-pubescent), adolescence, then variations within adulthood, including parental and old aged. However, a cornerstone of psychoanalytic theory is that these age-related 'states of mind' are not be experienced chronologically: for example, people older than toddlers have temper tantrums, though it is *typical* of a child in early childhood to have an experience of rage in the face of a situation that is out of his/her control that is referred to as a 'temper tantrum'.

Other examples: (1) Ordering, collecting and classifying are activities typical of the 'latency' state of mind; it is appropriate for an eight year old to develop their systems and arrangements and acquire knowledge; this state of mind is found in adults pursuing interests in, for example, mathematics, music technology or family genealogy; (2) Infancy is a state of mind characterised by the struggle for survival and the dependency on others, where experience oscillates from extreme fear (of annihilation) to utter comfort (of protection).

Contrastingly, (3), an adult (parental) state of mind is one that can think for others, for example, by imagining the infant's hunger/discomfort or by recognising the structures being organised within the latency child's art or play.

Intuiting another person's state of mind is not the same as knowing what is in their mind. Witnessing a person's temper tantrum, may suggest to the observer that, at that point in time, the person was in a toddler 'state of mind', but this does not mean the observer has any knowledge of what provoked the temper or what the person maybe thinking about.

Application to classroom observation:

There are two related applications of consideration of states of mind to the job of observing colleagues teach:

1. The observer considers the state of mind of the teacher being observed
2. The observer considers the state of mind of various pupils and relates pupils' states of mind to that of the teacher.

Teachers (experienced or in training) can adopt various states of mind even within one lesson; here are illustrations of three states of mind an observing teacher might encounter:

- The teacher is fearful of annihilation (e.g. due to anxiety about lack of preparation or hostility of the class). He clasps his arms round his chest and spends many minutes at one desk talking (equals being comforted by) to a pupil who appears to be listening. This partially illustrates an infant state of mind.

- The teacher is thoroughly planned and has clear structure for the lesson and anticipates that learning will take place given the sequence of tasks she has organised; she is not comfortable with digressions or disruptions and if there are too many of these, she loses the thread of the plan. This partially illustrates a latency state of mind.

- The teacher anticipates what the pupils will do with the tasks he's set though he is pleased and intrigued by responses he had not predicted or seen before; he resists filling in weekly progress charts for his pupils as he does not believe learning is linear. This partially illustrates an adult state of mind.

Teachers have obvious parental functions, related to protection and nurture, particularly for the younger pupils or pupils with additional to typical needs due to SEN or disability. In practice, of course, how parental functions are realised is complicated and depends very much on context. However, a young teacher who does not have children, can experience the 'state of mind' of a more mature adult. In the context of the mathematics classroom, it is possible to think for others in the sense of having a parental function, for example, by anticipating pupils' responses but not get 'thrown' when the responses are unexpected.

A more complicated skill for an observer to develop is to consider both a pupil's state of mind as well as that of the teacher being observed and see how they fit together. For example, if a pupil is in an infant or toddler state, verbal directions and explanations from the teacher are not going to be digestible by the pupil (though the sound of the teacher's voice might be comforting or frightening); if the teacher is super-organised and structured, as in latency, the adolescent pupils might rebel.

The first experience many subject leaders will have had of observing other teachers will have been as a mentor (or school-based tutor) to teachers in training. Observations of colleagues will differ from observations of trainees in that the subject-leader's observations can relate to personal and school-based priorities rather than QTS requirements.

Conclusion

One of the queries a reader of this chapter might have is "how do I distinguish pupils with additional to typical needs from other pupils when I don't have notification of any 'special need'?" By developing an interest in conditions associated with additional needs, like those discussed in the 'disability and difference' section of this chapter, and working with these young people and specialist advisors as well as observing carefully, a holistic picture will emerge. Then you'll start to spot characteristics of those diagnosed in other pupils. Such observation may well prompt thinking about providing some different or additional provision for those pupils. Another possible query is "given the personalisation agenda, I don't think of any pupil as 'typical', why should I conceptualise a category of 'additional to typical'?" In this chapter, 'typical' is used to indicate those in the central region of a bell curve, assuming a near normal distribution of the condition. The word is not used in the sense of not respecting individuality.

There are bound to be other queries and questions. Working with diversity – and the notion of 'additional to typical' is an aspect of social diversity – is an important social challenge of the world we live in. A central message of this chapter is that there are various ways of thinking about other people, including pupils with various and challenging needs. The task of the subject leader is first to prepare him/herself and then to support the other mathematics teachers in their own preparation of themselves for their encounters with their diverse range of pupils and to approach their task skilfully with interest and compassion.

Further Reading

Web references:
The Warnock report

- *http://www.sen.ttrb.ac.uk/viewarticle2.aspx?contentId=13852* (accessed 30.01.09)

- *http://www.publications.parliament.uk/pa/cm200506/cmselect/cmeduski/478/47805.htm* (accessed 30.01.09)

NHS direct (ADHD)

- *http://www.nhs.uk/conditions/Attention-deficit-hyperactivity-disorder/Pages/Introduction.aspx?url=Pages/What-is-it.aspx* (accessed 22.05.09)

Ann Dowker's research briefing "What works for children with mathematical difficulties"

- *www.dcsf.gov.uk/research/data/uploadfiles/RB554.pdf* (accessed 22.05.09)

Ofsted report

- *http://www.ofsted.gov.uk/Ofsted-home/Publications-and-research/Documents-by-type/Thematic-reports/Mathematics-understanding-the-score* (accessed 26.03.09)

References

Ahmed, A. (1987) *Better Mathematics*. London: HMSO. (There is now a 2007 update of this work).

Baron-Cohen, B. (1997) *Mindblindness: Essay on Autism and the Theory of Mind*. Cambridge, MA.: The MIT Press.

Dweck, C. (2000) *Self-theories: Their Role in Motivation, Personality, and Development*. Hove, E Sussex: Psychology Press.

Mason, J. (2002) *Researching your own practice : the discipline of noticing*. London: RoutledgeFalmer.

Waddell, M. (2002) *Inside lives: psychoanalysis and the growth of the personality*. London: Karnac.

11
USING ICT TO ENHANCE PROFESSIONAL PRACTICE

Dave Miller

This chapter is one of two with a focus on using ICT. The focus of this chapter is on how and why teachers use ICT; in the next chapter, the focus changes to pupils' use of ICT. This chapter will encourage you to audit the way that teachers in your department currently use ICT and what your current vision is of effective ICT use. It will then look at ways that you can augment your vision of how teachers can use ICT. Finally it will look at developing a plan for putting that new vision into practice.

ICT plays an increasing role in many of today's classrooms. Research has shown that in the best cases:

- As technology was embedded, schools' national test outcomes improved beyond expectations.
- Effective use of presentation technologies led to greater interaction between teachers and learners.
- Effective use of ICT personalised learning by enabling greater learner choice within the curriculum, improved assessment for learning and more learner-directed teaching.
- Technology facilitated more effective assessment for learning by making it easier for learners to be more involved in target-setting and for teachers to give individualised feedback. (Somekh, 2007)

From the above list, you will see how important it is that your department makes the most of the possibilities offered by ICT. For you as a subject leader, 'getting to grips' with ICT may seem like an endless task; new resources, software packages and hardware are being produced all the time. This chapter is designed to help you begin to feel that you are able to make good decisions in planning for teaching and learning with ICT. First you will establish what you have in place at the moment and then you will begin thinking about where you and your department want to be by developing or enhancing a vision for effective use of ICT. In order to help develop your vision the chapter will include research on the use of ICT, issues arising from an Ofsted report of 2008, and a discussion on how you might overcome some of the common barriers to using ICT confidently and effectively.

Why use ICT?

The resource base to support teaching and learning of mathematics has grown enormously in recent years. Resources such as video, animation, photographs, and graphing tools offer ways to make mathematics more interesting and engaging and also present ideas from several points of view. Exploration is important as a way of developing understanding of mathematical ideas and ICT offers many innovative environments for exploration. ICT enables good ideas that work well for one group of pupils to be more easily recycled in a variety of ways to meet the needs of different pupils. If ideas and their outcomes are efficiently saved on the computer the first time they are used, teachers will be able to retrieve and develop them in subsequent years. For example; a short mathematical film from the ATM website could be used to try to provoke mathematical thinking and the outcomes of that lesson could be saved along with notes in an 'I wish I had ...' section; or an interactive resource tailored to students' needs may be created using a dynamic geometry package and again saved in an appropriate area along with ideas for tailoring the idea further for other pupils. ICT use is important outside the classroom as well, teachers are expected to use ICT to support an increasing number of professional roles, from taking the register to writing reports.

Because of the perceived benefits of ICT to enhance teachers' work, there is a widespread agreement within the teaching community and the government that ICT is an essential tool for the teaching profession. Teachers are expected to be, at the very least, competent users of ICT themselves. Technology enables teachers to source and produce resources that are high-quality and tailored to the needs of their classes and many of these will be ICT based.

Using ICT effectively?

Despite the widespread availability of ICT resources, the situation 'on the ground' gives rise to concerns about whether teachers are using ICT as effectively as they might in the classroom. ICT is frequently used in a very limited and limiting way. Some departments use ICT primarily (or even solely) to modify behaviour, rather than facilitate learning. Departments that have access to a room with a bank of computers have been known to use this facility as a 'fun' alternative to a regular classroom lesson, or as a reward for completing other work. Facilities such as the 'computer room' or a set of laptop computers can be used much more effectively with a little research and some advice and planning.

Research has repeatedly shown that when ICT is used well it significantly improves both teaching and learning:

> There is increasingly strong evidence to show that, used effectively, technology can help to narrow the gap between the highest and lowest achievers, can help more people to continue successfully in learning; and can motivate and support those who are disaffected and disengaged.
> (Becta, 2007)

This report is not alone in showing highly positive outcomes from the use of ICT and in suggesting that ICT implementation in mathematics (and other subjects) is highly desirable. Achieving the improvements indicated is dependent on 'effective use' of ICT – but what does this mean? How do mathematics teachers recognise and understand what is meant by 'effective' use of ICT? One way to probe the effectiveness of the use of ICT in a lesson is to answer these two questions as fully and honestly as possible:

- If the teacher had not used ICT, would it have made a significant difference from the point of view of the *teaching*?

- If the teacher had not used ICT, would it have made a significant difference from the point of view of the *learning*?

Effective ICT use will make a significant difference to the learning that goes on, improving the pace of the lesson, allowing a concept to be demonstrated more clearly, involving the pupils in the thinking and the activity of the lesson and allowing the teacher and the pupils themselves to recognise that understanding is increasing.

The Vision – an e-mature department

The term 'e-mature' has been used, for example by Becta, to indicate a department that has made a plan based on where the teachers were and where they wanted to be and has gone a long way to achieving planned outcomes. An e-mature mathematics department will have recognised that ICT is merely a tool to support practice. The person who has taken the lead on ICT will have audited the quality, appropriateness and distribution of technology within the department and its availability to facilitate effective teaching, learning and collaboration. Leaders of e-mature departments encourage risk, creativity and experimentation, and they allow members of their department autonomy to experiment with different working patterns and innovative teaching styles. Such leadership will develop effective practitioners who:

- are ICT confident and competent.

- are positive about the learning benefits of ICT.

- use ICT effectively beyond the teaching environment.

- know how and when to use ICT effectively to enhance teaching and learning but, most importantly, also know when not to use ICT.

- are confident in the use of a range of digital and non-digital resources, moving seamlessly between different types of teaching environments.

- are willing to collaborate with others and share examples of good practice.

- evaluate the impact of using new technologies, reviewing and adapting their practice to reflect changing technology, pedagogy and practice.

This will take time, especially if you are starting from a situation where ICT is rarely used. All lasting change takes time to instigate. Somekh et al (2007) found that more e-mature departments made quicker improvement than those who were less so. They also found that,*"there was a dip in performance until the ICT became embedded and staff developed the requisite skills"*. Managing the implementation of ICT requires *"a strong vision, an extended planning phase, staged investment and support throughout"* and that *"schools needed to build sustainability – of both resources and pedagogic change – into their change management strategies from the start."*

Developing an e-mature department

There is likely to be significant variation between teachers in your department, both in terms of their experience of using ICT personally and their use of ICT in the classroom. This variation will be the result of a variety of factors including, amongst others:

- the beliefs and attitudes of the subject leader and how s/he supports mathematics staff in their use of ICT in its widest sense.
- the beliefs and attitudes of the individual teachers.
- the leadership of the school and, as a result, how ICT is perceived generally by staff.
- the resources in the mathematics classrooms and elsewhere in the school, including the level of access to such resources both within and outside the department.
- the level and type of CPD that the mathematics department have followed, as individuals, for example on their Initial Teacher Education course, or together as a department.
- the way that ICT systems are managed within the school and how this might help or hinder staff and pupil use of ICT.
- the access that pupils might have to ICT either away from school or in non-teaching time at school.

Each of these factors can help overcome problems created by others. For example, if a department is made up of teachers determined to use a wide range of technological resources to help pupils learn mathematics then overcoming problems with access to ICT resources becomes a priority and creative solutions are often found. However a negative influence from any of these factors can, by itself, lead to a situation where teachers do not use ICT to enhance their teaching and if several of them are exerting a negative influence their impact can be crippling. Therefore before the department moves forward you will need to find out both about each of the above factors and about anything that is currently planned to change the impact of these factors. Even with the best ideas and the best intentions, you will almost certainly come across a number of barriers as soon as you try to change your department's practice. There are two main types of barriers: those that arise out of 'people considerations' and those that arise out of 'technical considerations'.

- 'People considerations' refer to concerns such as: the confidence of staff to use ICT; knowing where to find suitable CPD; how to provide ongoing support and coaching; if there is a technician with suitable expertise to support staff and enable staff to have a vision of how, where and to what extent ICT will support teaching.
- 'Technical considerations' refer to concerns such as: whether there is sufficient hardware in terms of computers, interactive whiteboards, data loggers and other ICT tools; knowledge of how to use the hardware provided; the ability to access technical help when required; and the provision of and ability to use suitable software.

Some subject leaders feel that they are in a hopeless situation. They cannot change everything and everything about technology costs money, often in quantities that they have no access to. If you do feel frustrated, then remember why you are reading this chapter – in order to use ICT to improve your pupils' mathematical understanding and their interest in mathematics. This is an important and achievable goal. It is also useful to remember that large scale change has to start somewhere and starting with small changes such as a laptop loaded with free shareware resources such as Geogebra can start the ball rolling and you could soon be implementing a much wider ICT agenda.

One key thing to remember when encouraging your department to integrate ICT effectively into their practice is that, although everyone (including you!) has a different starting point depending upon experience and confidence, it is not necessary to master every aspect of the available technology to be an effective practitioner. Piggott in her research on ICT adoption notes:

> There is evidence (Preston et al (1999), Cox (1999), Gobbo and Girardi (2001), Mumtaz (2000)) that it is not necessary to know a lot of ICT to use it effectively in the classroom. However, it is necessary to have found aspects of ICT that the teacher can feel confident with, e.g. a particular piece of software + a teaching/learning convergence + the appropriate curriculum and resource opportunity. (Piggott 2006)

Confidence is achieved through the interplay of both 'people considerations' and 'technical considerations'. Allowing staff to negotiate their own 'ICT comfort zone' which they can then expand in a planned and manageable way is effective in helping teachers new to using aspects of ICT. Even the most ICT-confident teacher has favourite pieces of software and websites that they use frequently and may need reminders to explore further to find new solutions to teaching difficult topics. Teachers establish their own comfort zones by developing confidence in the technology that they want to use. That confidence is developed more quickly when both the hardware and software is robust, appropriate and stable, and technical support is available that is able to respond to immediate problems, otherwise teachers rightly will be reluctant to experiment.

Many teachers may want to use more ICT but are intimidated by what they perceive to be complicated and lengthy set up procedures. This fear is exacerbated if they do not know what to do if things go wrong. Ideally, staff should be able to access resources quickly and easily, by following a small number of straightforward and memorable steps. In your role as a subject teacher you will need to empathise with each of your staff and consider if they are justified in any reluctance they have to use the ICT available and what can be done to reduce any barriers. Use of ICT is greatly enhanced by a technological infrastructure in school that allows both practitioners and learners to access learning resources efficiently using a diversity of access devices from a variety of locations.

With these considerations in mind, the next part of this chapter looks at how to get started with developing all teachers' confidence in some aspect of ICT and how to take the next step towards becoming a truly ICT literate, e-mature department.

Auditing your Department

The first step to creating and sustaining an e-mature department is to take an audit of provision and practice. Once you know your 'baseline' you can use your knowledge of the wider perspectives, national ICT developments and ICT-related research to begin to answer the questions: 'What *must* be in our department?', 'What *should* be in our department?' and 'What *could* be in our department?' From your answers to these questions you will be in a position to determine a vision for using ICT within your department.

There are many factors and facets to the use of ICT in a mathematics department, so it is useful to start with some guidelines. Becta's self-review framework (Becta 2009) offers you a route for assessing and improving your department's use of ICT. The on-line framework asks you to assess how e-mature your department is by exemplifying good practice and to create an action plan for improvement. As you read the details on-line for each of the eight categories below, review your own department's practice – are there any categories in which you would rate yourself particularly well or poorly? It might be useful to try and think of particular examples for each statement, rather than simply answering 'yes' or 'no'.

The eight categories in the Becta self review documents	
	Do teachers in your department…
1. Leadership and management	• Develop and communicate a shared vision for ICT?
	• Plan a sustainable ICT strategy?
2. Curriculum	• Plan and lead a broad and balanced ICT curriculum?
	• Review and update the curriculum in the light of developments in technology and practice?
	• Ensure pupils' ICT experiences are progressive, coherent, balanced and consistent?
3. Learning and teaching	• Plan the use of ICT to enhance learning and teaching?
	• Meet pupils' expectations for the use of ICT?
	• Encourage teachers to work collaboratively in identifying and evaluating the impact of ICT on learning and teaching?
4. Assessment	• Assess the capability of ICT to support pupils' learning?
	• Use assessment evidence and data in planning learning and teaching across the whole curriculum?
	• Assess the learning when ICT has been used?

11. USING ICT TO ENHANCE PROFESSIONAL PRACTICE

The eight categories in the Becta self review documents	
5. Professional development	• Identify and address the ICT training needs of individual staff? • Provide quality support and training activities for all staff in the use of ICT sharing effective practice? • Review, monitor and evaluate professional development as an integral part of the development of your school?
6. Extending opportunities for learning	• Understand the needs of your pupils and community in their extended use of ICT? • Ensure provision is enhanced through informed planning resulting in quality of use of ICT? • Review, monitor and evaluate opportunities to extend learning beyond the classroom?
7. Resources	• Ensure learning and teaching environments use ICT effectively and in line with strategic needs? • Purchase, deploy and review appropriate ICT resources that reflect your school improvement strategy? • Manage technical support effectively for the benefit of pupils and staff?
8. Impact on pupil outcomes	• Demonstrate how pupils can make good progress in ICT capability? • Demonstrate awareness of how the use of ICT can have a wider positive impact on pupils' progress? • Review pupil attitudes and behaviour and how the use of ICT can impact positively on pupil achievement?

In order to gather as much information as possible you could also think back to, or find out about, your department's last inspection report. Were there any comments on the use of ICT in your department? Do you feel that any of their comments are still valid? Were there any departments in your school that were praised for their use of ICT? What might you learn from them that you could apply to your mathematics department?

Auditing individuals

All teachers are expected to develop confidence in use of ICT in support of their teaching. This is important both from the point of view of the learner and of the teacher. The professional standards for teachers (TDA) make this requirement clear:

- *QTS & Core Standard 17*: Know how to use skills in literacy, numeracy and ICT to support their teaching and wider professional activities.

- *Scope - Pedagogic practice*: Identifying and knowing where you can make effective use of your ICT skills in teaching and wider professional activities.

Each department is different; at one end of the spectrum you have many e-mature teachers and now feel highly optimistic in terms of moving your ICT vision forward, but at another extreme you may consider that there is very little that you can do and you have no 'assets' other than yourself. In reality most departments lie somewhere between these extremes, so there will be something 'going for you'. Imagine a department called together for a departmental meeting about the use of ICT. Three staff speak openly about using ICT in their lessons, but it is very clear they have very different opinions about using ICT:

- *David*: "I want to use more ICT in the classroom, but I just don't have the time to find new pieces of software and websites. I tend to use the same few things over and over again."

- *Surinder*: "I would like to use ICT, but it always takes so long to load something up and find what I want. It works OK for a few minutes, but then something goes wrong and I don't know what to do. It's safer to stick to the whiteboard."

- *Sam*: "ICT is great! I've got a second degree in programming in BOF+, and can write my own programs. We need to spend thousands of pounds upgrading to the latest version of my favourite piece of software, because I use it every lesson!"

How might you as a subject leader help these members of staff as individuals, as well as helping the department as a whole? You may choose to discuss issues such as these with your department – you could use these questions as a starting point:

- Does our use of ICT enhance our teaching and the pupils' learning?
- Do we actively plan to use ICT in our lessons regularly? At what stage in the planning process do we include it – is it an optional extra for individual teachers or a core part of our schemes of work?
- Do we evaluate our use of ICT and have a shared understanding of what is meant by 'effective' use?
- Do we share good practice in ICT with each other to promote effective use in the department?
- What barriers are holding us back from more effective use of ICT in the classroom?
- How might we remove these barriers?

Think about the implications of your answers for your department. What do you need to do to understand and develop effective practice?

Developing an augmented vision

Having discussed 'what currently is' and to some extent 'what must be' this section of the chapter is design to help you decide 'what should be', and 'what could be'. You will have a general vision of how you would like to see your department develop its use of ICT. By reading this section you will enhance or augment your vision. Clearly your local circumstances will have a major influence on the nature and scope of what is desirable and what is possible within your department. The last section of the chapter will help you consider in some depth, how your augmented vision for the department, will be implemented and managed.

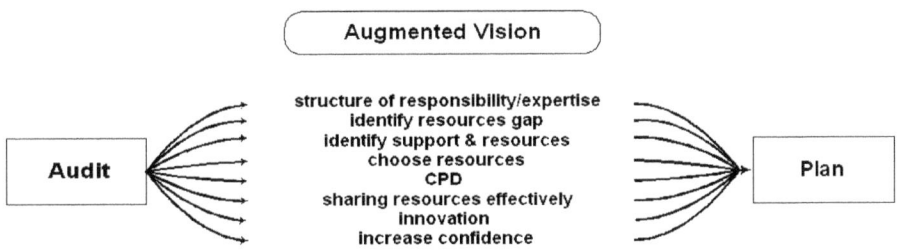

It is important to be aware, when discussing ICT, that you are likely to be limited to those developments that you know about – since you 'do not know what you do not know' – you are 'unconsciously incompetent' (Dubin 1962). This may mean that you and your colleagues, although fully competent as teachers, may not realise or have any experience many of the possibilities afforded by ICT. If you feel that, to an extent, the 'unconscious incompetence' may be hindering your progress, you might like to involve someone from outside the department in a needs analysis: a colleague from a department that is more e-mature, an Advanced Skills teacher from another school, a Local Authority advisor or a fellow teacher from one of the subject associations.

So what is there that is within your control that might help you move forward? Typically, for mathematics, you will have influence on some or all of:

- the level and quality of staffing
- an annual budget – with 'a tradition' in how this has been spent/allocated
- resources in each classroom
- resources elsewhere
- CPD allowance for staff
- examination expenditure
- opportunities to make bids for additional 'internal' funding/ resourcing
- opportunities to make bids for external funding

Clearly you need to make decisions for all aspects of mathematics provision and ICT is just one element of this provision, so how do you decide what to do?

One way is to align your direction with wider initiatives. We have already given an indication of external 'drivers' that demand development of ICT use within schools and departments, and sometimes demands can change quickly, such as with the unexpected cessation of KS3 tests in 2008. It follows that there will be advantages in considering a strategy for developing the department so that it will move forward to meet the emerging agenda, putting things in place gradually before they become expected or compulsory.

If your department currently has little expertise it might be tempting to send teachers on a course to develop their skills, but if, when they return they have no access to the hardware and software that they need will their enthusiasm last? If you expect your department to use ICT in their lessons but they do not have laptops that can move between home and school, is it realistic to expect staff to plan all their lessons using ICT at school? What is the school's policy with regard to using teachers own equipment at school? Should teachers be expected to use their own ICT resources? Should you invest in a wide range of software packages and site licences, or invest in upgrading the department's hardware? As subject leader you will need to think very carefully about where to start.

One theme present in research findings is the idea of working together: a lot of problems that arise when leading staff in ICT can be reduced by encouraging your department to work as a team. For example, in the hypothetical situations outlined in the section above, David might be able to help Surinder to master one or two pieces of software – perhaps she would like to do a peer observation to see him at work, and then he could observe her teaching once she has established an ICT comfort zone. Sam might be more capable at ICT than you – so delegate! You could ask him to find or write, simple applications that are robust, and place them in a shared area, although remember this may need some negotiation of copyright ownership.

Augmenting your vision through professional development
It is highly likely that your ideas for developing the ICT use in the department will involve some aspect of professional development and along with all staff, the mathematics department has an entitlement to regular professional development. Recent findings suggest that a collaborative approach to CPD might be beneficial, a report concludes:

> In all but one of the fifteen studies included, collaborative CPD was linked with improvements in teaching and learning. ... For instance, there were improvements in teachers' behaviour, beliefs and approaches to teaching and the use of resources. These changes were influenced by collaborative practices such as joint planning and team teaching and required time for problems to be identified and overcome ... students showed improvements in performance, approaches to learning, attitudes and levels of participation.

> The review identified the positive contributions made by aspects of collaborative CPD, for instance, the use of expertise external to the school, peer observation, feedback and peer support .... Some other contributory factors of note were dedicated time, interventions that built on what teachers already knew, opportunities for action research and use of research literature. (Cordingley et al 2005)

CPD can show you what is available or raise your expectations of what it is possible to do in the classroom. Other CPD can show you or your staff how to make the best use of a particular piece of equipment or software. What you choose will depend on where you are and what you already know. Whatever your needs you will be able to find CPD that enhances your current vision of how ICT can be used in the mathematics department.

Augmenting your vision - equipping the classroom

Parallel to any staff development, you will need to ensure that your department is furnished with appropriate technology. Competent staff without appropriate technology will soon become frustrated. A potentially useful equipment list, including both software and hardware, can be found in Appendix 1. This list contains items you might have thought about but others you may not have considered and which may be used to extend your vision of how your mathematics classrooms could be equipped. Some video retrieval websites such as TeacherTube and YouTube contain images and videos that add greatly to the learning experience in mathematics. For example, there is a video clip from the film 'Ma & Pa' (*http://www.youtube.com/watch?v=Bfq5kju627c*) which can be included to good effect when teaching arithmetic algorithms.

Augmenting your vision – as part of whole school development

It is the responsibility of the senior leadership team, to respond to Becta's expectation:

> to ensure that we have the right technology, connectivity, content and managed services in place right across the system to enable and support learning wherever and whenever it takes place"; "to ensure everyone in the education and training workforce is capable and confident in using technology effectively to achieve better results for learners" and "to find much better ways of identifying and spreading the most effective practice, so that every learner can benefit. (Becta 2007)

This is important because research shows that:

- The involvement of ICT changed the working practices of teachers and extended the roles of administrative staff and technicians.

- Well co-ordinated and sustained professional development opportunities were important in developing ICT skills and confidence of all staff and embedding the use of ICT. Informal, on-the-job training was very effective when supported by in-school champions.

- Where new technologies were introduced into all of a school's classrooms at the same time, a culture of sharing and mutual support developed as the whole staff faced the task of embedding the technology into their pedagogy. Collective need led to collective solutions being found and shared.

- Access to reliable technology and daily use led to rapid improvements in teachers' skills and improved management of workloads.

- Shared server areas and virtual learning environments made it easier for teachers to find, store, share, create and re-use resources and lesson plans. This ensured long-term value from the initial high investment by the workforce. (Somekh, 2007)

The development of ICT may well call for school-wide change and a willingness on behalf of the senior management team to both find and commit the money that system wide improvements require. Given the government's recent commitment to providing ICT funding, situations where there is no existing ICT infrastructure are less common. Many schools have already responded to the government's expectation that by 2010 every school will have a high quality, integrated learning and management system.

The Becta report also comments on 'the digital divide' between those that have easy computer and internet access at home and those that do not.

> the majority of students now have access to computers at home; loaning ICT equipment to learners helps to bridge the digital divide; and ICT made it much easier to share assessment information with parents via school websites or learning platforms". However, they also found that "increasing home access to ICT and the internet was operationally difficult for schools. It was very time consuming and required careful planning."
>
> (Somekh et al 2007)

Although the 'digital divide' is a whole school issue, there are ways to work around this in mathematics departments; for example, you might choose to provide all pupils with access to a graphic calculator whenever required – however, this would have consequences both in terms of cost, and in terms of having to devise resources and a scheme of work that integrates graphic calculators appropriately.

However, if the school itself is slow in developing ICT use, there are still implications for mathematics departments. Since mathematics teachers can make such a pronounced difference with ICT, they may wish to develop ahead of the rest of the school in the use of technologies such as class sets of laptops or interactive whiteboards. Consider how relevant you found your ICT-based learning resources, when you completed your audit of the department. How easy are they to access and manage and do you consider them to be of high quality? If your school has bought packages for use across the curriculum, how well do they meet the needs of the mathematics department? Some schools, for example, have bought packages that provide revision-type materials across several subjects. However, such packages may undermine your work as subject leader, for example by dividing mathematics into small unrelated chunks when you have decided to lead your department to teach connected, relational thinking. Such packages, although they may offer short term benefits, might also encourage 'teaching to the test' when the department is working to develop wide thinking and exploration, a fuller understanding of mathematics concepts and an ability and willingness on the part of pupils to study mathematics further.

An example of augmenting your vision - the use of Interactive Whiteboards

Ofsted commented on the use of IWBs in their 2008 report. In two key paragraphs inspectors noted that teachers used the presentational advantages of 'high-quality diagrams and relevant software to support learning through, for example, construction of graphs or visualisation of transformations' but that *'too often teachers used them simply for PowerPoint presentations with no interaction by the pupils'*. (Ofsted, 2008, para. 57). They also commented in the same paragraph that *'many of the curricular and guidance documents seen did not draw sufficient attention to the potential of interactive whiteboards'*, though it is not clear whether they refer to mathematics department or other sources. Finally, as well as noting generally on how *'teachers underused practical resources and games to develop pupils' understanding of mathematical ideas and help them to make connections between different topics'*, they commented that *'a negative effect of IWBs was a reduction in pupils' use of practical equipment: software is no replacement for hands-on experience'*.

At this point you might ask yourself and others in the department these key questions:

- Why do you or don't you have interactive whiteboards in your department?
- How might an interactive whiteboard be used to enhance the teaching and learning of mathematics?"

If you have IWBs in place, then you might ask teachers in the department to consider "How interactive are your lessons?" They might like to find their own 'Interactivity Quotient' by accessing published IWB maths training materials: *http://www.iwbmathstraining.co.uk/index.php?option=com_2j_tabs&Itemid=23*.

Teachers need to develop an appropriate pedagogy alongside their use of IWBs (Miller et al 2008). Over the last eight years, Dave Miller has worked extensively with teachers, undertaken research into and provided professional development related to interactive whiteboard use in mathematics classrooms. Alongside finding problems, they also found some very good practice where teachers used IWBs to work interactively. They found that the IWB has the potential to provide considerable enhancements for mathematics teaching, when teachers were well-versed in using IWBs to support interactive lessons.

There is extensive literature on the use of the IWB in teaching mathematics (for example see *www.iwbmaths.co.uk/research* and *www.keele.ac.uk/depts/ed/iaw/index.htm*). It is clear that there are many positive benefits that come from using an IWB interactively for both teachers and pupils where teachers have received appropriate professional development to understand the pedagogic possibilities made available by an IWB.

The General Teaching Council for England produce regular 'Research of the Month' reports. The question asked in its report for September 2008 was "What is good interactive whole class teaching and how can interactive whiteboards help?" and its brief answer was as follows:

> The researchers found that whole class teaching was typically characterised by traditional question and answer sequences directed by the teacher, with 64% of talk time being taken by teachers and with boys involved more than girls. True interactive teaching, which was more helpful to learning, was characterised by a more equal distribution of dialogue between the teacher and pupils. Pupils were generally very positive about their experience of IWBs, especially in providing a new mode for learning which chimed with pupils' increasing exposure to new technology. But the introduction of IWBs did not, by itself, automatically change the way teachers taught or interacted with pupils. (General Teaching Council 2008)

At its best, the IWB can be used 'at the board, on the desk, in the head', that is, interesting and creative mathematics is developed from teacher activities 'at the board', followed up by related pupil activities 'on the desk', (or *vice versa*) in order to help pupils understand the ideas 'in the head'. (Miller et al. 2008)

In the best lessons, IWB software is used as the 'managing medium' for the lesson, with all the electronic resources stored in the one IWB file. This improves lesson management as teachers do not need to search the computer for, for example., an Excel file. Activities can be designed to incorporate ideas 'at the board', 'on the desk', 'in the head' – often making use of virtual manipulatives which are electronic versions of pieces of apparatus, such as a protractor or a geoboard. Pupils have real apparatus on their desk to facilitate the board-desk link. Interaction, both pupil-teacher, and pupil-pupil, comes from questioning of pupils (for examples of appropriate questions see Watson and Mason, 1998) and discussion between pupils. Interaction is encouraged and the use of linear presentations, such as those usually created in presentation software like PowerPoint, is not relevant to such activities and rarely used.

As an example, an 'at the board', 'on the desk', 'in the head' lesson on Bearings might start with some class work. The pupils are invited to work on their desks matching compass bearings to the eight main compass directions. The teacher then introduces a map of the runways at Birmingham airport, downloaded from Google Earth, and showing the figures painted on each runway; the pupils are asked to try to interpret the figures. Work 'on the desk' follows, with pupils offering interpretations of why the runways have the figures written in the way shown. After a time, a consensus is reached. The pupils then watch a Teachers TV programme showing how bearings are used in the 'real' world, which incidentally includes an answer to the runway figures. The pupils have an opportunity to use maps and create their own journeys involving bearings. The teacher's main role in this lesson is not exposition, or even explanation, it is to ask the right questions to help pupils use what they are seeing, listening to and doing to build knowledge about bearings.

Further examples and explanations can be found at: *www.ncetm.org.uk/ mathemapedia/BoardDeskHead*. Other examples of this approach, starting from work at the desk, use the 'Improving learning in mathematics' materials developed by the Standards Unit (DfES 200x). IWB versions of all these have been created (*www.iwbmathstraining.co.uk*) so that when there is discussion of, for example, card sorting activities, 'cards' are available on the IWB so that they can be moved around to help with the discussion. The website points out that these IWB resources supplement the original materials rather than replace the desk work done independently by pupils. More similar materials are available at *www.iwbmaths.co.uk*.

The interactive whiteboard – training materials and resources

It is becomingly increasingly easy to train teachers in the use of interactive whiteboards - many sites offer tips, tricks and training for free. The manufacturers of the two main types of IWB used in secondary schools in England (Promethean and Smart) have good online materials available to help both inexperienced IWB users and those who wish to extend their knowledge

11. USING ICT TO ENHANCE PROFESSIONAL PRACTICE

to learn to use their software to good effect. They also both offer video training materials on either TeacherTube or YouTube.

Extensive sets of resources for use on the IWB are available free of charge online, but do be aware that the quality is variable. There are many copies of, for example, Pythagoras' theorem being 'well demonstrated' using 3, 4, 5 triangles and measuring approaches that show the squares drawn on the sides, but nothing that constitutes a proof. There are also plenty of examples for consolidating pupils ideas about Pythagoras' Theorem, often separated into 'find the hypotenuse' examples and 'find a shorter side' examples. Fortunately there are some examples that offer more exploratory approaches but these are harder to find. It is important to ensure that your choices with regard to resources are 'fit for purpose', and that they support and challenge, rather than limit, pupils' mathematical thinking.

Developing a plan

From a vision to a plan - the road to success

You will now have a good idea of your vision augmented by the ideas discussed in the previous section. This vision will probably include a notion of how mathematics classrooms should be equipped, how they might 'feel' for both pupils and staff and how far you have to 'travel' in terms of where you are and where you want to be. You may well have an idea about where you might find support for the vision and where there might be potential difficulties in terms of pupils, mathematics and other staff, parents and the school leadership.

When turning this vision into a plan, you will have to consider what you need to achieve in terms of the immediate, short-, mid- and long-term so that your vision might be achieved. It will help if you and your department have a shared vision, but there may be decisions, such as those concerning personnel, that you may not be able to share. It is also important that your vision is shared with the school leadership team, who might be the key to helping you achieve this vision and may be able to offer you advice as to how best argue your case.

In creating a plan, you will consider which parts of your vision might be achieved more easily than others because of, for example, the school development plan. The staff may be keen to use IWBs immediately if you can find the money; but they may have to wait until the senior management team agree to provide additional resources.

Whatever your vision, it is important to keep a healthy perspective. If something does not go well, reflect why that might be the case, and use it to inform future practice. But when something goes well, share it, celebrate the small victories and use it to encourage others.

Your plan to equip your teachers

There are many ways to equip your teachers with the knowledge that they need to use ICT effectively, here are three that you might like to consider to start with:

- *Departmental Workshops*: A number of organisations are beginning to offer ready-made, structured professional development sessions that are designed to be used with entire departments in schools without the use of outside help. The NCETM, for example, offer 'Departmental Workshops', including a module on Interpreting Statistical Data that you might use to support work in ICT. (These resources can be found at *www.ncetm.org.uk/Default.aspx?page=13&module=res&mode=100&resid=10848*.)

  They all have a similar format with clear objectives and provide a variety of activities including 'hooks for learning' for you to consider how they might enhance the pupils' learning experience. You would need to find at least two hours for the whole department (ideally including part-time members and regular supply and support staff) to undertake one of these. The department would need to meet and follow through the processes and then decide on meaningful outcomes that should be followed up at a later (named) date.

- *Paired or Small Group Directed Tasks*: As an alternative model, you might choose to split the department into small teams of two or more, each of which could work together on a specific task, such as integrating the use of geometrical software into the scheme of work (while other pairs of staff work on different developments). A lot of materials exist that can provide starting points, for example the book "Developing thinking in geometry" (Johnston-Wilder & Mason, 2005) or the "Getting started with interactive geometry" series from the Association of Teachers of Mathematics. Over an agreed period of time, the group could try out the activities and/or software, as well as planning, teaching and evaluating together some lessons that use the ideas and materials. The group should then feed back to the department. This approach would be a good way to investigate and disseminate the Bowland Maths materials (*www.bowlandmaths.org.uk/*).

- *Outside Expertise*: A third model might use outside expertise as a means to move the department forward more quickly. For example you might buy in experts in IWB materials and pedagogy who would work with the department for a day using a SPORE (Skills, Pedagogy, Opportunity, Reflection and Evolution) approach (Miller, Averis and Glover, 2008). Your department would get to learn new IWB skills, such as how to create a 'magic window' and will be provided with examples of use for these skills. They will think about using different teaching approaches, consider their pedagogy, and reflect how they might make opportunities in the curriculum to use these approaches in the near future. If you use this model, it is valuable to plan a time when the department can reflect on this classroom use, for example in the next department meeting in three weeks. This will give you time to consider as a department how to evolve as a consequence of the new learning, as well as sharing good practice and specific examples.

There are other ways in which teachers in the department can develop their expertise. Shared file areas can be an excellent way for departments to develop as a community, saving time, effort and sharing motivating to develop their use of ICT. Most school networks allow you to set up a folder which all staff can easily access. Encourage your staff to add their own tried and tested resources to the folder, and mention new additions at departmental meetings to keep the folder at the front of everyone's mind. If it is appropriate, you might like to insist at first that everyone adds at least one Powerpoint slideshow or flipchart each term. You could share a 'website of the week' (with brief notes on how it might be useful) each Monday, with staff members taking it in turns to come up with ideas. The possibilities are endless, but you will find it easier to lead a department in their development of ICT if your staff members are making the journey together. This joint development can be included when planning professional development.

Your plan to equip your classroom

In making a plan to equip your classrooms for effective use of ICT you will need to consider what ICT and other equipment you have already and what you would need for your ideal mathematics classroom. The 'Five dimensions of the effective classroom' found in Johnston-Wilder and Pimm (2005) originally taken from Hiebert et al (1997) provide a background against which to decide on what equipment you might need and how it would aid development within each of these dimensions.

Five dimensions of the effective classroom		
Dimension		Examples of how equipment may be used in this dimension
1. Nature of classroom task	Make mathematics problematic Connect with where pupils are Leave behind something of mathematical value	Dynamic geometry package to problematise mathematics. Internet access to make maths real
2. Role of the teacher	Select tasks with goals in mind Share essential information Establish classroom culture	Goals set and displayed on ticker tape setting Essential information displayed on IWB Laptops to facilitate collaborative working

Five dimensions of the effective classroom		
3. Social culture of the classroom	Ideas and methods are valued Pupils choose and share their methods Mistakes are learning sites for everyone Correctness resides in mathematical argument	Lap tops allow choice of what to work on and how to work Mini whiteboards and manipulables offer choice of ways of working. Ideas transferred to main screen allow all to participate in knowledge building discussions
4. Mathematical tools as learning supports	Meaning for tools must be constructed by each user Used with purpose – to solve problems Used for recording, communicating and thinking	Access to computers as individual or in pairs using software such as grid algebra allows tool use to construct meanings
5. Equality and accessibility	Tasks are accessible to all pupils Every pupil is heard Every pupil contributes	IWB and mini whiteboards can allow all to be heard

Developing firm plans

Because of the particular nature of ICT any plan to develop into an e-mature department will need to cover at least 5 years. Over those years you can plan how to develop teachers' confidence, and how to save in some areas in order to be able to spend the sums of money you may need for high value equipment or site licences in order to realise your vision of a fully equipped, e-mature, mathematics department. However you will also need to put in place less expensive but still essential CPD and processes for sharing and developing of expertise and resources. There will be other ideas that are needed to realise your plan, such as co-coaching (see Chapter 6) or using a shared area on the school computer network. You will need to consider which areas of expertise must be worked on first and how they are to be developed. If, as a department, you want to develop the use of graphing software do you all need to 'go on a course' or will one person attend a course, then practice and evaluate the ideas they have used in their classroom, perhaps using the action research ideas in Chapter 7, before disseminating to the whole department? There is not, of course, one right answer to such questions and many decisions will need to be made depending on the personnel in your department, the equipment already in place and the interests and expertise that already exists.

11. USING ICT TO ENHANCE PROFESSIONAL PRACTICE

It will be vital for all teachers to develop expertise in some of the ideas listed in Appendix 1, but it will be sufficient for just some of the teachers to become 'experts' in others. For example, a teacher who cannot use Word or Excel may be unable immediately to use the reporting system or the data collection tools that most schools use; enabling them to develop expertise in these pieces of software must be considered a priority. Some of the macro-use within Excel may be considered 'advanced use', in which only some teachers who are interested will develop expertise

Another important consideration is that the department will not have the time to develop expertise in all areas at once. If all members in the department already use graphing software then you might consider developing the use of videos to demonstrate mathematical concepts but you would not do both at once. If individual teachers become 'experts' in different ways of using ICT then many more ideas can be explored in your school context. Those that are evaluated as worth disseminating can be supported to develop across teachers in a way that suits the department and eventually everyone be confident in their use.

In general expertise in using ICT develops along a continuum such as that shown below.

A teacher:

knows that the idea exists	knows what the idea could do	makes personal use of the idea	uses the idea with pupils	allows the pupils to explore what they can do with the idea.

⟵——————————⟶ **Developing expertise** ——————————⟶

In order to help you make your plan consider each way of using ICT in Appendix 1 and decide:

- How important is this idea to my department?
- What will having expertise in this area allow the department to do that it cannot do without the ICT?
- What level of expense will be incurred in developing the idea?
- Is outside expertise needed or can the department support one another in developing this idea?
- At what stage does the department want to develop that expertise? immediately? this year? next year? later?
- Who needs to develop the expertise? All teachers, some or just those interested?
- What action will be needed by yourself as subject leader or by others in the department, to make sure that this ICT expertise is developed and disseminated?

From your responses to the ideas in Appendix 1, you may be ready to make a five-year plan which will, no doubt, be amended many times as personnel and other circumstances change. It would be appropriate to think of this as your vision of an e-mature department. This plan is aspirational, as you will want your department to be working towards being the best that it can be. Naturally this plan will be part of your department development plan and the use of ICT will inform and be informed by the developments that the department is making in other areas.

Once you have made your five-year plan, you will be able to make step by step plans that show the actions you need to take and decide on the timescale of implementing each action, in order to reach the goals you have set yourself. You will probably need a detailed one-year plan that shows what you want to achieve term by term this year. Always remember to set out what you want to achieve first and then decide how to work towards it, as this will ensure that you get where you want to be.

What we can expect to happen next?

A recent research report on ICT implementation and its use by teachers shows the kinds of outcomes that can be expected as a result of developing expertise in ICT. If you still needed any encouragement to develop a vision and make a plan then these outcomes may convince you. They were:

- As technology was embedded, schools' national test outcomes improved beyond expectations.

- Effective use of presentation technologies led to greater interaction between teachers and learners.

- Effective use of ICT personalised learning by enabling greater learner choice within the curriculum, improved assessment for learning and more learner-directed teaching.

- Technology facilitated more effective assessment for learning by making it easier for learners to be more involved in target-setting and for teachers to give individualised feedback. (Somekh, 2007)

ICT takes time to develop within a department but saves time in the long run. As we have seen, routine use of ICT enables teachers to share resources and to more easily save, re-cycle or develop resources from year to year or class to class, therefore saving time. The huge potential of ICT for interesting, engaging and involving the pupils will be sufficient reason for most teachers to want to develop their expertise. Some barriers, such as reliability and access to hardware, will need to be overcome before teachers can be expected to spend their precious time developing their use of ICT resources. Most subject leaders will find that once such barriers begin to be surmounted, teachers are willing to share existing expertise and develop more, in order to reap the benefits enjoyed by e-mature departments.

Throughout this chapter the focus has been on how mathematics teachers might develop their use of ICT within and outside their lessons to support pupils' understanding in and enthusiasm for mathematics. You should now have a wider background on the issues that are relevant in order for you to develop a vision of ICT use in mathematics – and this will be further informed by the next chapter in this book on pupils' use of ICT, and other chapters in this book for example Chapter 8, where ICT has a role. In addition, you should now have plans of how you might achieve this vision so that your pupils will benefit from their mathematics teachers' enhanced use of ICT.

References

Becta (2009) Self-review framework. Becta Schools, available at *http://schools.becta.org.uk/index.php?section=srf&rid=11966* accessed on 30th July 2009.

Becta (2008) Harnessing Technology: Next Generation Learning 2008-14. Becta: A summary available at: *http://schools.becta.org.uk/index.php?section=lv&&catcode=ss_lv_str_gov_03&rid=15463*.

Cordingley P, Bell M, Thomason S, Firth A (2005) The impact of collaborative continuing professional development (CPD) on classroom teaching and learning. Review: How do collaborative and sustained CPD and sustained but not collaborative CPD affect teaching and learning? In: *Research Evidence in Education Library*. London: EPPI-Centre, Social Science Research Unit, Institute of Education, University of London.

Cox, M.J. (1999) Motivating pupils through the use of ICT. in Leask, M. & Pachler, N. (Eds.) *Learning to Teach using ICT in the Secondary School*. London: Routledge.

Dubin, P. (1962) *Human Relations in Administration*. Englewood Cliffs, NJ.: Prentice Hall.

General Teaching Council for England (GTC) (2008). Interactive teaching and interactive whiteboards. Available at: *http://www.gtce.org.uk/research/romtopics/rom_curriculum/interactive_whiteboards_sep08/*.

Gobbo, C., & Girardi M., (2001) Teachers' beliefs and integration of information and communications technology in Italian schools. *Technology, Pedagogy and Education*, Vol. 10 Issues 1 and 2.

Hiebert, J., Carpenter, T. P., Fennema, E., Fuson, K.C., Wearne, D., Murray, H., Human, P., & Olivier, A. (1997). *Making sense: Teaching and learning mathematics with understanding*. Portsmouth, NH.: Heinemann.

Johnston-Wilder, S. & Mason, J. (2005) *Developing thinking in geometry*. London: Sage Publications.

Johnston-Wilder, S. and Pimm, D. (2005) *Teaching Secondary Mathematics with ICT*. Maidenhead, Berks: Open University Press

Miller, D., and Glover, D. (2008) Interactive whiteboard: Research Literature website found at *http://www.iwbmaths.co.uk/Research/index.html*.

Miller, D.J., Glover, D., & Averis, D. (2008). Enabling enhanced mathematics teaching with interactive whiteboards: Final Report for the National Centre for Excellence in the Teaching of Mathematics. *http://www.keele.ac.uk/depts/ed/iaw/docs/ncetmreport/ncetmreport.pdf*

Mumtaz, S. (2000). Factors affecting teachers' use of information and communications technology: a review of the literature. *Journal of Information Technology for Teacher Education*, 9(3).

National Centre for the Excellence in the Teaching of Mathematics, (2008) Departmental workshop'. Available at *http://www.ncetm.org.uk/Default.aspx?page=13&module=res&mode=100&resid=10848*

Ofsted. (2008) Mathematics: Understanding the score. London: HMSO. Available at: *http://www.ofsted.gov.uk/content/download/7137/73098/file/Mathematics%20-%20understanding%20the%20score.pdf*

Piggott, J. (2006). *An investigation into the nature of mathematical enrichment: a case study of implementation.* Thesis submitted for Doctor in Education, Institute of Education, University of London.

Preston, C., Cox, M. & Cox, K. (2000). *Teachers as Innovators: An evaluation of the Motivation of Teachers to use Information and Communications Technologies.* South Croydon: MirandaNet.

Somekh, B., Underwood, J., Convery, A., Dillon, G., Jarvis, J., Lewin, C., Mavers, D., Saxon, D., Sing, S., Steadman, S., Twining, P., Woodrow, W. (2007) Evaluation of the ICT Test Bed project: Final Report. Becta. Available at:

http://www.evaluation.icttestbed.org.uk/files/test_bed_evaluation_report_2006.pdf

TDA *http://www.tda.gov.uk/teachers/professionalstandards/standards/knowledgeunderstanding/litnumict/qts.aspx* Accessed on 1.2.09

Watson A. and Mason, J. (1998) *Questions and Prompts for Mathematical Thinking.* Derby: Association of Teachers of Mathematics

11. USING ICT TO ENHANCE PROFESSIONAL PRACTICE

Appendix 1

Idea/ software/ equipment	Example	Urgent/ 1 year/ 5 year/ never	All, some or few	Use within department	Action Needed
Word processor	Word Open office			Reports Personal use Resource creation	
Spreadsheets	Excel Open office			Data sources and analysis	
Communication software	Outlook Thunderbird Skype			e-mail within department and teacher-pupil, pupil-teacher	
Research Tools	Internet Explorer Firefox Google Yahoo			Investigations History of Maths	
Interactive whiteboard	Prometheus Smartboard				
Graphing software	Autograph Sketchpad				
Dynamic Geometry Software	Cabri Geogebra				
Videos	You Tube Teacher TV				
Video/ still cameras				Pupil use to explore concepts	
Editing software	Paint shop				
Grid Algebra					
Educational packages	Bowland Maths				

Appendix 1 (*continued*)

Images	Google Earth				
Mind mapping software	Mindmap				
Commercial mathematics packages	My Maths				
CAD packages	Autocad				
Graphic Calculators					

12
USING ICT TO ENHANCE LEARNING IN MATHEMATICS

Sue Johnston-Wilder

This chapter is placed last because it is perhaps the hardest. It is about helping you gain a vision for enhancing pupils' learning with ICT, a vision that will lead to change: a change in the way that lessons are constructed, a change in the way that pupils are expected to learn and a change in the role that a teacher is expected to take in the classroom. Since so many changes may be needed to gain fully from ICT, it is no wonder that effective pupil use of ICT is rare in mathematics lessons (Ofsted 2008). This chapter is about what you can do within the constraints under which many departments work to get the best out of ICT, unlocking its potential as a tool for your pupils, a tool with which to think and to learn.

Research has established that ICT, in the hands of pupils, has the potential to make an important difference to their learning of mathematics. Some of the reasons for schools not tapping into that potential are outside the gift of the department. However, much can be done by a determined, inspired department in which teachers have a clear vision of the possibilities and a realistic timeline. Particular opportunities for development often arise through those many teachers who have recently undertaken in-service training in using ICT, from the many NQTs who bring experience of recent developments on PGCE courses or from teachers who have attended mathematics subject knowledge courses that include learning with ICT. Such teachers may have been through a transforming experience, seeing what ICT can do in the hands of learners, and therefore bring to departments a willingness to wrestle with the bigger issues of how to incorporate that vision into departmental and school-level planning and policy.

Teachers need to learn to act and think differently because pupils learn differently using computers. This is perhaps the most difficult aspect of the use of ICT for teachers. Teachers need opportunities to develop an understanding of what the new learning opportunities look like before they can identify the changes in classroom practice that are needed to access these opportunities. Later in the chapter, you will consider in some detail six learning entitlements for pupils that are made possible when using ICT to learn mathematics. This leads to the crucial purpose of this chapter, which is to enable you to envision what learning with ICT might look like in your classroom and in your department, so that you can begin to identify the necessary changes in practice.

Inevitably, there will be some barriers to change, in particular, teachers' lack of experience, the confidence that such experience brings and the lack of suitable resources. Chapter 11 will have helped you to identify how you can begin to overcome these barriers with other teachers. In this chapter, I focus on the pupils' use of ICT and the difference that ICT can make to their learning 'in their hands'. However, pupils can also present their own barriers. If your pupils are unused to exploring and trying ideas out as part of their mathematical learning, then they may find some aspects of using ICT to learn difficult. It will take some explanation and experimentation before pupils rediscover their willingness to explore, make sense and learn.

Ultimately, making change in pedagogical practice at this level takes time, and perhaps the time required to make these changes is one of the factors that mitigates most against teachers making good and effective use of ICT. You may need to plan for change over a period of between 3 and 5 years as you seek to develop the necessary expertise amongst the teachers in your department and the pupils you teach, to enable all of them to work effectively with packages such as Autograph or dynamic geometry software.

'IT works!'

'IT works!' is the title of a 1994 report by NCET, the pre-cursor to Becta, about the evidence of the impact of ICT on learning. The new mathematics curriculum (QCA 2008b), produced and published in England for Key Stage 3, ages 11-14, also reflects the experience that ICT works. One intention of the new curriculum was to place the learning of subjects, including mathematics, in the context of the whole learning experience, and to make time for teachers and learners to focus on developing learning skills. An important part of this is to develop the functional skills and confidence required to use ICT when working on everyday tasks and problems. But ICT also provides learning experiences that are effective in developing ways of thinking and talking about mathematics and in promoting Personal Learning and Thinking Skills (PLTS). The new KS3 curriculum expects mathematics departments to provide pupils with a range of curriculum opportunities 'that are integral to their learning and enhance their engagement with the concepts, processes and content of the subject' including:

> (g) become familiar with a range of resources, including ICT, so that they can select appropriately

Curriculum developments for older pupils reflect similar beliefs that ICT works in the hands of learners. The new AS 'Use of Mathematics' (QCDA 2009) incorporates an expectation that learners will use the opportunities afforded by ICT, both throughout their course and in its assessment, to build their understanding of advanced mathematical skills, and concepts such as algebra and calculus. This is also true for diplomas (QCA 2008a), where the approach to learning mathematics is that mathematical skills need to be applied to solving problems in context and that ICT is an essential tool for doing so.

However, the recent history of the use of ICT in education in schools suggests that simply requiring that these curriculum opportunities are made available to learners may not be enough. If we look at the NCET (1994) report 'IT Works!', we can see that, although ICT has changed over the years, many of the issues remain the same and, if anything, are now more pertinent as the education agenda in England moves [back] towards a consideration of personalised learning and AfL and the new mathematics curriculum (QCA 2008b).

The evidenced claims in 1994 were that use of IT resulted in:

- flexibility to meet individual needs
- more enthusiasm and confidence, safe and non-threatening
- encouragement for those who otherwise do not enjoy or worse fail
- reduction in the risk of failure
- encouragement of reflection and modification of responses
- a shift in focus from technique to interpretation
- access to information
- access to ideas through alternative presentations
- interactivity, motivation, stimulation
- trying out ideas, risk-taking, development of autonomy and mathematical resilience, power, to try out different ideas, to take risks
- different approaches and different kinds of thought
- a special role helping pupils with SEN to achieve more
- a review of teaching approach and understanding of learning.

The same report identified that teachers need to be able to design meaningful tasks in the context of ICT, requiring pupils to work more independently of teachers in the classroom, both individually and in groups. In particular, teachers need to recognise when to intervene and when to allow pupils to continue. In order to develop the necessary skills and to recognise the opportunities afforded by the new technology, the report focussed on the teachers' need for access to the ICT. Though the focus in 1994 was on teachers requiring access to hardware, the argument still applies today in the context of both hardware and software. The purpose of looking at the history in this way is to remind ourselves that change takes time, and is not easy, and that we need to set realistic goals which recognise the time and effort that will be needed to implement the desired change.

Although the number of computers available has increased over the years and pupil access has increased (at least in theory), pupils' use of ICT in learning mathematics appears to have decreased since 2002. Ofsted writes:

> Several years ago, inspection evidence showed that most pupils had some opportunities to use ICT as a tool to solve or explore mathematical problems (Ofsted 2001; Ofsted 2002). This is no longer the case; mathematics makes a relatively limited contribution to developing pupils' ICT skills. Moreover, despite technological advances, the potential of ICT to enhance the learning of mathematics is too rarely realised. (Ofsted 2008, para 54).

Ofsted also noted that the reduction in use of graphic calculators in the early 2000s has resulted in teachers 'missing opportunities to exploit the power of hand-held technology in promoting students' understanding' (Ofsted 2008, para 59).

The failure to take up and develop the use of ICT as a tool for learning seems to be a problem peculiar to mathematics; Becta noted that ICT is used less in mathematics than in many other subject areas. 'This was also noted in ImpaCT2 (Harrison et al 2002), where 67 per cent of pupils at KS3 never or hardly ever used ICT in mathematics, although at KS4 the figure was over 80 per cent' (Becta 2006, p 32).

Consideration of the possibilities for promoting 'Deep Learning' through the appropriate use of ICT leads to an important additional insight regarding the opportunities afforded in the new curriculum. Sims (2006) offers a helpful working definition: 'Deep learning is secured when, through personalisation, the conditions for student learning are transformed.' Implicit to the concept of deep learning is that learning must be an active process, where learners search for patterns and principles while using evidence and logic (Entwistle 2000). As we will see, good ICT use is about allowing all pupils to reach for understanding and engage in true 'deep', relational learning.

What stops IT working with pupils?

Let us be honest – there are many reasons why mathematics teachers do not allow pupils to use technology as a tool in the classroom or seek to foster its use in pupils' homes. Here are some reasons that teachers give and that researchers find:

Computers do not fit into the normal routine/lack of time: The computer adds complexity – the mathematics can get lost in the classroom discourse as teachers and some pupils struggle to master the technology. Computer based activities may not easily fit into a teacher's normal routine (Monaghan 2004). As a result, incorporating ICT means that the planning often takes longer; furthermore, using ICT can cause lessons to stray from the lesson plan, as unexpected things happen. Also, as Monaghan noted, in preparing lessons, teachers 'spent abnormally high amounts of time selecting or designing suitable tasks for technology-based lessons' (2004, p 347)

ICT is not assessed: In terms of assessment of mathematics, it was alarming to me when a senior examiner of A level mathematics said 'pupils don't think when they have technology in their hand' and concluded that therefore ICT should not be allowed in examinations. ICT, used effectively, has been shown to be a tool that clearly supports mathematical thinking, although the tasks have to be appropriate and the pupils well prepared. Thinking with ICT might be further encouraged with increased use of assessment. However, proposed changes to assessment mean that this barrier may begin to reduce.

Lack of vision: A serious barrier to the effective use of ICT is the teachers' lack of vision and understanding of what ICT can offer as tool to express thinking. Teachers lack experience of learning with ICT – they are unconsciously incompetent (Dubin 1962); that is, they do not know what they do not know.

Most of the successes I have seen in persuading teachers to try out ICT in their teaching have arisen from opportunities they have had to learn mathematics with ICT first.

The change in teachers' roles: When using ICT effectively the teacher's facilitator role is increased. One teacher, Kate Graham, wrote, having recently experienced ICT as a learner, 'The potential of digital technologies to undermine accepted norms, as students' practice pushes at the boundaries of what constitutes valid mathematics, does not appear to have been recognised until recently.'

Lack of confidence: Many teachers simply lack confidence in using ICT. An apparently simple problem, such as a circle appearing elliptical on a poorly calibrated screen, can cause them to give up suddenly and revert to teaching in ways that they are more comfortable with. Building this confidence can take a long time but it is worth persevering.

The pupils are more at ease with ICT than their teachers: This can be very off-putting for teachers. Many pupils today are more literate about some aspects of computers than their teachers and the implications for CPD are significant. Teachers may need to discuss how they maintain their role of being 'in charge in the classroom', while acknowledging, and possibly learning to draw upon, pupils' greater facility with ICT.

Teaching pupils to use tools is more complex than was previously thought: The process of an artefact becoming a functioning mathematical tool in the hand of a pupil involves the pupil internalising its possibilities and constraints, amongst other things. This process is called instrumenting by some researchers (Ruthven 2003). Once instrumenting has happened, the pupil is more able to reflect on the task that involves the ICT and to do the mathematical thinking that will be required. Once again the issue of time is raised; it appears that pupils need to learn to use the ICT before they can learn any mathematics. However, by using carefully crafted tasks, which teachers need to learn to access or to create as part of a team, teachers can reveal the possibilities of the ICT tool gradually, while the pupils are still learning mathematics. Once pupils have learned about some of the possibilities and constraints of the ICT, the potential for mathematical thinking and learning will begin to emerge in practice and the results will be worth the time spent.

Barriers to change

Ofsted noted (Ofsted 2008, para 56) two main problems that prevented ICT from being used to enhance lessons. They were 'lack of ICT resources and weaknesses in identifying suitable activities at key points in schemes of work'. Using ICT tools can be a form of expression and development of thinking, but is usually not seen as such by teachers of mathematics. Ofsted noted that in mathematics lessons:

> The fundamental issue for teachers is how better to develop pupils' mathematical understanding. Too often, pupils are expected to remember methods, rules and facts without grasping the underpinning concepts, making connections with earlier learning and other topics, and making sense of the mathematics so that they can use it independently. The nature

of teaching and assessment, as well as the interpretation of the mathematics curriculum, often combine to leave pupils ill equipped to use and apply mathematics. Pupils rarely investigate open-ended problems which might offer them opportunities to choose which approach to adopt or to reason and generalise. Most lessons do not emphasise mathematical talk enough; as a result, pupils struggle to express and develop their thinking. ... The majority of pupils had too few opportunities to use and apply mathematics, to make connections across different areas of the subject, to extend their reasoning or to use ICT. (Ofsted 2008)

One place in which Ofsted noted an increase of ICT use by pupils, both in school and at home, is in the use of individual online help. Many schools have bought into commercial packages that can be accessed online, assessed by the package and the results communicated to teachers. However, Ofsted comments that 'the benefit is often short lived. Few programs have conceptual explanations or demonstrations and most examples practised immediately before the self-assessment are similar to those in the assessment itself'. (Ofsted 2008, para 60)

In summary, almost all of the barriers to the use of ICT come down to time. There is a lack of realistic awareness of how long it takes teachers to become fully developed in use of ICT and how much time is needed for CPD and opportunities to experiment. When a 3 – 5 year planning model is suggested it usually causes surprise, but this is what will be needed to move from a department that rarely uses ICT to one that is using ICT as an effective tool to help pupils learn mathematics.

What enables teachers to use ICT with pupils?

There are many ways of enabling teachers to use ICT with pupils. One way is to offer a vision of what that use will look like; such a vision will be presented later in this chapter. A further and important enabler is effective CPD. For example, the Teaching Advanced Mathematics (TAM) course run jointly between MEI and four universities (MEI 2008) supports teachers in learning mathematics with ICT and then teaching with ICT; participating teachers found that they were able to use ICT with their classes and, in a session, they noted the following learning gains:

- A developing conviction of a result prior to proof
- That it was easier to investigate
- The feedback given by ICT helped their pupils develop autonomy
- The pupils were given help with visualising
- Interactivity increased
- More discussion was generated
- Lessons became more dynamic
- The pupils used multiple representations
- The number of cases explored increased

- Pupils were required to predict, then given rapid feedback
- Self-assessment was facilitated
- Speed of production increased
- Interactive Whiteboards were used to promote community of learners working with misconceptions
- Pupils became presenters
- Videos and cameras were used to articulate mathematical thinking.

These are important developments in terms of pupil motivation as well as learning. Teachers need also to know how to introduce the more powerful tools to pupils gradually, with carefully crafted tasks; this involves teachers accessing existing resources which they may not yet know about or working together as part of a team, to develop resources that reveal the possibilities of the ICT tool gradually, while the pupils still learn mathematics.

How can you as subject leader allow your teachers to experience learning with ICT so that they begin to understand what a powerful tool it can be?

A model for learning mathematics with ICT

This section considers the pedagogy of teaching and learning with ICT. As we have seen, there is a danger of teachers imposing their familiar pedagogic thinking when using ICT. To help teachers to understand what they are looking for as they change their practice, first NCET and now Becta have worked with the subject associations to develop a model of pupil entitlement to describe what may realistically be expected of pupils learning differently because they have access to ICT:

The model describes what pupils do when using ICT that they do not do to such a great extent without ICT. There are six ingredients to the model:

- learning from feedback;
- observing patterns;
- seeing connections;
- working with dynamic images;
- exploring data;
- teaching the computer.

    Source: Becta 2009

The above are all ingredients which involve pupils being active – this relates closely to current thinking about deep learning. Deep learning is about pupils being actively engaged in their own learning, searching for, observing and working to generate patterns and understand mathematical principles, as required by the new National Curriculum. Compare this with the quote from Entwistle (2000):

> In the deep approach, the intention to extract meaning produces active learning processes that involve relating ideas and looking for patterns and

principles on the one hand (a holist strategy ...), and using evidence and examining the logic of the argument on the other (serialist). (page 4)

The following list gives more detail about the above entitlements.

1. Learning from feedback

Computers often provides fast and reliable feedback, which is non-judgemental and impartial. This can encourage pupils to make their own conjectures and to test out and modify their ideas.

2. Observing patterns

The speed of computers and calculators enables pupils to produce many examples when exploring mathematical problems. This supports their observation of patterns and the making and justifying of generalisations.

3. Seeing connections

Computers enable formulae, tables of numbers and graphs to be linked readily. Changing one representation and seeing changes in the others helps pupils to understand the connections between them.

4. Working with dynamic images

Pupils can use computers to manipulate diagrams dynamically. This encourages them to visualise the geometry as they generate their own mental images.

5. Exploring data

Computers enable pupils to work with real data, which can be represented in a variety of ways. This supports interpretation and analysis.

6. Teaching the computer

When pupils design an algorithm (a set of instructions) to make a computer achieve a particular result, they are compelled to express their commands unambiguously and in the correct order; they make their thinking explicit as they refine their ideas.

Source: Becta 2009

When comparing the entitlements with the *deep learning* of Entwistle, it is interesting to note that the notion of pattern-seeking features explicitly as one of the six entitlements. Further, pupils work actively in all six entitlements.

To this list, one might add new possibilities to articulate mathematics, using ICT to teach or communicate mathematics to others – for example, by making a video – but the focus in the Becta model is why the thinking is different, and the possibility of changing the pupils' experience in a transformative way, because the data the pupil has to think with is different.

It is important now that you should gain an understanding of these entitlements, so that you can envision what they look like in practice, identifying the changes that you and the teachers in your department may have to make, and consider how to overcome barriers to introducing them in class. To help you, I have included a copy of the entitlements with examples in Appendix 1 – and below I have added an example of how they appear when using a piece of ATM software called Grid Algebra. But first, imagine a lesson on definitions and properties. Imagine the pupils are working on a screen which has 5 shapes. The pupils are invited to move the shapes by dragging the vertices. Initially the shapes all look as if they are squares, but as the pupils move them around, they change in different way. One stays a square, although it can change size, but it transpires the others are a rhombus, a rectangle, a kite and a cyclic quadrilateral; pupils discover the constraints on the shapes by exploring possible movements – you can see examples on the website MathsNet (*www.mathsnet.net/dynamic/index.html*).

Pupils are thinking while they are manipulating these dynamic images and so they are better prepared to discuss definitions of quadrilaterals on the basis of their shared experience. The pupils can then be invited to construct one of the objects; the mathematics involved might include perpendicular and parallel lines, or transformation geometry, depending on how the teacher has set up the task, and the pupil would be able to assess their work by the way the resulting shape behaved when it was dragged about.

Grid Algebra as an example

Here we will examine the way that the 6 entitlements above are realised as pupils use Grid Algebra as a learning tool. Grid Algebra is based on the notion of journeys in the multiplication grid. In Grid Algebra, the feedback is a consequence of what you drag and where you drag it.

The following screen shot shows a multiplication grid in which only the rows have been pre-determined; an x has been dragged onto the grid.

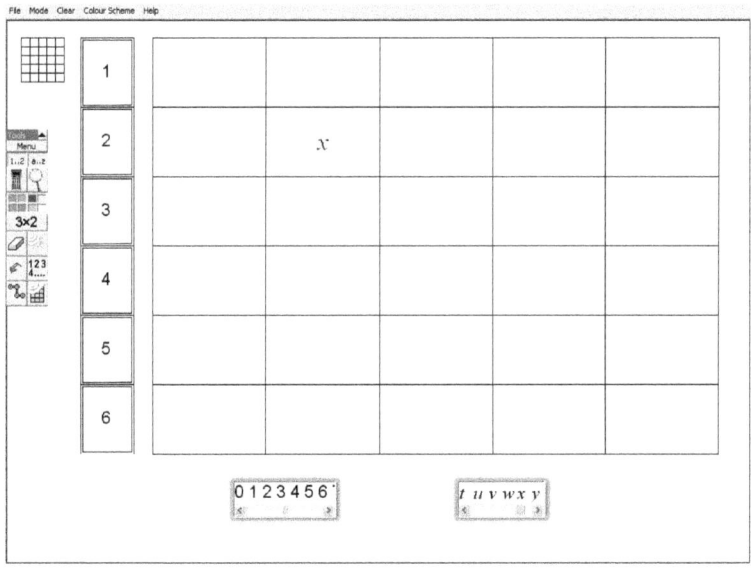

All the pupils can know about x from the grid is that it is a number in the 2 times table. If x is dragged horizontally, 2 is added for every cell it moves to the right and subtracted each time it moves to the left. If x is dragged vertically, it is multiplied and divided, in a way appropriate to which row of the multiplication table is involved.

1		$\frac{x}{2}$			
2	$x-2$	x		$x+4$	
3					
4		$2x$			
5					
6					

Numbers can be added into the grid to set up equations. For example, any multiple of 3 could be dragged into the shaded box.

Equivalent expressions are the outcome of equivalent journeys. Thus the pupil can take x to the box with the darker outline in the screen below either via $4x$ or via $x+2$ or via $x+3$.

1		x		
2	$\frac{4x+8}{2}-6$			$\frac{4x+8}{2}$
3				
4		$4x$		$4x+8$
5				
6	$3\left(\frac{4x+8}{2}-6\right)$			

$4x+8 = 4(x+2)$
$ = 4(x+3)-4$

12. USING ICT TO ENHANCE LEARNING IN MATHEMATICS

The nature of the **feedback** in this software is that, when the pupil makes a move, the software represents the move algebraically. The pupil can make predictions and test them out and there is a tendency for the pupil to become better at making predictions as they gain experience with the tool. If given time to explore, the pupil begins to see **patterns** from the beginning (if you move to the right in the 3 row, one step adds 3, two steps add 6 and so on), but the level of pattern development extends into algebraic notion, and from experience thus far, makes the algebra amore accessible (see Lugalia 2008). The pupil sees **connections** between the kinaesthetic movement and the algebraic representation. The images are **dynamic** in that the pupil can change the elements on screen and observe the consequences. In general, '**exploring data**' is about data in the traditional sense, but here the data are the elements generated by the pupil, which the pupil makes sense of as they generate more cases to think with. The software comes with many such screens built in, such as this one in which the pupil would be expected to answer $b-3$.

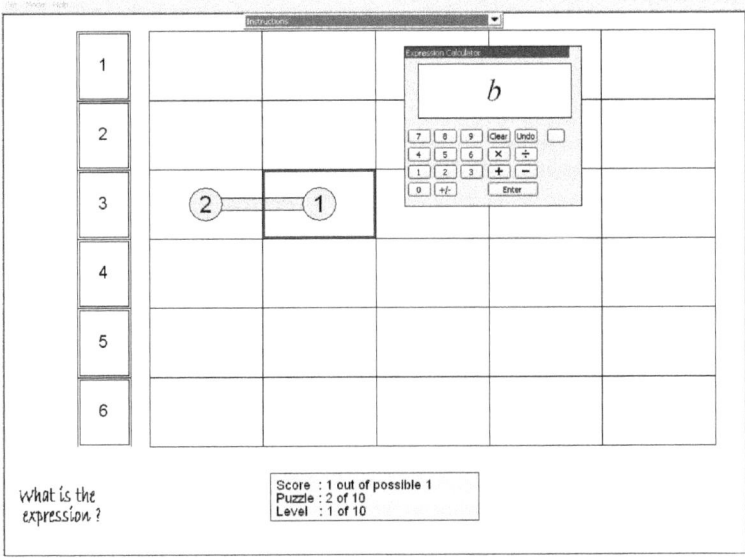

It is worth noting here that the package that comes with Grid Algebra offers teachers pre-written, carefully crafted tasks, and lesson plans that help the teacher enable the pupils to stay with a piece of curriculum mathematics while learning about the full potential of the tool.

ICT offers an environment for exploration that is usually far more visual and dynamic than the traditional learning environments to which the learner is exposed. This sometimes creates opportunities for pupils who otherwise struggle to do well. Von Glasersfeld said that, 'visual feedback is a far more powerful didactic tool than instructions that refer to details of the action which, normally, are dimly or not at all perceived by the actor himself' (von Glasersfeld 1983, p 11). ICT offers learners the chance to explore and play with images and, if the environment of this exploration is carefully chosen, as it has been in Grid Algebra, pupils will be required to think mathematically due to the nature of their exploration or 'play'.

There are many similar learning environments for learning, some using open software tools and some more restricted, often known as applets (with the intended meaning of small applications – see the National Library of Virtual Manipulatives *nlvm.usu.edu/* and the Entering into Symbols project *www.itee.uq.edu.au/~rduke/eis.html* for some examples.) Think of a pupil struggling to understand pie charts or bar charts and then think of exposing that pupil to Furbles (*www.furbles.co.uk*) where creatures can be created by deciding the parameters. The creatures play hide-and-seek in pie charts and bar charts and pupils will play for hours in this environment and gain a very different experience of statistical diagrams on which to build their future understanding.

What pupils need and therefore what teachers have to do!

> We need to improve pupils' use of ICT as a tool for learning mathematics. (Ofsted 2008)

'The presence of computers goes beyond first impact when it alters the nature of the learning process; for example, if it shifts the balance between the transfer of knowledge to students and the production of knowledge by students.' (Harel et al 1991). This major change in classroom dynamics is essential to allow the harnessing of the full power of ICT to help pupils develop understanding.

Through experience of working on tasks using ICT, pupils can learn to use aspects of the ICT as tools to support their thinking. As they do so, they can develop mental tools to think with, which emulate the images presented in the ICT tools and which have the potential to help make mathematical ideas accessible. Pupils need time to work with these new tools, using them to work on solving mathematical problems, and to develop different understandings of the mathematics they are learning. In order to enable them to have appropriate opportunities to develop and exercise the mental tools promoted by the use of ICT, the pupils need teachers who understand what it is to think with ICT tools, and tasks that take account of the opportunities offered by the ICT.

Simply introducing technology into the classroom does not, in itself, 'radically improve the learning and teaching' (Hoyles et al 2004, p 311). Pupils need to learn to use the tools and learn to think with the tools. Teachers will have to take on a new role, because, as discussed previously there is another source of feedback in the class. As Monaghan's (2004) study found, teacher and pupils can work more in collaboration, with less time taken up by 'whole class exposition' and an increased quality of task-based interactions.

The teacher becomes the person who knows what the technology adds to the mathematical thinking, the task setter and then the facilitator. The teacher learns when to intervene and when to give pupils time to think and work with the software. The teacher remains the mathematical expert but often the pupils become more expert in 'driving the software'.

In order to act in this way, the teacher must understand what it means to learn with ICT tools. Many teachers only really understand when they have had the chance to be a learner using ICT tools to think with. An intending teacher on a pre-PGCE mathematics subject knowledge course said to me: 'I can't see the point of the examples I have seen of pupils using ICT in mathematics classes and yet my own learning has been transformed on this course by using Autograph.' For this person, their personal experience of working with Autograph has the potential to provide them with insight into learning mathematics with ICT.

In terms of setting tasks, the teacher needs to consider carefully the role of ICT and the relationship between the technical and conceptual demands of the task in which ICT is used. Both the design of the task and the characteristics of the software the teacher makes available to the pupil afford and constrain the nature of the mathematical expression possible and how mathematical meaning is conveyed (Hoyles et al 2004). For example, consider the difference for the learner between articulating mathematics using a spreadsheet such as Excel and graphing software such as Autograph. One starts with data and relationships between cells; it helps to demonstrate the relationship between input and output at the level of the cell. The other uses notation similar to the function notation of school mathematics. Pupils need to learn to work with both.

The design of tasks, and the way in which they use the characteristics of the tools, is critical (Hoyles et al 2004). At best, ICT-based lessons provide a natural platform for the development, articulation and understanding of mathematical concepts. Sometimes the underlying mathematics may be altered by the software; for example, when working on angles in a polygon using Logo, the focus of attention turns to the outer angle of the polygon as the turtle moves around the shape. Pupils learn the 'total turtle trip theorem' that the total turn is $360°$, whereas other ICT tools may encourage a focus on the triangles within a polygon.

In terms of lesson planning, a key challenge for the teacher is to plan lessons in which pupils use technology to facilitate the development of their mathematical knowledge without becoming stuck with technical barriers. This involves the teacher knowing just enough about the software to recognise the learning opportunities, and developing enough confidence to call upon pupils' expertise in the software to help with technicalities. Teachers using ICT are effective when confident and comfortable with technology 'as an enabling addition to their pedagogical armoury'. (Bramald and Higgins 1999, p.97)

So, in an ideal world, teachers need time for:

- personal use,
- beginning use with pupils,
- more considered use with pupils;
- innovation.

Achieving this takes planning and support. Teachers will gradually learn to think and act differently. This can feel risky when teachers are under pressure. They can be supported through coaching (Ch 6) and be persuaded to experiment through a departmental focus on action research (Ch 7).

Because of the time that is needed for teachers to become confident in using one item of ICT with their pupils, it is unreasonable for teachers to be asked to become familiar with many pieces of software or other resources at the same time. Consequently, if you wish to introduce several ICT based mathematical learning tools, it is essential to plan for this over an extended period. This fits with the notion of the development of a 5 year plan to achieve a vision of a department that uses ICT effectively to enable pupils to learn mathematics.

Developing Expertise

Becta takes the view that all teachers must develop the skills and capabilities they need to use technology to meet the needs of learners and understand how technology supports personalised approaches to learning. Therefore Becta aims to provide teachers with access to 'as good a range and quality of support, tools and resources as possible, in the same way that these things are available to other professions, to help enhance teachers' status and build professional expertise'. (Becta 2008b, p 11)

The Subject Leader's role in developing this expertise is to:

- work to motivate all staff to develop skills in the use of ICT
- cultivate a culture of continuous development of ICT skills
- make sure that all teachers in the department can access a wide range of multimedia and digital resources
- work to enable ICT to be used in a wide range of learning spaces in the school and with variety of different group sizes
- encourage teachers in the department to create, use, efficiently store and adapt teaching resources
- support teachers in planning work for and monitoring the progress of groups and individuals.

Although all the above ideas are important, it is planning the continuous development of ICT skills that will lead to all the other parts of the role beginning to happen.

Department audit of learning with ICT

All development of expertise starts with an audit. There are many parts to this audit:

- What resources are already available in the department?
- What tools do you want to be available to your pupils?
- What do your teachers need to do to be able to use ICT effectively with your pupils?
- What skills do the pupils need to develop to be able to use ICT effectively?

What resources are already available in the department?

In order to make a plan for improving the pupils' use of ICT in the mathematics department, the first step will be to really know what is already available. So a subject leader's first step will be to review all the resources that are available to be used by the mathematics department. To do this fully, you will need to document everything, including calculators, especially graphic calculators. You might find sample software that has been sent to the school for review over the years. You may find many resources that can be used to make decisions for future purchases. Then look at the list of programmes centrally available on your school's system. Ask yourself which can be used for increasing mathematical learning?

What tools do you want to be available to your pupils?
Having completed the audit above, you will be in a position to identify any gaps and to consider how you will find the budget to fill those gaps. The following table of suggested resources will help you to identify what you already have access to and therefore where there may be gaps in your provision.

Source	Resource	Purpose
Bowland mathematics (free)	Professional development materials Case study materials for use with pupils	INSET resource Tasks that use ICT to support mathematical learning
Becta	'Hard to teach' topics	Resources to share and discuss with colleagues, about maths teachers using ICT
ATM	'Getting Started with Dynamic Geometry' 'Reaching the Core of AS'	Examples of well-crafted tasks
Autograph website	Autograph resources	Support in using graphing software
OU	Bronze/ Silver/ Gold ICT awards and related materials	Examples of well-crafted tasks
Adrian Oldknow website	Support for importing pictures and working with graphs, importing video clips and working into graphs	Support with using ICT to articulate mathematical thinking
Other Websites	• Mathsnet website • Nrich website • Applets website	Ideas

What do your teachers need to do to be able to use ICT effectively with your pupils?
The first step in answering this question is to consider the current levels of expertise of your staff. If you have read chapter 11 you will have already

thought about this, but this time think specifically about their expertise in facilitating pupils' use of ICT.

Level 1, 'Acquainted'	Level 2, the 'Personal User'	Level 3, the 'Classroom User'	Level 4, the 'Critical User'
represents having met and used the tool enough to know what it is. This is the level assumed in this chapter.	describes individuals who have used the tool to explore some mathematics for themselves and who are aware of some of the processes involved in using with pupils.	describes someone who has ideas for appropriate use of the tool with pupils learning mathematics at school level, and who has had the opportunity to work through and reflect on a variety of tasks designed to explore the power of the tool for enhancing the teaching and learning of mathematics.	refers to someone who feels able to identify some pitfalls and problems that may arise when using the tool with pupils, and who has some knowledge of educational research findings related to the tool.

⟵——————— Developing expertise ———————⟶

If all your staff are currently at Level 1, then you may need to bring in expertise from outside in order to get the use of ICT started with the pupils in your school. However, it is more likely that some of your staff are at each of those levels and therefore the ideas of coaching and mentoring explained in Chapter 6 may be appropriate to enable the expertise in your department to be shared with the less confident teachers. It may also be appropriate to use the principles of action research, as described in Chapter 7, to develop and disseminate skills in using ICT with the pupils.

Ask staff what experience they have and what they would like to develop. Do not forget to include your own skills and knowledge.

- Are they confident in using spreadsheets, Autograph or other graphing software, dynamic geometry packages etc.?
- Are there some ways of using ICT that they know about already, but their skills would need updating before being used in a classroom?

Once you know the answers to the above questions you will have to reflect on:

- Who can share their ideas and knowledge with another teacher or the whole department?

12. USING ICT TO ENHANCE LEARNING IN MATHEMATICS

- Who can or would like to work in a peer-coaching partnership to develop the use of specific software in lessons?
- Who is really keen to use some specific software and would benefit from some outside training?

The answers to these questions will help you begin to make a plan of how to use the existing expertise in your department and whether you need help from outside. Not all teachers need to, or will want to, develop the same expertise at the same time but once expertise is developing you will want the department to share what they know and can do.

When experimenting with a new pedagogical approach of a new piece of software, it is worth thinking about co-teaching. Co-teaching means that two – or more – teachers will plan a lesson or series of lessons together. They may each teach part of the lesson and be both present to answer the pupils' questions, or they may decide that one will teach and the other will observe how the pupils react and the learning that they demonstrate. The lesson will be followed by review and reflection by all of the teachers involved; lessons will be learned, changes will be made and put into practice and gradually a high quality outcome will be achieved.

Developing knowledge together – an example: If using ICT or asking the pupils to work collaboratively is new to some of your department, or if you want to introduce a new piece of software such as dynamic geometry to improve the way that your pupils learn from ICT, you may decide to work together as a department to increase your expertise. There are several resources available online to do this. You might decide to use *Bowland Mathematics PD Module 2* – 'Fostering and Managing Collaborative Work' which is available at *www.bowlandmathematics.org.uk/*. This module will support you as you study how to enable pupils to work together collaboratively using ICT. Other material that you might consider is the National Secondary Strategy material on using group work available from: *www.standards.dfes.gov.uk/secondary/keystage3/downloads/sec_pptl043304u10groupwork.pdf*.

Working together as a department, using resources such as those above, will have several benefits. The teachers will be using ICT to learn for themselves and this, as we have seen, is a powerful way to introduce ICT as a learning environment. The other benefit is that good practice will be shared in a natural way, your teachers will support one another with examples from their own practice and there is a high likelihood that the conversation will continue informally. This is an example of how you may cultivate a culture of continuous development of ICT skills.

What skills do the pupils need to develop to be able to use ICT effectively?
The skills that your pupils will need to develop will depend on the way that your department currently works. If you already expect pupils to explore mathematical ideas, to think mathematically and to articulate the learning that they have developed, then ICT will just be another environment for them to use. However, many pupils may need to learn to work collaboratively and may

need clear ground rules in order to work together to learn. Other pupils may need to learn to explore using more prosaic materials, such as paper and pencil, before they learn how to explore in an ICT-based learning environment.

However, as has been discussed earlier, there are times when pupils will need to learn the technicalities of the ICT environment before they can use it to develop mathematical thinking. There are many ways to make sure this happens using as little time as possible. You might decide to build the use of graphing software, dynamic geometry and spreadsheets into the Year 7 scheme of work, recognising that this will have time implications but that pupils will then be able quickly to settle to tasks involving the use of this software in later years. Another idea is to use older pupils as coaches to help younger pupils develop expertise. This has the advantage of providing many hands to help the younger pupils get to grips with the technicalities of a piece of software. It also will mean that the older pupils will reprise or consolidate their own knowledge and will be ready to take bigger steps in exploring the environment themselves. A certain amount of liaison with the ICT department will be helpful. You might assume that skills such as cutting and pasting screen shots of mathematics specific software into Word is skill that would be learned in ICT, but many heads of mathematics find pupils vary enormously in such skills.

Discussion

Thinking back to the expectations embedded in the NCET (1994) report, and progress since 1994, what is needed now is realistic planning at the level of department, with well-informed subject leaders who are aware of the difficulty of what they are doing, and the rewards.

The TAM teachers (MEI 2008), having used ICT to learn some mathematics, and having acquired an understanding of what ICT added to their learning, brought some issues about using ICT with learners to their next TAM session. They raised concerns about the amount of learner time needed for pupils to learn to drive software such as Autograph/Cabri/Sketchpad/Excel. As CPD providers, we acknowledged that the research says it is hard, discussed Ruthven's article on instrumenting, and discussed the possibility of staged use, including tasks such as the task related to definitions and properties of quadrilaterals described on page 191. We also discussed the teachers' experience that it was harder for teachers of mathematics to access a computer room with a whole class than it used to be, because use of computer rooms across subjects has increased; we considered how mathematics teachers could encourage pupils to use home computers or to access library computers to undertake ICT-based homework tasks.

In summary, you need to plan to:

- work together on mathematics with ICT or send teachers on courses such as TAM to learn mathematics at their own level, so they have a chance to reflect on their own learning with ICT;
- allow the teachers to raise their own issues through the use of an audit relating to the teaching and learning of mathematics with ICT and start

from where they are;

- support teachers to explore research evidence relevant to the previously identified issues and encourage them to explore their own use of ICT through action research and with the structure of a long term plan.

Look at ATM's online journal, MTi, for inspiration, watch the energy involved when pupils work with ICT effectively, whether in mathematics or in other subjects, capture the vision, and take a step towards putting 21st century tools into the hands of your learners. Keep in mind that Ofsted inspectors wish to see innovation and experimentation, and say as much in the many reports about the lack of use of ICT. Tell the world what you and your teachers have tried, in articles for the professional journals, and become a leader beyond your school. Better still, inspire the next generation of pupils to see mathematics as relevant and interesting.

Further reading

Becta (2009) Secondary Mathematics with ICT: A pupil's entitlement to ICT in secondary mathematics. Coventry: Becta. Accessed on 31/08/09.

www.teachernet.gov.uk/_doc/13781/entitlement_sec_mathematics.doc

Clark-Jeavons, A. (2005) *Exciting ICT in Mathematics*. Stafford: Network Educational Press.

Clark-Wilson, A., (2008) *Evaluating TI-Nspire in secondary mathematics classrooms*. Chichester: University of Chichester. Accessed on 31/08/09.

www.chiuni.ac.uk/teachered/documents/Clark-Wilson_2008_TI-Nspire_Final_Report_v6.Dec08.pdf

Deaney, R., Ruthven, K., & Hennessy, S. (2003) 'Pupil perspectives on the contribution of information and communication technology to teaching and learning in the secondary school'. *Research Papers in Education* 18 (2) 141-165. Accessed on 31/08/09. dx.doi.org/10.1080/0267152032000081913

Edwards J and Wright D *Integrating ICT into the Mathematics Classroom*. Derby: Association of Teachers of Mathematics.

Harel, I. & Papert, S. (1991) Situating Constructionism. retrieved November 28th 2006. Accessed on 31/08/09. *www.papert.org/articles/SituatingConstructionism.html*

Of course, the whole book is well worth reading if you can get hold of it.

Hennessy, S., Ruthven, K., & Brindley, S. (2005) 'Teacher perspectives on integrating ICT into subject teaching: Commitment, constraints, caution and change.' *Journal of Curriculum Studies* 37 (2) 155-192. Accessed on 31/08/09. dx.doi.org/10.1080/0022027032000276961

Hoyles, C., Noss, R. & Kent, P. (2004) On the Integration of Digital Technologies into Mathematics Classrooms. *International Journal of Computers for Mathematical Learning.* 9(3), 309-326.

Johnston-Wilder, S. and Pimm, D. (2005) *Teaching Secondary Mathematics with ICT*. Maidenhead, Berks.: Open University Press.

Monaghan, J. (2004) 'Teachers' Activities in Technology-based Mathematics Lessons'. *International Journal of Computers for Mathematical Learning*, 9(3), pp 327-357.

Oldknow A (Ed.) (2004) *ICT and Mathematics: A Guide to Learning and Teaching Mathematics 11-19 Using ICT*. Leicester: Mathematical Association

Taylor R. and Oldknow A. (2004) *Teaching Mathematics Using ICT* (with CD-ROM)

References

Becta (2003) *What the research says about using ICT in Mathematics*. Coventry: Becta.

Becta (2006) *The impact of ICT in schools – a landscape review*. Coventry: Becta.

Becta (2008a) *How Technology supports 14-19 reform: an essential guide*. Coventry: Becta.

Becta (2008b) *Harnessing technology: next generation learning, 2008-14, a summary*. Coventry: Becta.

Becta (2009) *Secondary Mathematics with ICT: A pupil's entitlement to ICT in secondary mathematics*. Coventry: Becta.

Becta (in press) *ICT and Deep Learning 14-19*. Coventry: Becta.

Bramald R, and Higgins, S. (1999) Mathematics, ICT and effective teaching. Making the Difference : *Proceedings of the 22nd annual conference of the Mathematics Education Research Group of Australasia*, J. M. Truran and K. M. Truran (Eds), pp 91-98.

Dubin, P. (1962) *Human Relations in Administration*. Englewood Cliffs, NJ.: Prentice Hall.

Entwistle, N. (2000) 'Promoting deep learning through teaching and assessment: conceptual frameworks and educational contexts'. TLRP Conference, Leicester. Accessed on 31/08/09. *www.leeds.ac.uk/educol/documents/00003220.doc*

Geraniou, E., Mavrikis, M., Hoyles, C. and Noss, R (2008) 'A constructionist approach to mathematical generalisation' in Joubert, M. (Ed.) (2008) *Proceedings of the British Society for Research into Learning Mathematics* 28(2), pp 37-42.

Accessed on 31/08/09. *www.bsrlm.org.uk/IPs/ip28-2/BSRLM-IP-28-2-07.pdf*

Hoyles, C., Noss, R. and Kent, P. (2004) 'On the integration of digital technologies into mathematics classrooms', *International Journal of Computers for Mathematical Learning*, 9 (3), pp 309–326.

Jones. K. (2005) 'Graphing Calculators in the teaching and learning of Mathematics: a research bibliography.' *MicroMath*, 21(2), pp 31-33.

Lugalia M. (2008) 'Using Grid Algebra', *Mathematics Teaching* 214, p 39. Accessed on 31/08/09. *www.atm.org.uk/journal/archive/mt214files/ATM-MT-214-39-39.pdf*

MEI (2008) 'A Gateway to Teaching Advanced Mathematics' Accessed on 31/08/09. www.mei.org.uk/files/pdf/TAM_Report.pdf

Monaghan, J. (2004) 'Teachers' Activities in Technology-based Mathematics Lessons'. *International Journal of Computers for Mathematical Learning*, 9(3), pp 327-357.

NCET (1994) 'IT works!' Accessed on 31/08/09. *web.archive.org/web/19980130203900/www.ncet.org.uk/publications/it-works/*

QCA (2008a) *The Diploma and its pedagogy*. London: QCA.

QCA (2008b) The National Curriculum for England, Key Stages 3 and 4, Mathematics, Accessed on 31/08/09. *http://curriculum.qcda.gov.uk/key-stages-3-and-4/index.aspx*

QCDA (2009) GCE AS use of mathematics, Accessed on 31/08/09. *www.qcda.gov.uk/6903.aspx*

Rodd, M. & Monaghan, J. (2002) 'Graphic Calculator Use in Leeds Schools: fragments of practice.' *Journal of Information Technology in Teacher Education*, 11(1), pp 93-108.

Ruthven, K. (2002) 'Instrumenting mathematical activity: Reflections on key studies of the educational use of computer algebra systems'. *International Journal of Computers for Mathematical Learning* 7(3), 275-291.

Sims, E. (2006) *Deep Learning – 1*. Millbank, London: SSAT.

Von Glasersfeld, E. (1991). *Radical Constructivism in Mathematics Education*. Dordrecht: Kluwer Academic Publishers.

Von Glasersfeld, E. (1983) 'Learning as Constructive Activity' In: J. C. Bergeron & N. Herscovics (Eds) *Proceedings of the 5th Annual Meeting of the North American Group of Psychology in Mathematics Education*, Vol. 1. Montreal: PME-NA.

Appendix

In the seven pages that follow, we reproduce the short form of Becta (2009) Secondary Mathematics with ICT: A pupil's entitlement to ICT in secondary mathematics. Coventry: Becta.

 Secondary Mathematics with ICT: A pupil's entitlement to ICT in secondary mathematics

There are six major opportunities for learners to benefit from the use of ICT in mathematics:

- Learning from feedback
- Observing patterns
- Seeing connections
- Developing visual imagery
- Exploring data
- 'Teaching' the computer.

These opportunities may be developed through a wide range of ICT – standard and graphic calculators, spreadsheets, interactive software on CD or online – as illustrated in the examples below.

Learning from feedback

Feedback is the fundamental way in which ICT supports learning in mathematics. Through feedback learners notice patterns and see connections, and explore, making mistakes and seeing the consequences of their decisions. Other opportunities, including working with dynamic images, exploring data and teaching the computer also support the learner through various forms of feedback. Through ICT resources, feedback is not only quick, but also reliable, non-judgemental and impartial.

National Curriculum Key Processes: Analysing

Pupils should be able to take account of feedback and learn from mistakes.

Using calculators

A basic example of learning from feedback with ICT is pupils adopting an exploratory approach through using trial and improvement to solve equations with calculators or a spreadsheet.

Exploring a microworld

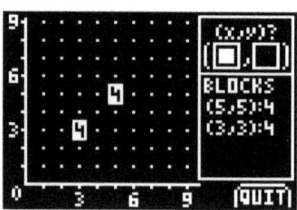

Year 7 students used a small software program (or microworld) running on a handheld device to help develop their problem-solving skills and practise their understanding of co-ordinates. The aim of the program was that they should try to find the rhino hidden in a grid.

This example uses an application for Texas Instruments graphical calculators, a free download from http://www.education.ti.com.

Exploring y=mx + c

A group of Year 10 students had the opportunity to obtain a good understanding of the connections between the equation for a straight line and its graph as they were able to generate many examples through varying the values of the constants and observing the effect on the graph. Using graphical calculators made this activity easily accessible to the students without elaborate preparations by the teacher.

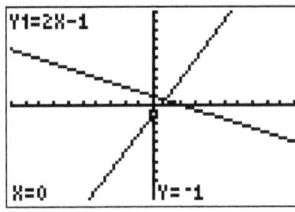

Observing patterns

The speed of computers and calculators enables pupils to produce many examples when exploring mathematical problems. This supports their observation of patterns and the making and justifying of generalisations based on the facility to look at sufficient cases.

National Curriculum Key Processes: Analysing

Pupils should be able to explore the effects of *varying values* and looking for invariance and covariance. *This involves changing values to explore a situation, including the use of ICT.*

National Curriculum Key Processes: Interpreting and evaluating

Pupils should be able to be aware of the strength of empirical *evidence* and appreciate the difference between evidence and proof. *This includes evidence gathered when using ICT to explore cases.*

Generalising about transformations

In a geometric context, Year 7 pupils dragged a point around the screen and watched the movements of a second point. They made conjectures about the geometric relationships between the pairs of points and added geometric construction lines and performed transformations to confirm or refute their thinking.

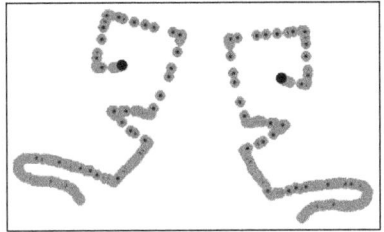
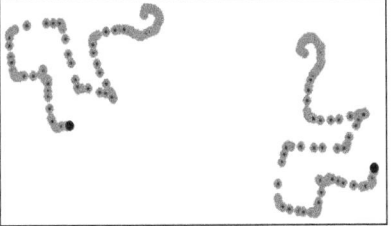

Number grids

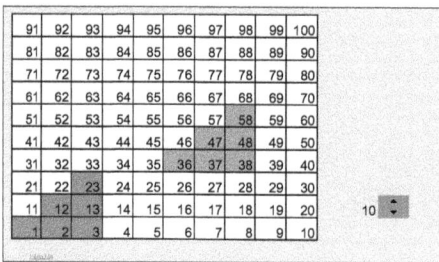

There are various software packages which allow many examples to be explored quickly so that learners can observe patterns in their results. This process will help them to explain what is happening.

Some Year 8 learners used a simple number grid which could be redrawn by increasing or decreasing the counter. They explored the sums of the numbers within the shaded shape for different grids.

This example uses *Number grid*, a free downloadable Excel resource from the Flexcel project.

http://www.maths-it.org.uk/index.php

Seeing connections

The computer enables formulae, tables of numbers and graphs to be linked readily. Changing one representation and seeing changes in the others helps pupils to understand the connections between them. Within a spreadsheet an algebraic formula can be used to generate a table of numbers and this can then be graphed. Alternatively, graphing software or a graphic calculator allows the graph to be drawn directly from the formula and values can be traced. Working through a medium which enables pupils to switch effortlessly between these representations enhances their conceptual development.

National Curriculum Key Processes: Analysing

Pupils should be able to make connections within mathematics. For example, realising that an equation, a table of values and a line on a graph can all represent the same thing or understanding that an intersection between two lines on a graph can represent the solution to a problem.

Connections between formulae, tables of numbers and graphs

Using a handheld device, Year 9 pupils entered data, plotted graphs and matched functions for a given quadratic number sequence based on a growing pattern made from square tiles.

This example, which uses the TI-Nspire handheld is included in the Teachers' TV programme *Hard to Teach – Secondary Maths Using ICT*. (http://www.teachers.tv/video/29853)

Progression idea

Year 10 pupils made explicit links between a trial and improvement strategy to find the roots of a quadratic equation alongside the graphical representation of this by plotting a scattergraph of their trials and seeing how the points got closer to the x-axis.

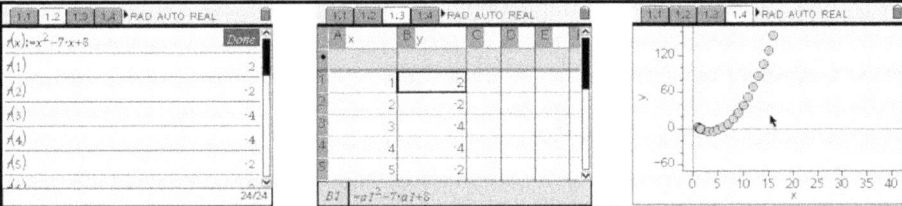

Working with dynamic images

Pupils can use computers to manipulate diagrams dynamically. This not only supports learning by producing actual diagrams and graphs, it also encourages pupils to develop the capability to generate their own mental images. The facility to generate many examples also helps pupils to notice 'what changes and what remains the same' and enables them to formulate and test their conjectures.

National Curriculum Key Processes: Analysing

Pupils should be able to visualise and work with dynamic images.

Using dynamic number lines

These Year 7 students used a dynamic number line to understand the meaning of variables. As they dragged the point *n* along the number line, the position of point *a* changed, according to the previously defined relationship.

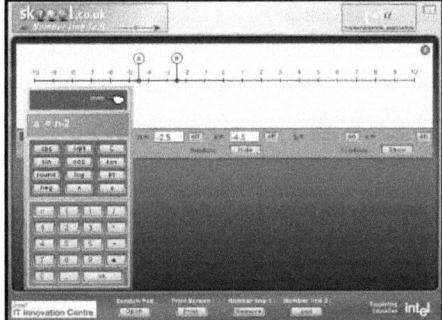

This example used the Number line tool from The Mathematical Toolkit, a free piece of software that can be downloaded or run from the London Grid for Learning. (www.lgfl.net).

The same example can be designed in most dynamic geometry software packages.

Using dynamic geometry software

Some Year 9 students explored a circle theorem by constructing an appropriate dynamic figure and used geometrical reasoning to make conclusions and reported them to others.

This is shown in the Teachers' TV programme *Hard to Teach – Secondary Maths Using ICT*. (http://www.teachers.tv/video/29853)

Progression idea

Students could use a dynamic number line to explore when two different functions share the same values of *x* and *y*. For example, for which values of x are the values of *y* the same for the functions $y = 2x$ and $y = x^2$?

Exploring graphs dynamically

These Year 10 students used a new software development which enabled the graph of a function to be dragged, allowing them to simultaneously observe changes in its parameters.

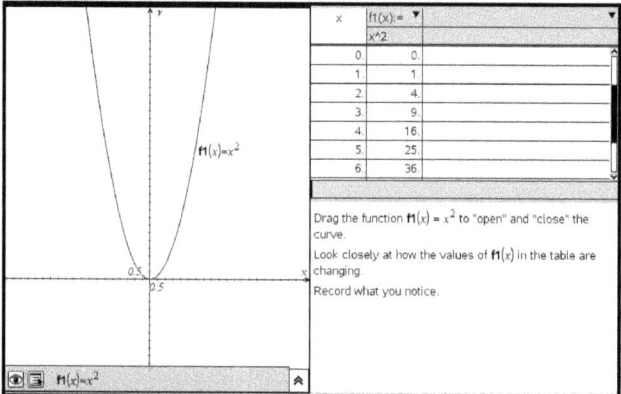

This example uses TI-Nspire software or handheld.

(http://www.ti-nspire.com)

Exploring data

Computers also enable pupils to work with real data which can be represented in a variety of ways, which supports interpretation and analysis.

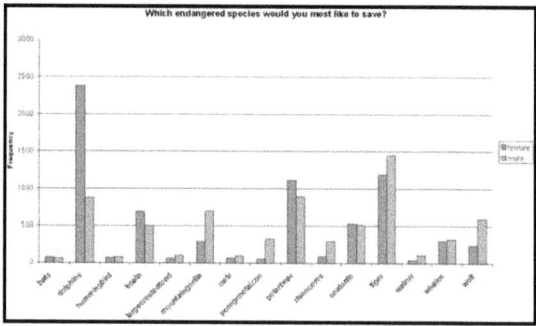

Some Year 7 pupils had recently taken part in an online survey, one of whose questions required them to decide which endangered species they would most like to save. They were then able to compare and contrast their views with pupils from another part of the country, using a range of graphs and statistical calculations.

The survey was part of the free Census at School project.
http://www.censusatschool.ntu.ac.uk

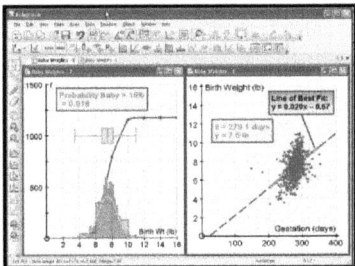

Existing databases provide access to much larger sets of data. For example, these Y10 pupils used a database of 1174 babies to explore the distribution of baby weights, and, after creating a range of standard diagrams, measured the probability of a baby over 10 lbs. They then investigated the relationship between gestation length and baby weight.

The database is freely available from

http://www.tsm-resources.com/useful-files.html

Using a motion detector

These Year 9 pupils planned a 'walk' to match a given distance/time graph and then tested their plan using the motion detector and a whole-class display.

An example of a motion detector being used is shown in the Teachers' TV programme *New Maths Technology – In the Classroom*. (http://www.teachers.tv/video/154)

'Teaching' the computer

When pupils design an algorithm (a set of instructions) to make a computer achieve a particular result, they must express themselves unambiguously and in the correct order. They are beginning to model particular behaviours or develop a set of rules. This engagement with a 'formal system' sets up the opportunity for developing a mathematical habit of mind, to develop their skills of algebraic thinking.

'Teaching the computer' encourages pupils to formalise their mathematical thinking, define conditions, sequence actions and express their ideas clearly. When the computer carries out the instructions it has been given, pupils need to observe the effect, and if necessary refine and improve the procedure they taught the computer.

Logo

For example, when Year 7 students devised a simple Logo program to draw a hexagon, they needed to decide on the sequence of actions carried out by the 'turtle' and the angle turned.

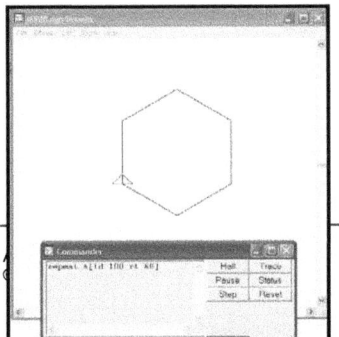

MSW Logo is a free software package available from http://www.softronix.com

They also needed to use the correct syntax. This is not just a technical matter; it gave the pupils an opportunity to engage in a 'formal' system for a real purpose – to draw a shape. In this context pupils were also able to be creative, pursued their own goals and developed a sense of authorship.

Spreadsheet formulae

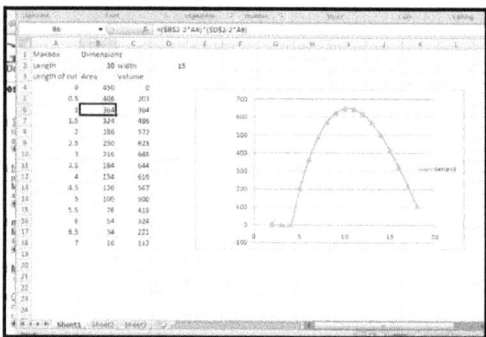

The opportunity to 'teach a computer' arises whenever pupils use formulae in a spreadsheet. It is important, in this context, that pupils are given the opportunity to do this for themselves.

For example, these Year 10 pupils taught a spreadsheet to display the volume of a box, in the Maxbox investigation, which assisted their understanding of symbolic representations.

Programming graphical calculators

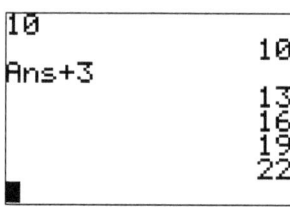

Most graphical calculators have a programming facility which is easily accessible. For example, some Year 8 pupils produced a range of programs, from simple ones which carried out basic calculations automatically to ones which could generate random numbers or sequences. In doing so they generalised and expressed their ideas in a formal language.

Progression idea

Pupils could build on the logo procedures for drawing a hexagon to try to tessellate them. By trying out the procedures and 'debugging' them, they will engage with a rich mathematical environment, working with geometry, algebra and logic.

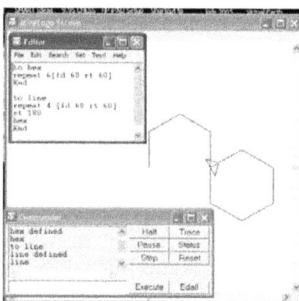

EPILOGUE

Clare Lee and Sue Johnston-Wilder

The book has been designed to help you to grow and expand your vision of what your mathematics department might become and to help you see what actions will be needed to achieve that vision. There will be many facets to that vision and now is the time to acknowledge that you as a new or aspiring subject leader cannot do everything at once. So you will need to prioritise. It may be that your first priority is to:

- boost the confidence and professionalism of your teachers so you may decide to use a programme of coaching to introduce problem-solving in Year 7 as explained in Chapter 6. The coaching will build the department's self-reliance and help them to articulate the expertise that they already have whilst enabling Year 7 to experience a new and exciting way to learn mathematics and to know that mathematics is about joy and rigour as discussed in Chapter 2.
- spend the money that has been allocated to build ICT use within the school. The department may need to work together through the ideas and lists in Chapter 11 in order to make good choices to enable your pupils to benefit from ICT use in the ways described in Chapter 12.
- make effective use of Assessment for Learning as detailed in Chapter 8. Your teachers are mostly experienced but see AfL as collecting data for checking progress. Using a collaborative action research project as detailed in Chapter 7 may be the way to widen your teachers' expectations of their ability to find out exactly what each and every pupil in their classes are learning and how to help them learn even more.

Whether the pressure to change comes from outside the department; from a National Strategy initiative, a Local Authority focus, an Ofsted report or from inside the department, for example, ideas that your staff want to develop together, your department will need to meld as a team to improve learning or change the way that teaching is approached . Changes and improvements will always need to be made; the more that you work to make sure everyone in the department takes ownership of those changes and improvements the more lasting they are likely to be. Therefore effective subject leaders will include their departments in prioritising and possibly rejecting some initiatives and making their own agreed department development plan, taking account of school and other pressures but ultimately setting their own priorities for action.

You as a subject leader will sometimes feel that you have so many competing pressures on you and your department that you do not know which way to turn. This is where developing a support network will be vital. Now is the time to take action to develop a support network. You are a valuable resource and can provide support and ideas for others while they provide the same for you. How you develop this support network is up to you. Chapter 1 gave some ideas, for example, joining subject associations and working as a mentor for trainee teachers for your local Higher Education Institute. In Chapter 6 the Heads of Department spoke of how important taking a masters level education course at their local university had been for them, in provoking a change in outlook as well as providing a support network of like-minded individuals.

Those mathematics teachers that initiate or take up the support offered by the networks described above to increase their professional skills can now take up an offer to have those skills recognised as a Chartered Mathematics Teacher. This is an important step forward in promoting the skills of accomplished mathematics teachers and resonates with the vision of effective mathematics teaching discussed in this book.

The Chartered Mathematics Teacher (CMathTeach) designation 'reflects the balance between teaching skills (pedagogy) and mathematics knowledge that is necessary for a professional teacher to educate and inspire today's students.' The CMathTeach designation will identify you as being at the forefront of your profession, and encapsulates standards of professional excellence across mathematics teaching. It will benchmark you at the same level as, for example, a Chartered Mathematician or a Chartered Engineer. The CMathTeach designation is incorporated within the Royal Charter of the Institute of Mathematics and is awarded by the Chartered Mathematics Teacher Registration Authority. The Authority is composed of representatives from all the recognised mathematics education organisations, ATM, MA etc. To apply for the CMathTeach designation you must be a member of at least one those organisations and also satisfy the requirements in the following four areas: Pedagogy, Mathematics, Experience and Continuing Professional Development

A journey of a thousand miles starts with the first step – in reading this book we think you will be prepared to take that first step.

The Mathematics Education Subject Organisations

ATM	The Association of Teachers of Mathematics
IMA	The Institute of Mathematics and its Applications
MA	The Mathematical Association
NANAMIC	The National Association for Numeracy and Mathematics In Colleges

INDEX

Action research...87
  Collaboration...89
  Collecting data...95
  Cycle...91-92
  Data collection tools...96-101
  Definition...89
  Problems...93
  Starting...95
  Tensions...90
  Triangulation...101
  Why use...88
  Writing up...102
Additional to Typical
  Needs...139-157
  Assessing teacher attitudes
    to...152-155
  Attention deficit disorders...144
  Beliefs about learning...147
  Diagnosis...141
  Difference...139
  Disability...139
      SEN, and...145
  Dyscalculia...142
  Dyslexia...142
  Dyspraxia...142
  Effort, notions of...149
  Historical perspective...139
  Low prior attainment...144
  Motivation...149
  Medical conditions...144
  Observing colleagues...152-155
  SEN...141
  Special Educational
    Needs...141
  Warnock Report...141

Ambadassor
  Subject leader role as...8
APP *see* Assessing Pupil
  Performance
Apprenticeship learning...41
  Learning strategies,
    applying...52
Assessment data, using...105-122
  Available...107-112
  Departmental collection...120
  Why use...112
Assessment for
  Learning...119,123-138
  Learning resources, pupils
    as...130
  Provide feedback...126
  Pupils as owners...132
  Success, providing vision
    of...128
  Systematic...124
Assessing Pupil
  Performance...119
Association of Teachers of
  Mathematics (ATM)...191
Associationism...33
ATM...191,201
Attention deficit disorders...144
Autograph...195

BECTA...160,161,164,184
  Model for learning...189,190
  Pupil's entitlement to
    ICT...204-210
  Self-review...164
Beginning teachers...7

Behaviourism...33,34-35
  Learning strategies,
  applying...47
Bernstein, Basil...34,43,53
Black, P et al...123
Boaler, J...42,134
Brown, M...20

Cardinality...51
Carr, W...87
Challenge...18
Class, social...43
Coaching...80
  Agreement...83
  Impact...84
  Principles...81-83
  Questioning...84
Cobb, P...55
Cognitive conflict...39,51
Collaboration
  Academic...30
  Inter-school...30
Collaborative working...28
Conjecturing...61
Constructivism...49
  Learning strategies,
  applying...50
Continuing Professional
Development...75-86
  And see CPD
Co-coaching...81
Cooper, Barry...21
Corey, Stephen...87
CPD...7,75-86
  Definition...78
  ICT...162,168
Cultural psychology...40
  Learning strategies,
  applying...50
Curiosity, engaging...18

Curriculum,
  Mathematics place in...8
  New...9,10

Data, assessment *see* Assessment data
Data collection tools, action
  research...96
  Documentary evidence...99
  Field notes and diaries...100
  Interviews...96
  Observations...99
  Surveys...98
  Triangulation...101
Davydov...50,51
Deep learning...186
Departmental meetings...75
  ICT...174
Differentiation...68
Digital divide...170
Dunne, M...21
Dweck, C...133,147
Dyscalculia...143
Dyslexia...142
Dyspraxia...142

e-mature...161
Enjoyment, subject...15,16
Entering into Symbols...194
Entwhistle, N...189
Environment, learning...11
Epistemology, genetic...36
Ethos, department...63
Experience, teacher...26
Experiencing mathematics...61
Exploring mathematics...61

Fisher Family Trust,
  data...107,109-110
  Using...110

Formative assessment *see* Assessment for Learning
Functional skills...10,20
  Context of...24
Furbles...194

Gattegno...39
Generalisation...51
Glaserfeld, Von...193
Grammar, strong...34
Graphic calculators...186
Grid algebra...191

Hardy, G.H.....17
Hoyles, C...195

ICT and learning
  Audit, department...196
  Barriers to change...187
  Barriers to learning...186
  Deep learning...186,189
  Effectiveness...184
  Model for...189
  Pupil needs...194
  Pupil skills required...200
  Tools, available...197
ICT in teaching...159-182
  Audit, departmental...164-165
  Audit, individuals...165-166
  Confidence...187
  Department, developing...162
  Digital divide...170
  Effect on role...187
  Effective use...160
  Equipment...169,173,175
  Interactive Whiteboards...170
  Plan, developing...173-177
    Checklist for...181
  Professional development...168,174
  School-wide development...169
  Shared network resources...175
  Vision, developing...166,188
  Why use...159
Information technology *see* ICT
Inquiry...29
Instrumental understanding...6,27
Instrumenting...187,200
Interactive Whiteboards...170
  Training materials...172
Investigative ethos...25
Invisible pedagogy...43

Joy...15-16
  Seizing the moment...26

Kemmis, S...87
Klein, M...154

LAT *see* Learning Achievement Tracker
Lave, Jean...42,52
Leadership
  ICT...196
  Mathematics outside department...72
  Negotiation...62
  Pedagogy...59-74
  Starting...61
Learner attitudes to mathematics...5,16
Learning Achievement Tracker...112
Learning and Skills Council...112
Lee, Clare...27
Lewin, Kurt...88
Linguistic code...43
Local Authority data...111
Logo...195
Low prior attainment...144

McNiff, J...90
Mason, J...39,126,153
Masters, role of...12
  Action research and...87
Mastery orientation...147
Mathematics
  Attitude to...5,6,11
  Creative subject, as...5
  Joy in...15-16
  Real world...20
  Rigour of...16
  Role as ambassador...9
  Thinking...20,61,70
Maturation...39
Mediation, cultural...38
Meetings, departmental...75
MEI...188
Mentoring...80
  Principles...81
Metaknowing...30
Miller, D...171
Monaghan, J...186
Monitoring programme, school...12
MTi...201

NCET...184
NCETM *see* National Centre for Excellence in Teaching Mathematics
National Centre for Excellence in Teaching Mathematics...12,30
National College of School Leadership...87
National Library of Virtual Manipulatives...194
Negotiation...62
Non-specialist teachers...7

Ofsted...12,112,115,148
  ICT...185,186,188
Online help...188
Organisation of learning...11
Outcomes, learning, agreeing...47

Pausing, role of...24,26
Pavlov...34
Pedagogy
  Good...60
  Leadership...59-74
Performance management...12
Performance orientation...147
Perks, Pat...29
Piaget...34,35-41
  Developmental psychology...38
  Generalisation...51
Piggott, J...163
Polya...39
Positivism *see* Behaviourism
Prestage, Stephanie...29
Prior attainment...11
Problem-solving...70
Procedural learning...27
Process skills, learners...10
Professional development *see* CPD

Questioning, coaching...84
  constructivism...47
RAISEonline, data...107-108
  Using...110
Real world mathematics...20
  Problems with...23
Recognition...26
Recruitment
  Beginning teachers...7
Reflection, critical...29
Reflexology...33

Relational understanding...6,27
Resources...11
Rigour...16
Rote learning...16
Rule-and-cue following...16
Ruthven, K...200

Schemes of work...54
Schon...88
SEF *see* Self-Evaluation Form
Self-Evaluation Form...115-117
SEN *see* Additional to Typical Needs
Setting....16,69
Situated cognition...42
Skemp, Richard...27,51
Skinner...34
Social reproduction...43
Sociology of education...43
   Learning strategies, applying...53
Software...11,186-201
   Audit...181
Somekh, B et al...161,167
Special Educational Needs *see* Additional to Typical Needs
Stenhouse, Lawrence...87,102
Subject associations...12
Subject leader *and see* Leadership
   Enjoyment of subject...15,16
   Learner attitudes to mathematics...5,11
   Outside department...72
   Supporting teachers...28,29
   Team attitudes, developing...5,6,63
      Inquiry, spirit of...31
Swedish National Agency for Education...16

Target setting
   Using assessment data...117
Teacher attitudes...5
   Enjoyment...16
   Goals...25
Teacher development...7
   ICT...161
   Mathematics, strength of...65
   Theory and...54
Teaching Advanced Mathematics...188,200
Team leadership....5,6,63
Theories, learning...33-44,57-57
Thorndike...34
Tracking data, internal...118
Training new teachers...7

Video...160
Visible pedagogy...43
Vygotsky...34,35-41,129
   Developmental psychology...40-41
   Generalisation...51

Waddell, M...153
Warnock Report...141
Watson...34
Wenger...52
William, D...124
Working inclusively...63

Zone of proximal development...40

Other Titles for Teachers from Tarquin

An Applet for the Teacher: Maths for the imagination
Alan Graham and Roger Duke   2010

978 1 899619 00 9
Applets are software applications that are particularly easy to use anywhere where you have a computer with an internet browser. It does not have to be online and requires just a simple piece of free Java software to be installed. Applets require limited memory resources, and are perfect for targeted, dynamic enrichment of lessons. The authors have worked together to design, create and test out a wide range of applets to support children's mathematical learning. As the maths educator, Alan has concentrated on how the applets can best meet the needs of learners; as technologist, Roger has actually created the applets. Overall, we have found them to be great fun to use and highly effective in helping learners to understand key topics in mathematics. This colourful and substantial book provides you with access to a selection of these applets, along with a wealth of advice and suggestions about how you can use them effectively with learners. Topics include: Matchbox Algebra; Tuckshop Kit; Fractions; a set for younger learners – subtraction, fractions and percentages and angles; and a set for older learners on subtraction, Monty Hall game show, number conversion and down the middle. Whether you are a classroom teacher, a parent wishing to help your child or just someone who wants to revisit their own mathematics in a fresh way, please use these applets fully and experience the fun of learning mathematics with understanding. Applets come at no extra cost.   **£15.00**

Designing and Using Mathematical Tasks
Open University Course Researching Mathematics Learning
Professor John Mason and Sue Johnston-Wilder

Paperback   978 1 899618 65 1 **£15.00**   Hardback   978 1 899618 60 6   **£65.00**
Mathematics seems, on the face of it, a cut and dried subject. But does being able to "do" mathematics mean being competent at techniques? Understanding how ideas and techniques fit together? Using basic principles in problem-solving? Something else…or all of these? This book addresses these questions through a definition of learning as transformation in the way that learners perceive or think. Learners increase their choice of actions and develop their powers to think mathematically and their competence and fluency in using specific techniques and language and their appreciation of how ideas fit together. This book forms part of the Open University course ME825 Researching Mathematics Learning.

Learning and Doing Mathematics
Professor John Mason
Second edition of a classic text   978 1 858530 49 9
Originally written for Open University students, then modified for students entering university generally, this book shows how to transform potential confrontations with problems into situations where users "own" the problem and develop solutions.   **£9.90**

Making Meaning in Mathematics
Ed Laurinda Brown   978 1 858531 02 1
This collection covers the proceedings of a BSLRM conference and provides a range of contributions that will be invaluable for those involved in mathematics education. Apart from good practical-based research reports using classroom observation and official data, readers will also find new perspectives on language, social learning and semiotics.   **£9.90**

Tarquin Publications, 99 Hatfield Road, St Albans, AL1 4JL
Tel: +44 01727 833866   Fax: +44 0845 456 6385   info@tarquinbooks.com

www.tarquinbooks.com

www.ingramcontent.com/pod-product-compliance
Ingram Content Group UK Ltd.
Pitfield, Milton Keynes, MK11 3LW, UK
UKHW020907010225
454546UK00007B/635